Anti-social Behaviour, Crime and Policing Act 2014

CHAPTER 12

Explanatory Notes are available separately

GRAN*GIS* UK Publishing

Adapted and published by GRANGIS (Grand Register Library).
Online: www.grangis.com
E-mail: contact@grangis.com

In this version:
ISBN: 979-8-88559-004-4

Note: This is the original version (as it was originally enacted). Title, sub-title and the generated date is as marked on the pages.

Anti-social Behaviour, Crime and Policing Act 2014

CHAPTER 12

ANTI-SOCIAL BEHAVIOUR, CRIME AND POLICING ACT 2014

PART 1

INJUNCTIONS

Injunctions

Contents of injunctions

Applications for injunctions

Interim injunctions

Variation and discharge

Breach of injunctions

Exclusion from home

Supplemental

PART 2

CRIMINAL BEHAVIOUR ORDERS

Criminal behaviour orders

Interim orders

Variation and discharge

Review of orders (under-18s)

Breach of orders

Supplemental

PART 3

DISPERSAL POWERS

PART 4

COMMUNITY PROTECTION

CHAPTER 1

COMMUNITY PROTECTION NOTICES

Community protection notices

Failure to comply with notice

Who may issue notices

Supplemental

CHAPTER 2

PUBLIC SPACES PROTECTION ORDERS

Public spaces protection orders

Enforcement

Supplemental

PART 5

RECOVERY OF POSSESSION OF DWELLING-HOUSES: ANTI-SOCIAL BEHAVIOUR GROUNDS

Absolute ground for possession: secure tenancies

Absolute ground for possession: assured tenancies

Discretionary grounds: secure and assured tenancies

Supplemental

PART 6

LOCAL INVOLVEMENT AND ACCOUNTABILITY

Community remedies

Response to complaints about anti-social behaviour

PART 7

DANGEROUS DOGS

PART 8

FIREARMS

PART 9

PROTECTION FROM SEXUAL HARM AND VIOLENCE

Protection from sexual harm

Child sexual exploitation at hotels

Violent offending

PART 10

FORCED MARRIAGE

PART 11

POLICING ETC

College of Policing

Review bodies for police remuneration etc

Anti-social Behaviour, Crime and Policing Act 2014

2014 CHAPTER 12

An Act to make provision about anti-social behaviour, crime and disorder, including provision about recovery of possession of dwelling-houses; to make provision amending the Dangerous Dogs Act 1991, the Police Act 1997, Schedules 7 and 8 to the Terrorism Act 2000, the Extradition Act 2003 and Part 3 of the Police Reform and Social Responsibility Act 2011; to make provision about firearms, about sexual harm and violence and about forced marriage; to make provision about the police, the Independent Police Complaints Commission and the Serious Fraud Office; to make provision about invalid travel documents; to make provision about criminal justice and court fees; and for connected purposes. [13th March 2014]

BE IT ENACTED by the Queen's most Excellent Majesty, by and with the advice and consent of the Lords Spiritual and Temporal, and Commons, in this present Parliament assembled, and by the authority of the same, as follows:—

PART 1

INJUNCTIONS

Injunctions

1 Power to grant injunctions

(1) A court may grant an injunction under this section against a person aged 10 or over ("the respondent") if two conditions are met.

(2) The first condition is that the court is satisfied, on the balance of probabilities, that the respondent has engaged or threatens to engage in anti-social behaviour.

(3) The second condition is that the court considers it just and convenient to grant the injunction for the purpose of preventing the respondent from engaging in anti-social behaviour.

(4) An injunction under this section may for the purpose of preventing the respondent from engaging in anti-social behaviour—
- (a) prohibit the respondent from doing anything described in the injunction;
- (b) require the respondent to do anything described in the injunction.

(5) Prohibitions and requirements in an injunction under this section must, so far as practicable, be such as to avoid—
- (a) any interference with the times, if any, at which the respondent normally works or attends school or any other educational establishment;
- (b) any conflict with the requirements of any other court order or injunction to which the respondent may be subject.

(6) An injunction under this section must—
- (a) specify the period for which it has effect, or
- (b) state that it has effect until further order.

In the case of an injunction granted before the respondent has reached the age of 18, a period must be specified and it must be no more than 12 months.

(7) An injunction under this section may specify periods for which particular prohibitions or requirements have effect.

(8) An application for an injunction under this section must be made to—
- (a) a youth court, in the case of a respondent aged under 18;
- (b) the High Court or the county court, in any other case.

Paragraph (b) is subject to any rules of court made under section 18(2).

2 Meaning of "anti-social behaviour"

(1) In this Part "anti-social behaviour" means—
- (a) conduct that has caused, or is likely to cause, harassment, alarm or distress to any person,
- (b) conduct capable of causing nuisance or annoyance to a person in relation to that person's occupation of residential premises, or
- (c) conduct capable of causing housing-related nuisance or annoyance to any person.

(2) Subsection (1)(b) applies only where the injunction under section 1 is applied for by—
- (a) a housing provider,
- (b) a local authority, or
- (c) a chief officer of police.

(3) In subsection (1)(c) "housing-related" means directly or indirectly relating to the housing management functions of—
- (a) a housing provider, or
- (b) a local authority.

(4) For the purposes of subsection (3) the housing management functions of a housing provider or a local authority include—

(a) functions conferred by or under an enactment;

(b) the powers and duties of the housing provider or local authority as the holder of an estate or interest in housing accommodation.

Contents of injunctions

3 Requirements included in injunctions

(1) An injunction under section 1 that includes a requirement must specify the person who is to be responsible for supervising compliance with the requirement.

The person may be an individual or an organisation.

(2) Before including a requirement, the court must receive evidence about its suitability and enforceability from—

(a) the individual to be specified under subsection (1), if an individual is to be specified;

(b) an individual representing the organisation to be specified under subsection (1), if an organisation is to be specified.

(3) Before including two or more requirements, the court must consider their compatibility with each other.

(4) It is the duty of a person specified under subsection (1)—

(a) to make any necessary arrangements in connection with the requirements for which the person has responsibility (the "relevant requirements");

(b) to promote the respondent's compliance with the relevant requirements;

(c) if the person considers that the respondent—

(i) has complied with all the relevant requirements, or

(ii) has failed to comply with a relevant requirement,

to inform the person who applied for the injunction and the appropriate chief officer of police.

(5) In subsection (4)(c) "the appropriate chief officer of police" means—

(a) the chief officer of police for the police area in which it appears to the person specified under subsection (1) that the respondent lives, or

(b) if it appears to that person that the respondent lives in more than one police area, whichever of the relevant chief officers of police that person thinks it most appropriate to inform.

(6) A respondent subject to a requirement included in an injunction under section 1 must—

(a) keep in touch with the person specified under subsection (1) in relation to that requirement, in accordance with any instructions given by that person from time to time;

(b) notify the person of any change of address.

These obligations have effect as requirements of the injunction.

4 Power of arrest

(1) A court granting an injunction under section 1 may attach a power of arrest to a prohibition or requirement of the injunction if the court thinks that—

- (a) the anti-social behaviour in which the respondent has engaged or threatens to engage consists of or includes the use or threatened use of violence against other persons, or
- (b) there is a significant risk of harm to other persons from the respondent.

"Requirement" here does not include one that has the effect of requiring the respondent to participate in particular activities.

(2) If the court attaches a power of arrest, the injunction may specify a period for which the power is to have effect which is shorter than that of the prohibition or requirement to which it relates.

Applications for injunctions

5 Applications for injunctions

(1) An injunction under section 1 may be granted only on the application of—

- (a) a local authority,
- (b) a housing provider,
- (c) the chief officer of police for a police area,
- (d) the chief constable of the British Transport Police Force,
- (e) Transport for London,
- (f) the Environment Agency,
- (g) the Natural Resources Body for Wales,
- (h) the Secretary of State exercising security management functions, or a Special Health Authority exercising security management functions on the direction of the Secretary of State, or
- (i) the Welsh Ministers exercising security management functions, or a person or body exercising security management functions on the direction of the Welsh Ministers or under arrangements made between the Welsh Ministers and that person or body.

(2) In subsection (1) "security management functions" means—

- (a) the Secretary of State's security management functions within the meaning given by section 195(3) of the National Health Service Act 2006;
- (b) the functions of the Welsh Ministers corresponding to those functions.

(3) A housing provider may make an application only if the application concerns anti-social behaviour that directly or indirectly relates to or affects its housing management functions.

(4) For the purposes of subsection (3) the housing management functions of a housing provider include—

- (a) functions conferred by or under an enactment;
- (b) the powers and duties of the housing provider as the holder of an estate or interest in housing accommodation.

(5) The Secretary of State may by order—

(a) amend this section;
(b) amend section 20 in relation to expressions used in this section.

6 Applications without notice

(1) An application for an injunction under section 1 may be made without notice being given to the respondent.

(2) If an application is made without notice the court must either—
(a) adjourn the proceedings and grant an interim injunction (see section 7), or
(b) adjourn the proceedings without granting an interim injunction, or
(c) dismiss the application.

Interim injunctions

7 Interim injunctions

(1) This section applies where the court adjourns the hearing of an application (whether made with notice or without) for an injunction under section 1.

(2) The court may grant an injunction under that section lasting until the final hearing of the application or until further order (an "interim injunction") if the court thinks it just to do so.

(3) An interim injunction made at a hearing of which the respondent was not given notice may not have the effect of requiring the respondent to participate in particular activities.

(4) Subject to that, the court has the same powers (including powers under section 4) whether or not the injunction is an interim injunction.

Variation and discharge

8 Variation or discharge of injunctions

(1) The court may vary or discharge an injunction under section 1 on the application of—
(a) the person who applied for the injunction, or
(b) the respondent.

(2) In subsection (1) "the court" means—
(a) the court that granted the injunction, except where paragraph (b) applies;
(b) the county court, where the injunction was granted by a youth court but the respondent is aged 18 or over.

(3) The power to vary an injunction includes power—
(a) to include an additional prohibition or requirement in the injunction, or to extend the period for which a prohibition or requirement has effect;
(b) to attach a power of arrest, or to extend the period for which a power of arrest has effect.

(4) If an application under this section is dismissed, the party by which the dismissed application was made may make no further application under this section without—

(a) the consent of the court, or
(b) the agreement of the other party.

(5) Section 3 applies to additional requirements included under subsection (3)(a) above as it applies to requirements included in a new injunction.

Breach of injunctions

9 Arrest without warrant

(1) Where a power of arrest is attached to a provision of an injunction under section 1, a constable may arrest the respondent without warrant if he or she has reasonable cause to suspect that the respondent is in breach of the provision.

(2) A constable who arrests a person under subsection (1) must inform the person who applied for the injunction.

(3) A person arrested under subsection (1) must, within the period of 24 hours beginning with the time of the arrest, be brought before—
(a) a judge of the High Court or a judge of the county court, if the injunction was granted by the High Court;
(b) a judge of the county court, if—
(i) the injunction was granted by the county court, or
(ii) the injunction was granted by a youth court but the respondent is aged 18 or over;
(c) a justice of the peace, if neither paragraph (a) nor paragraph (b) applies.

(4) In calculating when the period of 24 hours ends, Christmas Day, Good Friday and any Sunday are to be disregarded.

(5) The judge before whom a person is brought under subsection (3)(a) or (b) may remand the person if the matter is not disposed of straight away.

(6) The justice of the peace before whom a person is brought under subsection (3)(c) must remand the person to appear before the youth court that granted the injunction.

10 Issue of arrest warrant

(1) If the person who applied for an injunction under section 1 thinks that the respondent is in breach of any of its provisions, the person may apply for the issue of a warrant for the respondent's arrest.

(2) The application must be made to—
(a) a judge of the High Court, if the injunction was granted by the High Court;
(b) a judge of the county court, if—
(i) the injunction was granted by the county court, or
(ii) the injunction was granted by a youth court but the respondent is aged 18 or over;
(c) a justice of the peace, if neither paragraph (a) nor paragraph (b) applies.

(3) A judge or justice may issue a warrant under this section only if the judge or justice has reasonable grounds for believing that the respondent is in breach of a provision of the injunction.

(4) A warrant issued by a judge of the High Court must require the respondent to be brought before that court.

(5) A warrant issued by a judge of the county court must require the respondent to be brought before that court.

(6) A warrant issued by a justice of the peace must require the respondent to be brought before—

(a) the youth court that granted the injunction, if the person is aged under 18;

(b) the county court, if the person is aged 18 or over.

(7) A constable who arrests a person under a warrant issued under this section must inform the person who applied for the injunction.

(8) If the respondent is brought before a court by virtue of a warrant under this section but the matter is not disposed of straight away, the court may remand the respondent.

11 Remands

Schedule 1 (remands under sections 9 and 10) has effect.

12 Powers in respect of under-18s

Schedule 2 (breach of injunctions: powers of court in respect of under-18s) has effect.

Exclusion from home

13 Power to exclude person from home in cases of violence or risk of harm

(1) An injunction under section 1 may have the effect of excluding the respondent from the place where he or she normally lives ("the premises") only if—

(a) the respondent is aged 18 or over,

(b) the injunction is granted on the application of—

(i) a local authority,

(ii) the chief officer of police for the police area that the premises are in, or

(iii) if the premises are owned or managed by a housing provider, that housing provider, and

(c) the court thinks that—

(i) the anti-social behaviour in which the respondent has engaged or threatens to engage consists of or includes the use or threatened use of violence against other persons, or

(ii) there is a significant risk of harm to other persons from the respondent.

(2) For the purposes of this section a housing provider owns a place if—

(a) the housing provider is a person (other than a mortgagee not in possession) entitled to dispose of the fee simple of the place, whether in possession or in reversion, or

(b) the housing provider is a person who holds or is entitled to the rents and profits of the place under a lease that (when granted) was for a term of not less then 3 years.

Supplemental

14 Requirements to consult etc

(1) A person applying for an injunction under section 1 must before doing so—

(a) consult the local youth offending team about the application, if the respondent will be aged under 18 when the application is made;

(b) inform any other body or individual the applicant thinks appropriate of the application.

This subsection does not apply to a without-notice application.

(2) Where the court adjourns a without-notice application, before the date of the first on-notice hearing the applicant must—

(a) consult the local youth offending team about the application, if the respondent will be aged under 18 on that date;

(b) inform any other body or individual the applicant thinks appropriate of the application.

(3) A person applying for variation or discharge of an injunction under section 1 granted on that person's application must before doing so—

(a) consult the local youth offending team about the application for variation or discharge, if the respondent will be aged under 18 when that application is made;

(b) inform any other body or individual the applicant thinks appropriate of that application.

(4) In this section—

"local youth offending team" means—

(a) the youth offending team in whose area it appears to the applicant that the respondent lives, or

(b) if it appears to the applicant that the respondent lives in more than one such area, whichever one or more of the relevant youth offending teams the applicant thinks it appropriate to consult;

"on-notice hearing" means a hearing of which notice has been given to the applicant and the respondent in accordance with rules of court;

"without-notice application" means an application made without notice under section 6.

15 Appeals against decisions of youth courts

(1) An appeal lies to the Crown Court against a decision of a youth court made under this Part.

(2) On an appeal under this section the Crown Court may make—

(a) whatever orders are necessary to give effect to its determination of the appeal;

(b) whatever incidental or consequential orders appear to it to be just.

(3) An order of the Crown Court made on an appeal under this section (other than one directing that an application be re-heard by the youth court) is to be treated for the purposes of section 8 as an order of the youth court.

16 Special measures for witnesses

(1) Chapter 1 of Part 2 of the Youth Justice and Criminal Evidence Act 1999 (special measures directions in the case of vulnerable and intimidated witnesses) applies to proceedings under this Part as it applies to criminal proceedings, but with—

- (a) the omission of the provisions of that Act mentioned in subsection (2) (which make provision appropriate only in the context of criminal proceedings), and
- (b) any other necessary modifications.

(2) The provisions are—

- (a) section 17(4) to (7);
- (b) section 21(4C)(e);
- (c) section 22A;
- (d) section 27(10);
- (e) section 32.

(3) Rules of court made under or for the purposes of Chapter 1 of Part 2 of that Act apply to proceedings under this Part—

- (a) to the extent provided by rules of court, and
- (b) subject to any modifications provided by rules of court.

(4) Section 47 of that Act (restrictions on reporting special measures directions etc) applies with any necessary modifications—

- (a) to a direction under section 19 of that Act as applied by this section;
- (b) to a direction discharging or varying such a direction.

Sections 49 and 51 of that Act (offences) apply accordingly.

17 Children and young persons: disapplication of reporting restrictions

Section 49 of the Children and Young Persons Act 1933 (restrictions on reports of proceedings in which children and young persons are concerned) does not apply to proceedings under this Part.

18 Rules of court

(1) Rules of court may provide that an appeal from a decision of the High Court, the county court or a youth court—

- (a) to dismiss an application for an injunction under section 1 made without notice being given to the respondent, or
- (b) to refuse to grant an interim injunction when adjourning proceedings following such an application,

may be made without notice being given to the respondent.

(2) Rules of court may provide for a youth court to give permission for an application for an injunction under section 1 against a person aged 18 or over to be made to the youth court if—

- (a) an application to the youth court has been made, or is to be made, for an injunction under that section against a person aged under 18, and
- (b) the youth court thinks that it would be in the interests of justice for the applications to be heard together.

(3) In relation to a respondent attaining the age of 18 after proceedings under this Part have begun, rules of court may—

(a) provide for the transfer of the proceedings from the youth court to the High Court or the county court;

(b) prescribe circumstances in which the proceedings may or must remain in the youth court.

19 Guidance

(1) The Secretary of State may issue guidance to persons entitled to apply for injunctions under section 1 (see section 5) about the exercise of their functions under this Part.

(2) The Secretary of State may revise any guidance issued under this section.

(3) The Secretary of State must arrange for any guidance issued or revised under this section to be published.

20 Interpretation etc

(1) In this Part—

"anti-social behaviour" has the meaning given by section 2;

"harm" includes serious ill-treatment or abuse, whether physical or not;

"housing accommodation" includes—

(a) flats, lodging-houses and hostels;

(b) any yard, garden, outhouses and appurtenances belonging to the accommodation or usually enjoyed with it;

(c) any common areas used in connection with the accommodation;

"housing provider" means—

(a) a housing trust, within the meaning given by section 2 of the Housing Associations Act 1985, that is a charity;

(b) a housing action trust established under section 62 of the Housing Act 1988;

(c) in relation to England, a non-profit private registered provider of social housing;

(d) in relation to Wales, a Welsh body registered as a social landlord under section 3 of the Housing Act 1996;

(e) any body (other than a local authority or a body within paragraphs (a) to (d)) that is a landlord under a secure tenancy within the meaning given by section 79 of the Housing Act 1985;

"local authority" means—

(a) in relation to England, a district council, a county council, a London borough council, the Common Council of the City of London or the Council of the Isles of Scilly;

(b) in relation to Wales, a county council or a county borough council;

"respondent" has the meaning given by section 1(1).

(2) A person's age is treated for the purposes of this Part as being that which it appears to the court to be after considering any available evidence.

21 Saving and transitional provision

(1) In this section "existing order" means any of the following injunctions and orders—

(a) an anti-social behaviour injunction under section 153A of the Housing Act 1996;

(b) an injunction under section 153B of that Act (injunction against unlawful use of premises);

(c) an injunction in which anything is included by virtue of section 153D(3) or (4) of that Act (power to include provision banning person from premises or area, or to include power of arrest, in injunction against breach of tenancy agreement);

(d) an order under section 1 or 1B of the Crime and Disorder Act 1998 (anti-social behaviour orders etc);

(e) an individual support order under section 1AA of that Act made in connection with an order under section 1 or 1B of that Act;

(f) an intervention order under section 1G of that Act;

(g) a drinking banning order under section 3 or 4 of the Violent Crime Reduction Act 2006.

(2) The repeal or amendment by this Act of provisions about any of the existing orders specified in subsection (1)(a) to (d), (f) and (g) does not apply in relation to—

(a) an application made before the commencement day for an existing order;

(b) an existing order (whether made before or after that day) applied for before that day;

(c) anything done in connection with such an application or order.

(3) The repeal or amendment by this Act of provisions about an order specified in subsection (1)(e) does not apply in relation to—

(a) an individual support order made before the commencement day;

(b) anything done in connection with such an order.

(4) As from the commencement day there may be no variation of an existing order that extends the period of the order or of any of its provisions.

(5) At the end of the period of 5 years beginning with the commencement day—

(a) in relation to any of the existing orders specified in subsection (1)(a), (b) and (d) to (g) that is still in force, this Part has effect, with any necessary modifications (and with any modifications specified in an order under section 185(7)), as if the provisions of the order were provisions of an injunction under section 1;

(b) the provisions of this Part set out in subsection (6) apply to any injunction specified in subsection (1)(c) that is still in force as they apply to an injunction under section 1;

(c) subsections (2) to (4) cease to have effect.

(6) The provisions referred to in subsection (5)(b) are—

(a) section 1(7);

(b) sections 4(2) and 9 (if a power of arrest is attached);

(c) sections 6 to 8;

(d) section 10;

(e) section 11 and Schedule 1;

(f) section 12 and Schedule 2;
(g) section 18(1).

(7) In deciding whether to grant an injunction under section 1 a court may take account of conduct occurring up to 6 months before the commencement day.

(8) In this section "commencement day" means the day on which this Part comes into force.

PART 2

CRIMINAL BEHAVIOUR ORDERS

Criminal behaviour orders

22 Power to make orders

(1) This section applies where a person ("the offender") is convicted of an offence.

(2) The court may make a criminal behaviour order against the offender if two conditions are met.

(3) The first condition is that the court is satisfied, beyond reasonable doubt, that the offender has engaged in behaviour that caused or was likely to cause harassment, alarm or distress to any person.

(4) The second condition is that the court considers that making the order will help in preventing the offender from engaging in such behaviour.

(5) A criminal behaviour order is an order which, for the purpose of preventing the offender from engaging in such behaviour—
(a) prohibits the offender from doing anything described in the order;
(b) requires the offender to do anything described in the order.

(6) The court may make a criminal behaviour order against the offender only if it is made in addition to—
(a) a sentence imposed in respect of the offence, or
(b) an order discharging the offender conditionally.

(7) The court may make a criminal behaviour order against the offender only on the application of the prosecution.

(8) The prosecution must find out the views of the local youth offending team before applying for a criminal behaviour order to be made if the offender will be under the age of 18 when the application is made.

(9) Prohibitions and requirements in a criminal behaviour order must, so far as practicable, be such as to avoid—
(a) any interference with the times, if any, at which the offender normally works or attends school or any other educational establishment;
(b) any conflict with the requirements of any other court order or injunction to which the offender may be subject.

(10) In this section "local youth offending team" means—
(a) the youth offending team in whose area it appears to the prosecution that the offender lives, or
(b) if it appears to the prosecution that the offender lives in more than one such area, whichever one or more of the relevant youth offending teams the prosecution thinks appropriate.

23 Proceedings on an application for an order

(1) For the purpose of deciding whether to make a criminal behaviour order the court may consider evidence led by the prosecution and evidence led by the offender.

(2) It does not matter whether the evidence would have been admissible in the proceedings in which the offender was convicted.

(3) The court may adjourn any proceedings on an application for a criminal behaviour order even after sentencing the offender.

(4) If the offender does not appear for any adjourned proceedings the court may—
(a) further adjourn the proceedings,
(b) issue a warrant for the offender's arrest, or
(c) hear the proceedings in the offender's absence.

(5) The court may not act under paragraph (b) of subsection (4) unless it is satisfied that the offender has had adequate notice of the time and place of the adjourned proceedings.

(6) The court may not act under paragraph (c) of subsection (4) unless it is satisfied that the offender—
(a) has had adequate notice of the time and place of the adjourned proceedings, and
(b) has been informed that if the offender does not appear for those proceedings the court may hear the proceedings in his or her absence.

(7) Subsection (8) applies in relation to proceedings in which a criminal behaviour order is made against an offender who is under the age of 18.

(8) In so far as the proceedings relate to the making of the order—
(a) section 49 of the Children and Young Persons Act 1933 (restrictions on reports of proceedings in which children and young persons are concerned) does not apply in respect of the offender;
(b) section 39 of that Act (power to prohibit publication of certain matters) does so apply.

24 Requirements included in orders

(1) A criminal behaviour order that includes a requirement must specify the person who is to be responsible for supervising compliance with the requirement.

The person may be an individual or an organisation.

(2) Before including a requirement, the court must receive evidence about its suitability and enforceability from—

(a) the individual to be specified under subsection (1), if an individual is to be specified;

(b) an individual representing the organisation to be specified under subsection (1), if an organisation is to be specified.

(3) Before including two or more requirements, the court must consider their compatibility with each other.

(4) It is the duty of a person specified under subsection (1)—

(a) to make any necessary arrangements in connection with the requirements for which the person has responsibility (the "relevant requirements");

(b) to promote the offender's compliance with the relevant requirements;

(c) if the person considers that the offender—

(i) has complied with all the relevant requirements, or

(ii) has failed to comply with a relevant requirement,

to inform the prosecution and the appropriate chief officer of police.

(5) In subsection (4)(c) "the appropriate chief officer of police" means—

(a) the chief officer of police for the police area in which it appears to the person specified under subsection (1) that the offender lives, or

(b) if it appears to that person that the offender lives in more than one police area, whichever of the relevant chief officers of police that person thinks it most appropriate to inform.

(6) An offender subject to a requirement in a criminal behaviour order must—

(a) keep in touch with the person specified under subsection (1) in relation to that requirement, in accordance with any instructions given by that person from time to time;

(b) notify the person of any change of address.

These obligations have effect as requirements of the order.

25 Duration of order etc

(1) A criminal behaviour order takes effect on the day it is made, subject to subsection (2).

(2) If on the day a criminal behaviour order ("the new order") is made the offender is subject to another criminal behaviour order ("the previous order"), the new order may be made so as to take effect on the day on which the previous order ceases to have effect.

(3) A criminal behaviour order must specify the period ("the order period") for which it has effect.

(4) In the case of a criminal behaviour order made before the offender has reached the age of 18, the order period must be a fixed period of—

(a) not less than 1 year, and

(b) not more than 3 years.

(5) In the case of a criminal behaviour order made after the offender has reached the age of 18, the order period must be—

(a) a fixed period of not less than 2 years, or

(b) an indefinite period (so that the order has effect until further order).

(6) A criminal behaviour order may specify periods for which particular prohibitions or requirements have effect.

Interim orders

26 Interim orders

(1) This section applies where a court adjourns the hearing of an application for a criminal behaviour order.

(2) The court may make a criminal behaviour order that lasts until the final hearing of the application or until further order ("an interim order") if the court thinks it just to do so.

(3) Section 22(6) to (8) and section 25(3) to (5) do not apply in relation to the making of an interim order.

(4) Subject to that, the court has the same powers whether or not the criminal behaviour order is an interim order.

Variation and discharge

27 Variation or discharge of orders

(1) A criminal behaviour order may be varied or discharged by the court which made it on the application of—

(a) the offender, or

(b) the prosecution.

(2) If an application by the offender under this section is dismissed, the offender may make no further application under this section without—

(a) the consent of the court which made the order, or

(b) the agreement of the prosecution.

(3) If an application by the prosecution under this section is dismissed, the prosecution may make no further application under this section without—

(a) the consent of the court which made the order, or

(b) the agreement of the offender.

(4) The power to vary an order includes power to include an additional prohibition or requirement in the order or to extend the period for which a prohibition or requirement has effect.

(5) Section 24 applies to additional requirements included under subsection (4) as it applies to requirements included in a new order.

(6) In the case of a criminal behaviour order made by a magistrates' court, the references in this section to the court which made the order include a reference to any magistrates' court acting in the same local justice area as that court.

Review of orders (under-18s)

28 Review of orders

(1) If—

(a) a person subject to a criminal behaviour order will be under the age of 18 at the end of a review period (see subsection (2)),

(b) the term of the order runs until the end of that period or beyond, and

(c) the order is not discharged before the end of that period,

a review of the operation of the order must be carried out before the end of that period.

(2) The "review periods" are—

(a) the period of 12 months beginning with—

(i) the day on which the criminal behaviour order takes effect, or

(ii) if during that period the order is varied under section 27, the day on which it is varied (or most recently varied, if the order is varied more than once);

(b) a period of 12 months beginning with—

(i) the day after the end of the previous review period, or

(ii) if during that period of 12 months the order is varied under section 27, the day on which it is varied (or most recently varied, if the order is varied more than once).

(3) A review under this section must include consideration of—

(a) the extent to which the offender has complied with the order;

(b) the adequacy of any support available to the offender to help him or her comply with it;

(c) any matters relevant to the question whether an application should be made for the order to be varied or discharged.

(4) Those carrying out or participating in a review under this section must have regard to any relevant guidance issued by the Secretary of State under section 32 when considering—

(a) how the review should be carried out;

(b) what particular matters the review should deal with;

(c) what action (if any) it would be appropriate to take as a result of the findings of the review.

29 Carrying out and participating in reviews

(1) A review under section 28 is to be carried out by the chief officer of police of the police force maintained for the police area in which the offender lives or appears to be living.

(2) The chief officer, in carrying out a review under section 28, must act in co-operation with the council for the local government area in which the offender lives or appears to be living; and the council must co-operate in the carrying out of the review.

(3) The chief officer may invite the participation in the review of any other person or body.

(4) In this section "local government area" means—

(a) in relation to England, a district or London borough, the City of London, the Isle of Wight and the Isles of Scilly;

(b) in relation to Wales, a county or a county borough.

For the purposes of this section, the council for the Inner and Middle Temples is the Common Council of the City of London.

Breach of orders

30 Breach of order

(1) A person who without reasonable excuse—

(a) does anything he or she is prohibited from doing by a criminal behaviour order, or

(b) fails to do anything he or she is required to do by a criminal behaviour order,

commits an offence.

(2) A person guilty of an offence under this section is liable—

(a) on summary conviction, to imprisonment for a period not exceeding 6 months or to a fine, or to both;

(b) on conviction on indictment, to imprisonment for a period not exceeding 5 years or to a fine, or to both.

(3) If a person is convicted of an offence under this section, it is not open to the court by or before which the person is convicted to make an order under subsection (1)(b) of section 12 of the Powers of Criminal Courts (Sentencing) Act 2000 (conditional discharge).

(4) In proceedings for an offence under this section, a copy of the original criminal behaviour order, certified by the proper officer of the court which made it, is admissible as evidence of its having been made and of its contents to the same extent that oral evidence of those things is admissible in those proceedings.

(5) In relation to any proceedings for an offence under this section that are brought against a person under the age of 18—

(a) section 49 of the Children and Young Persons Act 1933 (restrictions on reports of proceedings in which children and young persons are concerned) does not apply in respect of the person;

(b) section 45 of the Youth Justice and Criminal Evidence Act 1999 (power to restrict reporting of criminal proceedings involving persons under 18) does so apply.

(6) If, in relation to any proceedings mentioned in subsection (5), the court does exercise its power to give a direction under section 45 of the Youth Justice and Criminal Evidence Act 1999, it must give its reasons for doing so.

Supplemental

31 Special measures for witnesses

(1) Chapter 1 of Part 2 of the Youth Justice and Criminal Evidence Act 1999 (special measures directions in the case of vulnerable and intimidated witnesses) applies to criminal behaviour order proceedings as it applies to criminal proceedings, but with—

(a) the omission of the provisions of that Act mentioned in subsection (2) (which make provision appropriate only in the context of criminal proceedings), and

(b) any other necessary modifications.

(2) The provisions are—

(a) section 17(4) to (7);

(b) section 21(4C)(e);

(c) section 22A;

(d) section 27(10);

(e) section 32.

(3) Rules of court made under or for the purposes of Chapter 1 of Part 2 of that Act apply to criminal behaviour order proceedings—

(a) to the extent provided by rules of court, and

(b) subject to any modifications provided by rules of court.

(4) Section 47 of that Act (restrictions on reporting special measures directions etc) applies with any necessary modifications—

(a) to a direction under section 19 of that Act as applied by this section;

(b) to a direction discharging or varying such a direction.

Sections 49 and 51 of that Act (offences) apply accordingly.

(5) In this section "criminal behaviour order proceedings" means proceedings in a magistrates' court or the Crown Court so far as relating to the issue whether to make a criminal behaviour order.

32 Guidance

(1) The Secretary of State may issue guidance to—

(a) chief officers of police, and

(b) the councils mentioned in section 29(2),

about the exercise of their functions under this Part.

(2) The Secretary of State may revise any guidance issued under this section.

(3) The Secretary of State must arrange for any guidance issued or revised under this section to be published.

33 Saving and transitional provision

(1) The repeal or amendment by this Act of provisions about any of the orders specified in subsection (2) does not—

(a) prevent an order specified in that subsection from being made in connection with criminal proceedings begun before the commencement day;

(b) apply in relation to an order specified in that subsection which is made in connection with criminal proceedings begun before that day;

(c) apply in relation to anything done in connection with such an order.

(2) The orders are—

(a) an order under section 1C of the Crime and Disorder Act 1998 (orders on conviction in criminal proceedings);

(b) an individual support order under section 1AA of that Act made in connection with an order under section 1C of that Act;

(c) a drinking banning order under section 6 of the Violent Crime Reduction Act 2006 (orders on conviction in criminal proceedings).

(3) As from the commencement day there may be no variation of an order specified in subsection (2) that extends the period of the order or of any provision of the order.

(4) At the end of the period of 5 years beginning with the commencement day—

(a) this Part has effect in relation to any order specified in subsection (2) that is still in force as if the provisions of the order were provisions of a criminal behaviour order;

(b) subsections (1) to (3) cease to have effect.

This Part, as it applies by virtue of paragraph (a), has effect with any necessary modifications (and with any modifications specified in an order under section 185(7)).

(5) In deciding whether to make a criminal behaviour order a court may take account of conduct occurring up to 1 year before the commencement day.

(6) In this section "commencement day" means the day on which this Part comes into force.

PART 3

DISPERSAL POWERS

34 Authorisations to use powers under section 35

(1) A police officer of at least the rank of inspector may authorise the use in a specified locality, during a specified period of not more than 48 hours, of the powers given by section 35.

"Specified" means specified in the authorisation.

(2) An officer may give such an authorisation only if satisfied on reasonable grounds that the use of those powers in the locality during that period may be necessary for the purpose of removing or reducing the likelihood of—

(a) members of the public in the locality being harassed, alarmed or distressed, or

(b) the occurrence in the locality of crime or disorder.

(3) In deciding whether to give such an authorisation an officer must have particular regard to the rights of freedom of expression and freedom of assembly set out in articles 10 and 11 of the Convention.

"Convention" has the meaning given by section 21(1) of the Human Rights Act 1998.

(4) An authorisation under this section—

(a) must be in writing,

(b) must be signed by the officer giving it, and

(c) must specify the grounds on which it is given.

35 Directions excluding a person from an area

(1) If the conditions in subsections (2) and (3) are met and an authorisation is in force under section 34, a constable in uniform may direct a person who is in a public place in the locality specified in the authorisation—

(a) to leave the locality (or part of the locality), and

(b) not to return to the locality (or part of the locality) for the period specified in the direction ("the exclusion period").

(2) The first condition is that the constable has reasonable grounds to suspect that the behaviour of the person in the locality has contributed or is likely to contribute to—

(a) members of the public in the locality being harassed, alarmed or distressed, or

(b) the occurrence in the locality of crime or disorder.

(3) The second condition is that the constable considers that giving a direction to the person is necessary for the purpose of removing or reducing the likelihood of the events mentioned in subsection (2)(a) or (b).

(4) The exclusion period may not exceed 48 hours.

The period may expire after (as long as it begins during) the period specified in the authorisation under section 34.

(5) A direction under this section—

(a) must be given in writing, unless that is not reasonably practicable;

(b) must specify the area to which it relates;

(c) may impose requirements as to the time by which the person must leave the area and the manner in which the person must do so (including the route).

(6) The constable must (unless it is not reasonably practicable) tell the person to whom the direction is given that failing without reasonable excuse to comply with the direction is an offence.

(7) If the constable reasonably believes that the person to whom the direction is given is under the age of 16, the constable may remove the person to a place where the person lives or a place of safety.

(8) Any constable may withdraw or vary a direction under this section; but a variation must not extend the duration of a direction beyond 48 hours from when it was first given.

(9) Notice of a withdrawal or variation of a direction—

(a) must be given to the person to whom the direction was given, unless that is not reasonably practicable, and

(b) if given, must be given in writing unless that is not reasonably practicable.

(10) In this section "public place" means a place to which at the material time the public or a section of the public has access, on payment or otherwise, as of right or by virtue of express or implied permission.

(11) In this Part "exclusion period" has the meaning given by subsection (1)(b).

36 Restrictions

(1) A constable may not give a direction under section 35 to a person who appears to the constable to be under the age of 10.

(2) A constable may not give a direction under section 35 that prevents the person to whom it is given having access to a place where the person lives.

(3) A constable may not give a direction under section 35 that prevents the person to whom it is given attending at a place which the person is—

- (a) required to attend for the purposes of the person's employment, or a contract of services to which the person is a party,
- (b) required to attend by an obligation imposed by or under an enactment or by the order of a court or tribunal, or
- (c) expected to attend for the purposes of education or training or for the purposes of receiving medical treatment,

at a time when the person is required or expected (as the case may be) to attend there.

(4) A constable may not give a direction to a person under section 35 if the person is one of a group of persons who are—

- (a) engaged in conduct that is lawful under section 220 of the Trade Union and Labour Relations (Consolidation) Act 1992 (peaceful picketing), or
- (b) taking part in a public procession of the kind mentioned in subsection (1) of section 11 of the Public Order Act 1986 in respect of which—
  - (i) written notice has been given in accordance with that section, or
  - (ii) written notice is not required to be given as provided by subsections (1) and (2) of that section.

(5) In deciding whether to give a direction under section 35 a constable must have particular regard to the rights of freedom of expression and freedom of assembly set out in articles 10 and 11 of the Convention.

"Convention" has the meaning given by section 21(1) of the Human Rights Act 1998.

37 Surrender of property

(1) A constable who gives a person a direction under section 35 may also direct the person to surrender to the constable any item in the person's possession or control that the constable reasonably believes has been used or is likely to be used in behaviour that harasses, alarms or distresses members of the public.

(2) A direction under this section must be given in writing, unless that is not reasonably practicable.

(3) A constable who gives a person a direction under this section must (unless it is not reasonably practicable)—

- (a) tell the person that failing without reasonable excuse to comply with the direction is an offence, and
- (b) give the person information in writing about when and how the person may recover the surrendered item.

(4) The surrendered item must not be returned to the person before the end of the exclusion period.

(5) If after the end of that period the person asks for the item to be returned, it must be returned (unless there is power to retain it under another enactment).

(6) But if it appears to a constable that the person is under the age of 16 and is not accompanied by a parent or other responsible adult, the item may be retained until the person is so accompanied.

(7) If the person has not asked for the return of the item before the end of the period of 28 days beginning with the day on which the direction was given, the item may be destroyed or otherwise disposed of.

38 Record-keeping

(1) A constable who gives a direction under section 35 must make a record of—

(a) the individual to whom the direction is given,

(b) the time at which the direction is given, and

(c) the terms of the direction (including in particular the area to which it relates and the exclusion period).

(2) A constable who withdraws or varies a direction under section 35 must make a record of—

(a) the time at which the direction is withdrawn or varied,

(b) whether notice of the withdrawal or variation is given to the person to whom the direction was given and if it is, at what time, and

(c) if the direction is varied, the terms of the variation.

(3) A constable who gives a direction under section 37 must make a record of—

(a) the individual to whom the direction is given,

(b) the time at which the direction is given, and

(c) the item to which the direction relates.

39 Offences

(1) A person given a direction under section 35 who fails without reasonable excuse to comply with it commits an offence.

(2) A person guilty of an offence under subsection (1) is liable on summary conviction—

(a) to imprisonment for a period not exceeding 3 months, or

(b) to a fine not exceeding level 4 on the standard scale,

(3) A person given a direction under section 37 who fails without reasonable excuse to comply with it commits an offence.

(4) A person guilty of an offence under subsection (3) is liable on summary conviction to a fine not exceeding level 2 on the standard scale.

40 Powers of community support officers

(1) Schedule 4 to the Police Reform Act 2002 (powers of community support officers) is amended as follows.

(2) In paragraph 2(6), for paragraph (aa) there is substituted—

"(aa) an offence under section 39 of the Anti-social Behaviour, Crime and Policing Act 2014;".

(3) For paragraph 4A of Schedule 4 there is substituted—

"4A Where a designation applies this paragraph to a person, that person has within the relevant police area the powers conferred on a constable by section 35 of the Anti-social Behaviour, Crime and Policing Act 2014.

4AB (1) Where a designation applies this paragraph to a person, that person has within the relevant police area the powers conferred on a constable by section 37 of the Anti-social Behaviour, Crime and Policing Act 2014.

(2) A designation may not apply this paragraph to a person unless a designation also applies paragraph 4A to that person."

41 Guidance

(1) The Secretary of State may issue guidance to chief officers of police about the exercise, by officers under their direction or control, of those officers' functions under this Part.

(2) The Secretary of State may revise any guidance issued under this section.

(3) The Secretary of State must arrange for any guidance issued or revised under this section to be published.

42 Saving and transitional provision

(1) The repeal by this Act of Part 4 of the Anti-social Behaviour Act 2003, and the repeal or amendment by this Act of provisions related to that Part, do not apply in relation to—

(a) an authorisation given under section 30(2) of that Act before the commencement day, or

(b) anything done in connection with such an authorisation.

(2) The repeal by this Act of section 27 of the Violent Crime Reduction Act 2006, and the repeal or amendment by this Act of provisions related to that section, do not apply in relation to—

(a) a direction given under that section before the commencement day, or

(b) anything done in connection with such a direction.

(3) In this section "commencement day" means the day on which this Part comes into force.

PART 4

COMMUNITY PROTECTION

CHAPTER 1

COMMUNITY PROTECTION NOTICES

Community protection notices

43 Power to issue notices

(1) An authorised person may issue a community protection notice to an individual aged 16 or over, or a body, if satisfied on reasonable grounds that—

(a) the conduct of the individual or body is having a detrimental effect, of a persistent or continuing nature, on the quality of life of those in the locality, and

(b) the conduct is unreasonable.

(2) In subsection (1) "authorised person" means a person on whom section 53 (or an enactment amended by that section) confers power to issue community protection notices.

(3) A community protection notice is a notice that imposes any of the following requirements on the individual or body issued with it—

(a) a requirement to stop doing specified things;

(b) a requirement to do specified things;

(c) a requirement to take reasonable steps to achieve specified results.

(4) The only requirements that may be imposed are ones that are reasonable to impose in order—

(a) to prevent the detrimental effect referred to in subsection (1) from continuing or recurring, or

(b) to reduce that detrimental effect or to reduce the risk of its continuance or recurrence.

(5) A person (A) may issue a community protection notice to an individual or body (B) only if—

(a) B has been given a written warning that the notice will be issued unless B's conduct ceases to have the detrimental effect referred to in subsection (1), and

(b) A is satisfied that, despite B having had enough time to deal with the matter, B's conduct is still having that effect.

(6) A person issuing a community protection notice must before doing so inform any body or individual the person thinks appropriate.

(7) A community protection notice must—

(a) identify the conduct referred to in subsection (1);

(b) explain the effect of sections 46 to 51.

(8) A community protection notice may specify periods within which, or times by which, requirements within subsection (3)(b) or (c) are to be complied with.

44 Occupiers of premises etc

(1) Conduct on, or affecting, premises (other than premises within subsection (2)) that a particular person—

(a) owns,

(b) leases,

(c) occupies,

(d) controls,

(e) operates, or

(f) maintains,

is treated for the purposes of section 43 as conduct of that person.

(2) Conduct on, or affecting, premises occupied for the purposes of a government department is treated for the purposes of section 43 as conduct of the Minister in charge of that department.

(3) This section does not treat an individual's conduct as that of another person if that person cannot reasonably be expected to control or affect it.

45 Occupier or owner unascertainable

(1) This section applies where—

(a) an authorised person has power to issue a community protection notice,

(b) the detrimental effect referred to in section 43(1) arises from the condition of premises or the use to which premises have been put, and

(c) the authorised person has made reasonable enquiries to find out the name or proper address of the occupier of the premises (or, if the premises are unoccupied, the owner) but without success.

(2) The authorised person may—

(a) post the community protection notice on the premises;

(b) enter the premises, or other premises, to the extent reasonably necessary for that purpose.

(3) The community protection notice is treated as having been issued to the occupier of the premises (or, if the premises are unoccupied, the owner) at the time the notice is posted.

(4) In this section "authorised person" has the same meaning as in section 43(1).

46 Appeals against notices

(1) A person issued with a community protection notice may appeal to a magistrates' court against the notice on any of the following grounds.

1. That the conduct specified in the community protection notice—

   (a) did not take place,

   (b) has not had a detrimental effect on the quality of life of those in the locality,

   (c) has not been of a persistent or continuing nature,

   (d) is not unreasonable, or

(e) is conduct that the person cannot reasonably be expected to control or affect.

2. That any of the requirements in the notice, or any of the periods within which or times by which they are to be complied with, are unreasonable.
3. That there is a material defect or error in, or in connection with, the notice.
4. That the notice was issued to the wrong person.

(2) An appeal must be made within the period of 21 days beginning with the day on which the person is issued with the notice.

(3) While an appeal against a community protection notice is in progress—

(a) a requirement imposed by the notice to stop doing specified things remains in effect, unless the court orders otherwise, but

(b) any other requirement imposed by the notice is of no effect.

For this purpose an appeal is "in progress" until it is finally determined or is withdrawn.

(4) A magistrates' court hearing an appeal against a community protection notice must—

(a) quash the notice,

(b) modify the notice (for example by extending a period specified in it), or

(c) dismiss the appeal.

Failure to comply with notice

47 Remedial action by local authority

(1) Where a person issued with a community protection notice ("the defaulter") fails to comply with a requirement of the notice, the relevant local authority may take action under subsection (2) or subsection (3) (or both).

(2) The relevant local authority may have work carried out to ensure that the failure is remedied, but only on land that is open to the air.

(3) As regards premises other than land open to the air, if the relevant local authority issues the defaulter with a notice—

(a) specifying work it intends to have carried out to ensure that the failure is remedied,

(b) specifying the estimated cost of the work, and

(c) inviting the defaulter to consent to the work being carried out,

the authority may have the work carried out if the necessary consent is given.

(4) In subsection (3) "the necessary consent" means the consent of—

(a) the defaulter, and

(b) the owner of the premises on which the work is to be carried out (if that is not the defaulter).

Paragraph (b) does not apply where the relevant authority has made reasonable efforts to contact the owner of the premises but without success.

(5) A person authorised by a local authority to carry out work under this section may enter any premises to the extent reasonably necessary for that purpose, except that a person

who is only authorised to carry out work under subsection (2) may only enter land that is open to the air.

(6) If work is carried out under subsection (2) or (3) and the relevant local authority issues a notice to the defaulter—

(a) giving details of the work that was carried out, and

(b) specifying an amount that is no more than the cost to the authority of having the work carried out,

the defaulter is liable to the authority for that amount (subject to the outcome of any appeal under subsection (7)).

(7) A person issued with a notice under subsection (6) may appeal to a magistrates' court, within the period of 21 days beginning with the day on which the notice was issued, on the ground that the amount specified under subsection (6)(b) is excessive.

(8) A magistrates' court hearing an appeal under subsection (7) must—

(a) confirm the amount, or

(b) substitute a lower amount.

(9) In this section "the relevant local authority" means—

(a) the local authority that issued the community protection notice;

(b) if the community protection notice was not issued by a local authority, the local authority (or, as the case may be, one of the local authorities) that could have issued it.

48 Offence of failing to comply with notice

(1) A person issued with a community protection notice who fails to comply with it commits an offence.

(2) A person guilty of an offence under this section is liable on summary conviction—

(a) to a fine not exceeding level 4 on the standard scale, in the case of an individual;

(b) to a fine not exceeding £20,000, in the case of a body.

(3) A person does not commit an offence under this section if—

(a) the person took all reasonable steps to comply with the notice, or

(b) there is some other reasonable excuse for the failure to comply with it.

49 Remedial orders

(1) A court before which a person is convicted of an offence under section 48 in respect of a community protection notice may make whatever order the court thinks appropriate for ensuring that what the notice requires to be done is done.

(2) An order under this section may in particular require the defendant—

(a) to carry out specified work, or

(b) to allow specified work to be carried out by or on behalf of a specified local authority.

(3) To be specified under subsection (2)(b) a local authority must be—

(a) the local authority that issued the community protection notice;

(b) if the community protection notice was not issued by a local authority, the local authority (or, as the case may be, one of the local authorities) that could have issued it.

(4) A requirement imposed under subsection (2)(b) does not authorise the person carrying out the work to enter the defendant's home without the defendant's consent.

But this does not prevent a defendant who fails to give that consent from being in breach of the court's order.

(5) In subsection (4) "the defendant's home" means the house, flat, vehicle or other accommodation where the defendant—

(a) usually lives, or

(b) is living at the time when the work is or would be carried out.

(6) If work is carried out under subsection (2)(b) and the local authority specified under that subsection issues a notice to the defaulter—

(a) giving details of the work that was carried out, and

(b) specifying an amount that is no more than the cost to the authority of having the work carried out,

the defaulter is liable to the authority for that amount (subject to the outcome of any appeal under subsection (7)).

(7) A person issued with a notice under subsection (6) may appeal to a magistrates' court, within the period of 21 days beginning with the day on which the notice was issued, on the ground that the amount specified under subsection (6)(b) is excessive.

(8) A magistrates' court hearing an appeal under subsection (7) must—

(a) confirm the amount, or

(b) substitute a lower amount.

50 Forfeiture of item used in commission of offence

(1) A court before which a person is convicted of an offence under section 48 may order the forfeiture of any item that was used in the commission of the offence.

(2) An order under this section may require a person in possession of the item to hand it over as soon as reasonably practicable—

(a) to a constable, or

(b) to a person employed by a local authority or designated by a local authority under section 53(1)(c).

(3) An order under this section may require the item—

(a) to be destroyed, or

(b) to be disposed of in whatever way the order specifies.

(4) Where an item ordered to be forfeited under this section is kept by or handed over to a constable, the police force of which the constable is a member must ensure that arrangements are made for its destruction or disposal, either—

(a) in accordance with the order, or

(b) if no arrangements are specified in the order, in whatever way seems appropriate to the police force.

(5) Where an item ordered to be forfeited under this section is kept by or handed over to a person within subsection (2)(b), the local authority by whom the person is employed or was designated must ensure that arrangements are made for its destruction or disposal, either—

(a) in accordance with the order, or

(b) if no arrangements are specified in the order, in whatever way seems appropriate to the local authority.

51 Seizure of item used in commission of offence

(1) If a justice of the peace is satisfied on information on oath that there are reasonable grounds for suspecting—

(a) that an offence under section 48 has been committed, and

(b) that there is an item used in the commission of the offence on premises specified in the information,

the justice may issue a warrant authorising any constable or designated person to enter the premises within 14 days from the date of issue of the warrant to seize the item.

(2) In this section "designated person" means a person designated by a local authority under section 53(1)(c).

(3) A constable or designated person may use reasonable force, if necessary, in executing a warrant under this section.

(4) A constable or designated person who has seized an item under a warrant under this section—

(a) may retain the item until any relevant criminal proceedings have been finally determined, if such proceedings are started before the end of the period of 28 days following the day on which the item was seized;

(b) otherwise, must before the end of that period return the item to the person from whom it was seized.

(5) In subsection (4) "relevant criminal proceedings" means proceedings for an offence under section 48 in the commission of which the item is alleged to have been used.

52 Fixed penalty notices

(1) An authorised person may issue a fixed penalty notice to anyone who that person has reason to believe has committed an offence under section 48.

(2) In subsection (1) "authorised person" means a person on whom section 53 (or an enactment amended by that section) confers power to issue fixed penalty notices under this section.

(3) A fixed penalty notice is a notice offering the person to whom it is issued the opportunity of discharging any liability to conviction for the offence by payment of a fixed penalty to a local authority specified in the notice.

(4) The local authority specified under subsection (3) must be—

(a) the local authority that issued the community protection notice to which the fixed penalty notice relates;

(b) if the community protection notice was not issued by a local authority, the local authority (or, as the case may be, one of the local authorities) that could have issued it.

(5) Where a person is issued with a notice under this section in respect of an offence—

(a) no proceedings may be taken for the offence before the end of the period of 14 days following the date of the notice;

(b) the person may not be convicted of the offence if the person pays the fixed penalty before the end of that period.

(6) A fixed penalty notice must—

(a) give reasonably detailed particulars of the circumstances alleged to constitute the offence;

(b) state the period during which (because of subsection (5)(a)) proceedings will not be taken for the offence;

(c) specify the amount of the fixed penalty;

(d) state the name and address of the person to whom the fixed penalty may be paid;

(e) specify permissible methods of payment.

(7) An amount specified under subsection (6)(c) must not be more than £100.

(8) A fixed penalty notice may specify two amounts under subsection (6)(c) and specify that, if the lower of those amounts is paid within a specified period (of less than 14 days), that is the amount of the fixed penalty.

(9) Whatever other method may be specified under subsection (6)(e), payment of a fixed penalty may be made by pre-paying and posting to the person whose name is stated under subsection (6)(d), at the stated address, a letter containing the amount of the penalty (in cash or otherwise).

(10) Where a letter is sent as mentioned in subsection (9), payment is regarded as having been made at the time at which that letter would be delivered in the ordinary course of post.

(11) In any proceedings, a certificate that—

(a) purports to be signed by or on behalf of the chief finance officer of the local authority concerned, and

(b) states that payment of a fixed penalty was, or was not, received by the dated specified in the certificate,

is evidence of the facts stated.

(12) In this section "chief finance officer", in relation to a local authority, means the person with responsibility for the authority's financial affairs.

Who may issue notices

53 Authorised persons

(1) A community protection notice or a fixed penalty notice may be issued by—

(a) a constable;

(b) the relevant local authority (see subsections (2) and (3));

(c) a person designated by the relevant local authority for the purposes of this section.

(2) For a community protection notice, "the relevant local authority" means the local authority (or, as the case may be, any of the local authorities) within whose area the conduct specified in the notice has, according to the notice, been taking place.

(3) For a fixed penalty notice, "the relevant local authority" means the local authority (or, as the case may be, any of the local authorities) within whose area the offence in question is alleged to have taken place.

(4) Only a person of a description specified in an order made by the Secretary of State for the purposes of subsection (1)(c) may be designated under that subsection.

(5) In Part 1 of Schedule 4 to the Police Reform Act 2002 (powers exercisable by community support officers), after paragraph 1ZA there is inserted—

"1ZB Power to issue community protection notices

1ZB A person shall have the power of a constable to issue a community protection notice under section 43 of the Anti-social Behaviour, Crime and Policing Act 2014 if—

(a) a designation applies this paragraph to that person, and

(b) the conduct specified in the notice has (according to the notice) been taking place within the relevant police area."

(6) In paragraph 1 of that Schedule (power of community support officers to issue fixed penalty notices), after paragraph (ab) of sub-paragraph (2) there is inserted—

"(ac) the power of a constable to issue a fixed penalty notice under section 52 of the Anti-social Behaviour, Crime and Policing Act 2014 (fixed penalty notice in respect of failure to comply with community protection notice);".

Supplemental

54 Exemption from liability

(1) A local authority exercising or purporting to exercise a power under section 47(2) is not liable to an occupier or owner of land for damages or otherwise (whether at common law or otherwise) arising out of anything done or omitted to be done in the exercise or purported exercise of that power.

(2) A person carrying out work under section 47(2), or a person by or on whose behalf work is carried out under section 49(2)(b), is not liable to an occupier or owner of land for damages or otherwise (whether at common law or otherwise) arising out of anything done or omitted to be done in carrying out that work.

(3) Subsections (1) and (2) do not apply—

(a) to an act or omission shown to have been in bad faith, or

(b) to liability arising out of a failure to exercise due care and attention.

(4) Subsections (1) and (2) do not apply so as to prevent an award of damages made in respect of an act or omission on the ground that the act or omission was unlawful by virtue of section 6(1) of the Human Rights Act 1998.

(5) This section does not affect any other exemption from liability (whether at common law or otherwise).

55 Issuing of notices

(1) A notice under this Chapter may be issued to a person by—

(a) handing it to the person,

(b) leaving it at the person's proper address, or

(c) sending it by post to the person at that address.

(2) A notice under this Chapter to a body corporate may be issued to the secretary or clerk of that body.

(3) A notice under this Chapter to a partnership may be issued to a partner or a person who has the control or management of the partnership business.

(4) For the purposes of this section and of section 7 of the Interpretation Act 1978 (service of documents by post) in its application to this section, the proper address of a person is the person's last known address, except that—

(a) in the case of a body corporate or its secretary or clerk, it is the address of the body's registered or principal office;

(b) in the case of a partnership or person having the control or the management of the partnership business, it is the principal office of the partnership.

(5) For the purposes of subsection (4) the principal office of a company registered outside the United Kingdom, or of a partnership carrying on business outside the United Kingdom, is its principal office within the United Kingdom.

(6) If a person has specified an address in the United Kingdom, other than the person's proper address within the meaning of subsection (4), as the one at which the person or someone on the person's behalf will accept notices of the same description as a notice under this Chapter, that address is also treated for the purposes of this section and section 7 of the Interpretation Act 1978 as the person's proper address.

56 Guidance

(1) The Secretary of State may issue—

(a) guidance to chief officers of police about the exercise, by officers under their direction or control, of those officers' functions under this Chapter;

(b) guidance to local authorities about the exercise of their functions under this Chapter and those of persons designated under section 53(1)(c).

(2) The Secretary of State may revise any guidance issued under this section.

(3) The Secretary of State must arrange for any guidance issued or revised under this section to be published.

57 Interpretation of Chapter 1

In this Chapter—

"conduct" includes a failure to act;

"local authority" means—

(a) in relation to England, a district council, a county council for an area for which there is no district council, a London borough council, the Common Council of the City of London or the Council of the Isles of Scilly;
(b) in relation to Wales, a county council or a county borough council;

"owner", in relation to premises, means—

(a) a person (other than a mortgagee not in possession) entitled to dispose of the fee simple of the premises, whether in possession or in reversion;
(b) a person who holds or is entitled to the rents and profits of the premises under a lease that (when granted) was for a term of not less then 3 years;

"premises" includes any land.

58 Saving and transitional provision

(1) The repeal or amendment by this Act of provisions about any of the notices specified in subsection (2) does not apply in relation to—

(a) a notice specified in that subsection served before the commencement day;
(b) anything done in connection with such a notice.

(2) The notices are—

(a) a litter abatement notice under section 92 of the Environmental Protection Act 1990;
(b) a litter clearing notice under section 92A of that Act;
(c) a street litter control notice under section 93 of that Act;
(d) a defacement removal notice under section 48 of the Anti-social Behaviour Act 2003.

(3) A community protection notice that contains no requirement that could not have been contained in one of the notices specified in subsection (2) may be issued in respect of conduct before the commencement day.

(4) Subsection (3) applies only during the period of 3 months beginning with the commencement day.

(5) In this section "commencement day" means the day on which this Chapter comes into force.

CHAPTER 2

PUBLIC SPACES PROTECTION ORDERS

Public spaces protection orders

59 Power to make orders

(1) A local authority may make a public spaces protection order if satisfied on reasonable grounds that two conditions are met.

(2) The first condition is that—

(a) activities carried on in a public place within the authority's area have had a detrimental effect on the quality of life of those in the locality, or

(b) it is likely that activities will be carried on in a public place within that area and that they will have such an effect.

(3) The second condition is that the effect, or likely effect, of the activities—

(a) is, or is likely to be, of a persistent or continuing nature,

(b) is, or is likely to be, such as to make the activities unreasonable, and

(c) justifies the restrictions imposed by the notice.

(4) A public spaces protection order is an order that identifies the public place referred to in subsection (2) ("the restricted area") and—

(a) prohibits specified things being done in the restricted area,

(b) requires specified things to be done by persons carrying on specified activities in that area, or

(c) does both of those things.

(5) The only prohibitions or requirements that may be imposed are ones that are reasonable to impose in order—

(a) to prevent the detrimental effect referred to in subsection (2) from continuing, occurring or recurring, or

(b) to reduce that detrimental effect or to reduce the risk of its continuance, occurrence or recurrence.

(6) A prohibition or requirement may be framed—

(a) so as to apply to all persons, or only to persons in specified categories, or to all persons except those in specified categories;

(b) so as to apply at all times, or only at specified times, or at all times except those specified;

(c) so as to apply in all circumstances, or only in specified circumstances, or in all circumstances except those specified.

(7) A public spaces protection order must—

(a) identify the activities referred to in subsection (2);

(b) explain the effect of section 63 (where it applies) and section 67;

(c) specify the period for which the order has effect.

(8) A public spaces protection order must be published in accordance with regulations made by the Secretary of State.

60 Duration of orders

(1) A public spaces protection order may not have effect for a period of more than 3 years, unless extended under this section.

(2) Before the time when a public spaces protection order is due to expire, the local authority that made the order may extend the period for which it has effect if satisfied on reasonable grounds that doing so is necessary to prevent—

(a) occurrence or recurrence after that time of the activities identified in the order, or

(b) an increase in the frequency or seriousness of those activities after that time.

(3) An extension under this section—

(a) may not be for a period of more than 3 years;

(b) must be published in accordance with regulations made by the Secretary of State.

(4) A public spaces protection order may be extended under this section more than once.

61 Variation and discharge of orders

(1) Where a public spaces protection order is in force, the local authority that made the order may vary it—

(a) by increasing or reducing the restricted area;

(b) by altering or removing a prohibition or requirement included in the order, or adding a new one.

(2) A local authority may make a variation under subsection (1)(a) that results in the order applying to an area to which it did not previously apply only if the conditions in section 59(2) and (3) are met as regards activities in that area.

(3) A local authority may make a variation under subsection (1)(b) that makes a prohibition or requirement more extensive, or adds a new one, only if the prohibitions and requirements imposed by the order as varied are ones that section 59(5) allows to be imposed.

(4) A public spaces protection order may be discharged by the local authority that made it.

(5) Where an order is varied, the order as varied must be published in accordance with regulations made by the Secretary of State.

(6) Where an order is discharged, a notice identifying the order and stating the date when it ceases to have effect must be published in accordance with regulations made by the Secretary of State.

Prohibition on consuming alcohol

62 Premises etc to which alcohol prohibition does not apply

(1) A prohibition in a public spaces protection order on consuming alcohol does not apply to—

(a) premises (other than council-operated licensed premises) authorised by a premises licence to be used for the supply of alcohol;

(b) premises authorised by a club premises certificate to be used by the club for the supply of alcohol;

(c) a place within the curtilage of premises within paragraph (a) or (b);

(d) premises which by virtue of Part 5 of the Licensing Act 2003 may at the relevant time be used for the supply of alcohol or which, by virtue of that Part, could have been so used within the 30 minutes before that time;

(e) a place where facilities or activities relating to the sale or consumption of alcohol are at the relevant time permitted by virtue of a permission granted under section 115E of the Highways Act 1980 (highway-related uses).

(2) A prohibition in a public spaces protection order on consuming alcohol does not apply to council-operated licensed premises—

(a) when the premises are being used for the supply of alcohol, or

(b) within 30 minutes after the end of a period during which the premises have been used for the supply of alcohol.

(3) In this section—

"club premises certificate" has the meaning given by section 60 of the Licensing Act 2003;

"premises licence" has the meaning given by section 11 of that Act;

"supply of alcohol" has the meaning given by section 14 of that Act.

(4) For the purposes of this section, premises are "council-operated licensed premises" if they are authorised by a premises licence to be used for the supply of alcohol and—

(a) the licence is held by a local authority in whose area the premises (or part of the premises) are situated, or

(b) the licence is held by another person but the premises are occupied by a local authority or are managed by or on behalf of a local authority.

63 Consumption of alcohol in breach of prohibition in order

(1) This section applies where a constable or an authorised person reasonably believes that a person (P)—

(a) is or has been consuming alcohol in breach of a prohibition in a public spaces protection order, or

(b) intends to consume alcohol in circumstances in which doing so would be a breach of such a prohibition.

In this section "authorised person" means a person authorised for the purposes of this section by the local authority that made the public spaces protection order (or authorised by virtue of section 69(1)).

(2) The constable or authorised person may require P—

(a) not to consume, in breach of the order, alcohol or anything which the constable or authorised person reasonably believes to be alcohol;

(b) to surrender anything in P's possession which is, or which the constable or authorised person reasonably believes to be, alcohol or a container for alcohol.

(3) A constable or an authorised person who imposes a requirement under subsection (2) must tell P that failing without reasonable excuse to comply with the requirement is an offence.

(4) A requirement imposed by an authorised person under subsection (2) is not valid if the person—

(a) is asked by P to show evidence of his or her authorisation, and

(b) fails to do so.

(5) A constable or an authorised person may dispose of anything surrendered under subsection (2)(b) in whatever way he or she thinks appropriate.

(6) A person who fails without reasonable excuse to comply with a requirement imposed on him or her under subsection (2) commits an offence and is liable on summary conviction to a fine not exceeding level 2 on the standard scale.

Restrictions on public rights of way

64 Orders restricting public right of way over highway

(1) A local authority may not make a public spaces protection order that restricts the public right of way over a highway without considering—

- (a) the likely effect of making the order on the occupiers of premises adjoining or adjacent to the highway;
- (b) the likely effect of making the order on other persons in the locality;
- (c) in a case where the highway constitutes a through route, the availability of a reasonably convenient alternative route.

(2) Before making such an order a local authority must—

- (a) notify potentially affected persons of the proposed order,
- (b) inform those persons how they can see a copy of the proposed order,
- (c) notify those persons of the period within which they may make representations about the proposed order, and
- (d) consider any representations made.

In this subsection "potentially affected persons" means occupiers of premises adjacent to or adjoining the highway, and any other persons in the locality who are likely to be affected by the proposed order.

(3) Before a local authority makes a public spaces protection order restricting the public right of way over a highway that is also within the area of another local authority, it must consult that other authority if it thinks it appropriate to do so.

(4) A public spaces protection order may not restrict the public right of way over a highway for the occupiers of premises adjoining or adjacent to the highway.

(5) A public spaces protection order may not restrict the public right of way over a highway that is the only or principal means of access to a dwelling.

(6) In relation to a highway that is the only or principal means of access to premises used for business or recreational purposes, a public spaces protection order may not restrict the public right of way over the highway during periods when the premises are normally used for those purposes.

(7) A public spaces protection order that restricts the public right of way over a highway may authorise the installation, operation and maintenance of a barrier or barriers for enforcing the restriction.

(8) A local authority may install, operate and maintain barriers authorised under subsection (7).

(9) A highway over which the public right of way is restricted by a public spaces protection order does not cease to be regarded as a highway by reason of the restriction (or by reason of any barrier authorised under subsection (7)).

(10) In this section—

"dwelling" means a building or part of a building occupied, or intended to be occupied, as a separate dwelling;

"highway" has the meaning given by section 328 of the Highways Act 1980.

65 Categories of highway over which public right of way may not be restricted

(1) A public spaces protection order may not restrict the public right of way over a highway that is—

(a) a special road;

(b) a trunk road;

(c) a classified or principal road;

(d) a strategic road;

(e) a highway in England of a description prescribed by regulations made by the Secretary of State;

(f) a highway in Wales of a description prescribed by regulations made by the Welsh Ministers.

(2) In this section—

"classified road", "special road" and "trunk road" have the meaning given by section 329(1) of the Highways Act 1980;

"highway" has the meaning given by section 328 of that Act;

"principal road" has the meaning given by section 12 of that Act (and see section 13 of that Act);

"strategic road" has the meaning given by section 60(4) of the Traffic Management Act 2004.

Validity of orders

66 Challenging the validity of orders

(1) An interested person may apply to the High Court to question the validity of—

(a) a public spaces protection order, or

(b) a variation of a public spaces protection order.

"Interested person" means an individual who lives in the restricted area or who regularly works in or visits that area.

(2) The grounds on which an application under this section may be made are—

(a) that the local authority did not have power to make the order or variation, or to include particular prohibitions or requirements imposed by the order (or by the order as varied);

(b) that a requirement under this Chapter was not complied with in relation to the order or variation.

(3) An application under this section must be made within the period of 6 weeks beginning with the date on which the order or variation is made.

(4) On an application under this section the High Court may by order suspend the operation of the order or variation, or any of the prohibitions or requirements imposed by the order (or by the order as varied), until the final determination of the proceedings.

(5) If on an application under this section the High Court is satisfied that—

(a) the local authority did not have power to make the order or variation, or to include particular prohibitions or requirements imposed by the order (or by the order as varied), or

(b) the interests of the applicant have been substantially prejudiced by a failure to comply with a requirement under this Chapter,

the Court may quash the order or variation, or any of the prohibitions or requirements imposed by the order (or by the order as varied).

(6) A public spaces protection order, or any of the prohibitions or requirements imposed by the order (or by the order as varied), may be suspended under subsection (4) or quashed under subsection (5)—

(a) generally, or

(b) so far as necessary for the protection of the interests of the applicant.

(7) An interested person may not challenge the validity of a public spaces protection order, or of a variation of a public spaces protection order, in any legal proceedings (either before or after it is made) except—

(a) under this section, or

(b) under subsection (3) of section 67 (where the interested person is charged with an offence under that section).

Failure to comply with orders

67 Offence of failing to comply with order

(1) It is an offence for a person without reasonable excuse—

(a) to do anything that the person is prohibited from doing by a public spaces protection order, or

(b) to fail to comply with a requirement to which the person is subject under a public spaces protection order.

(2) A person guilty of an offence under this section is liable on summary conviction to a fine not exceeding level 3 on the standard scale.

(3) A person does not commit an offence under this section by failing to comply with a prohibition or requirement that the local authority did not have power to include in the public spaces protection order.

(4) Consuming alcohol in breach of a public spaces protection order is not an offence under this section (but see section 63).

68 Fixed penalty notices

(1) A constable or an authorised person may issue a fixed penalty notice to anyone he or she has reason to believe has committed an offence under section 63 or 67 in relation to a public spaces protection order.

(2) A fixed penalty notice is a notice offering the person to whom it is issued the opportunity of discharging any liability to conviction for the offence by payment of a fixed penalty to a local authority specified in the notice.

(3) The local authority specified under subsection (2) must be the one that made the public spaces protection order.

(4) Where a person is issued with a notice under this section in respect of an offence—

(a) no proceedings may be taken for the offence before the end of the period of 14 days following the date of the notice;

(b) the person may not be convicted of the offence if the person pays the fixed penalty before the end of that period.

(5) A fixed penalty notice must—

(a) give reasonably detailed particulars of the circumstances alleged to constitute the offence;

(b) state the period during which (because of subsection (4)(a)) proceedings will not be taken for the offence;

(c) specify the amount of the fixed penalty;

(d) state the name and address of the person to whom the fixed penalty may be paid;

(e) specify permissible methods of payment.

(6) An amount specified under subsection (5)(c) must not be more than £100.

(7) A fixed penalty notice may specify two amounts under subsection (5)(c) and specify that, if the lower of those amounts is paid within a specified period (of less than 14 days), that is the amount of the fixed penalty.

(8) Whatever other method may be specified under subsection (5)(e), payment of a fixed penalty may be made by pre-paying and posting to the person whose name is stated under subsection (5)(d), at the stated address, a letter containing the amount of the penalty (in cash or otherwise).

(9) Where a letter is sent as mentioned in subsection (8), payment is regarded as having been made at the time at which that letter would be delivered in the ordinary course of post.

(10) In any proceedings, a certificate that—

(a) purports to be signed by or on behalf of the chief finance officer of the local authority concerned, and

(b) states that payment of a fixed penalty was, or was not, received by the dated specified in the certificate,

is evidence of the facts stated.

(11) In this section—

"authorised person" means a person authorised for the purposes of this section by the local authority that made the order (or authorised by virtue of section 69(2));

"chief finance officer", in relation to a local authority, means the person with responsibility for the authority's financial affairs.

Supplemental

69 Powers of community support officers

(1) In Part 1 of Schedule 4 to the Police Reform Act 2002 (powers exercisable by community support officers), for paragraph 5 there is substituted—

"5 Alcohol consumption in restricted areas

5 Where a designation applies this paragraph to any person, that person shall, within the relevant police area, have the powers of a constable under section 63 of the Anti-social Behaviour, Crime and Policing Act 2014 (consumption of alcohol in breach of prohibition in public spaces protection order)—

(a) to impose a requirement under subsection (2) of that section; and

(b) to dispose under subsection (5) of that section of anything surrendered to the person;

and that section shall have effect in relation to the exercise of those powers by that person as if the references to a constable were references to that person."

(2) In paragraph 1 of that Schedule (power of community support officers to issue fixed penalty notices), after paragraph (e) of sub-paragraph (2) there is inserted—

"(f) the power of a constable to issue a fixed penalty notice under section 68 of the Anti-social Behaviour, Crime and Policing Act 2014 (fixed penalty notice in respect of failure to comply with public spaces protection order)."

70 Byelaws

A byelaw that prohibits, by the creation of an offence, an activity regulated by a public spaces protection order is of no effect in relation to the restricted area during the currency of the order.

71 Bodies other than local authorities with statutory functions in relation to land

(1) The Secretary of State may by order—

(a) designate a person or body (other than a local authority) that has power to make byelaws in relation to particular land, and

(b) specify land in England to which the power relates.

(2) This Chapter has effect as if—

(a) a person or body designated under subsection (1) (a "designated person") were a local authority, and

(b) land specified under that subsection were within its area.

But references in the rest of this section to a local authority are to a local authority that is not a designated person.

(3) The only prohibitions or requirements that may be imposed in a public spaces protection order made by a designated person are ones that it has power to impose (or would, but for section 70, have power to impose) by making a byelaw in respect of the restricted area.

(4) A public spaces protection order made by a designated person may not include provision regulating, in relation to a particular public space, an activity that is already regulated in relation to that space by a public spaces protection order made by a local authority.

(5) Where a public spaces protection order made by a local authority regulates, in relation to a particular public space, an activity that a public spaces protection order made by a designated person already regulates, the order made by the designated person ceases to have that effect.

(6) If a person or body that may be designated under subsection (1)(a) gives a notice in writing under this subsection, in respect of land in relation to which it has power to make byelaws, to a local authority in whose area the land is situated—

(a) no part of the land may form, or fall within, the restricted area of any public spaces protection order made by the local authority;

(b) if any part of the land—

(i) forms the restricted area of a public spaces protection order already made by the local authority, or

(ii) falls within such an area,

the order has ceases to have effect (where sub-paragraph (i) applies), or has effect as if the restricted area did not include the land in question (where sub-paragraph (ii) applies).

72 Convention rights, consultation, publicity and notification

(1) A local authority, in deciding—

(a) whether to make a public spaces protection order (under section 59) and if so what it should include,

(b) whether to extend the period for which a public spaces protection order has effect (under section 60) and if so for how long,

(c) whether to vary a public spaces protection order (under section 61) and if so how, or

(d) whether to discharge a public spaces protection order (under section 61),

must have particular regard to the rights of freedom of expression and freedom of assembly set out in articles 10 and 11 of the Convention.

(2) In subsection (1) "Convention" has the meaning given by section 21(1) of the Human Rights Act 1998.

(3) A local authority must carry out the necessary consultation and the necessary publicity, and the necessary notification (if any), before—

(a) making a public spaces protection order,

(b) extending the period for which a public spaces protection order has effect, or

(c) varying or discharging a public spaces protection order.

(4) In subsection (3)—

"the necessary consultation" means consulting with—

(a) the chief officer of police, and the local policing body, for the police area that includes the restricted area;

(b) whatever community representatives the local authority thinks it appropriate to consult;

(c) the owner or occupier of land within the restricted area;

"the necessary publicity" means—

(a) in the case of a proposed order or variation, publishing the text of it;

(b) in the case of a proposed extension or discharge, publicising the proposal;

"the necessary notification" means notifying the following authorities of the proposed order, extension, variation or discharge—

(a) the parish council or community council (if any) for the area that includes the restricted area;

(b) in the case of a public spaces protection order made or to be made by a district council in England, the county council (if any) for the area that includes the restricted area.

(5) The requirement to consult with the owner or occupier of land within the restricted area—

(a) does not apply to land that is owned and occupied by the local authority;

(b) applies only if, or to the extent that, it is reasonably practicable to consult the owner or occupier of the land.

(6) In the case of a person or body designated under section 71, the necessary consultation also includes consultation with the local authority which (ignoring subsection (2) of that section) is the authority for the area that includes the restricted area.

(7) In relation to a variation of a public spaces protection order that would increase the restricted area, the restricted area for the purposes of this section is the increased area.

73 Guidance

(1) The Secretary of State may issue—

(a) guidance to local authorities about the exercise of their functions under this Chapter and those of persons authorised by local authorities under section 63 or 68;

(b) guidance to chief officers of police about the exercise, by officers under their direction or control, of those officers' functions under this Part.

(2) The Secretary of State may revise any guidance issued under this section.

(3) The Secretary of State must arrange for any guidance issued or revised under this section to be published.

74 Interpretation of Chapter 2

(1) In this Chapter—

"alcohol" has the meaning given by section 191 of the Licensing Act 2003;

"community representative", in relation to a public spaces protection order that a local authority proposes to make or has made, means any individual or body appearing to the authority to represent the views of people who live in, work in or visit the restricted area;

"local authority" means—

(a) in relation to England, a district council, a county council for an area for which there is no district council, a London borough council, the Common Council of the City of London (in its capacity as a local authority) or the Council of the Isles of Scilly;

(b) in relation to Wales, a county council or a county borough council;

"public place" means any place to which the public or any section of the public has access, on payment or otherwise, as of right or by virtue of express or implied permission;

"restricted area" has the meaning given by section 59(4).

(2) For the purposes of this Chapter, a public spaces protection order "regulates" an activity if the activity is—

(a) prohibited by virtue of section 59(4)(a), or

(b) subjected to requirements by virtue of section 59(4)(b),

whether or not for all persons and at all times.

75 Saving and transitional provision

(1) The repeal or amendment by this Act of provisions about any of the orders specified in subsection (2) does not apply in relation to—

(a) an order specified in that subsection made before the commencement day;

(b) anything done in connection with such an order.

(2) The orders are—

(a) a gating order under Part 8A of the Highways Act 1980;

(b) an order under section 13(2) of the Criminal Justice and Police Act 2001 (power of local authority to designate public place for restrictions on alcohol consumption);

(c) a dog control order under Chapter 1 of Part 6 of the Clean Neighbourhoods and Environment Act 2005.

(3) At the end of the period of 3 years beginning with the commencement day—

(a) this Chapter has effect in relation to any order specified in subsection (2) that is still in force as if the provisions of the order were provisions of a public spaces protection order;

(b) subsection (1) ceases to have effect.

This Part, as it applies by virtue of paragraph (a), has effect with any necessary modifications (and with any modifications specified in an order under section 185(7)).

(4) In this section "commencement day" means the day on which this Chapter comes into force.

CHAPTER 3

CLOSURE OF PREMISES ASSOCIATED WITH NUISANCE OR DISORDER ETC

Closure notices

76 Power to issue closure notices

(1) A police officer of at least the rank of inspector, or the local authority, may issue a closure notice if satisfied on reasonable grounds—

(a) that the use of particular premises has resulted, or (if the notice is not issued) is likely soon to result, in nuisance to members of the public, or

(b) that there has been, or (if the notice is not issued) is likely soon to be, disorder near those premises associated with the use of those premises,

and that the notice is necessary to prevent the nuisance or disorder from continuing, recurring or occurring.

(2) A closure notice is a notice prohibiting access to the premises for a period specified in the notice.

For the maximum period, see section 77.

(3) A closure notice may prohibit access—

(a) by all persons except those specified, or by all persons except those of a specified description;

(b) at all times, or at all times except those specified;

(c) in all circumstances, or in all circumstances except those specified.

(4) A closure notice may not prohibit access by—

(a) people who habitually live on the premises, or

(b) the owner of the premises,

and accordingly they must be specified under subsection (3)(a).

(5) A closure notice must—

(a) identify the premises;

(b) explain the effect of the notice;

(c) state that failure to comply with the notice is an offence;

(d) state that an application will be made under section 80 for a closure order;

(e) specify when and where the application will be heard;

(f) explain the effect of a closure order;

(g) give information about the names of, and means of contacting, persons and organisations in the area that provide advice about housing and legal matters.

(6) A closure notice may be issued only if reasonable efforts have been made to inform—

(a) people who live on the premises (whether habitually or not), and

(b) any person who has control of or responsibility for the premises or who has an interest in them,

that the notice is going to be issued.

(7) Before issuing a closure notice the police officer or local authority must ensure that any body or individual the officer or authority thinks appropriate has been consulted.

(8) The Secretary of State may by regulations specify premises or descriptions of premises in relation to which a closure notice may not be issued.

77 Duration of closure notices

(1) The maximum period that may be specified in a closure notice is 24 hours unless subsection (2) applies.

(2) The maximum period is 48 hours—

(a) if, in the case of a notice issued by a police officer, the officer is of at least the rank of superintendent, or

(b) if, in the case of a notice issued by a local authority, the notice is signed by the chief executive officer of the authority or a person designated by him or her for the purposes of this subsection.

(3) In calculating when the period of 48 hours ends, Christmas Day is to be disregarded.

(4) The period specified in a closure notice to which subsection (2) does not apply may be extended by up to 24 hours—

(a) if, in the case of a notice issued by a police officer, an extension notice is issued by an officer of at least the rank of superintendent, or

(b) if, in the case of a notice issued by a local authority, the authority issues an extension notice signed by the chief executive officer of the authority or a person designated by the chief executive officer for the purposes of this subsection.

(5) An extension notice is a notice which—

(a) identifies the closure notice to which it relates, and

(b) specifies the period of the extension.

(6) In this section "chief executive officer", in relation to a local authority, means the head of the paid service of the authority designated under section 4 of the Local Government and Housing Act 1989.

78 Cancellation or variation of closure notices

(1) This section applies where a closure notice is in force and the relevant officer or authority is no longer satisfied as mentioned in section 76(1), either—

(a) as regards the premises as a whole, or

(b) as regards a particular part of the premises.

(2) In a case within subsection (1)(a) the relevant officer or authority must issue a cancellation notice.

A cancellation notice is a notice cancelling the closure notice.

(3) In a case within subsection (1)(b) the relevant officer or authority must issue a variation notice.

A variation notice is a notice varying the closure notice so that it does not apply to the part of the premises referred to in subsection (1)(b).

(4) A cancellation notice or a variation notice that relates to a closure notice which was—

(a) issued by a local authority, and

(b) signed as mentioned in section 77(2)(b),

must be signed by the person who signed the closure notice (or, if that person is not available, by another person who could have signed as mentioned in section 77(2)(b)).

(5) A cancellation notice or a variation notice that relates to a closure notice which was—

(a) issued by a local authority, and

(b) extended under section 77(4)(b),

must be signed by the person who signed the extension notice (or, if that person is not available, by another person who could have signed the extension notice).

(6) In this section "the relevant officer or authority" means—

(a) in the case of a closure notice issued by a police officer and not extended under section 77(4)(a), that officer (or, if that officer is not available, another officer of the same or higher rank);

(b) in the case of a closure notice issued by a police officer and extended under section 77(4)(a), the officer who issued the extension notice (or, if that officer is not available, another officer of the same or higher rank);

(c) in the case of a closure notice issued by a local authority, that authority.

79 Service of notices

(1) A closure notice, an extension notice, a cancellation notice or a variation notice must be served by—

(a) a constable, in the case of a notice issued by a police officer;

(b) a representative of the authority that issued the notice, in the case of a notice issued by a local authority.

(2) The constable or local authority representative must if possible—

(a) fix a copy of the notice to at least one prominent place on the premises,

(b) fix a copy of the notice to each normal means of access to the premises,

(c) fix a copy of the notice to any outbuildings that appear to the constable or representative to be used with or as part of the premises,

(d) give a copy of the notice to at least one person who appears to the constable or representative to have control of or responsibility for the premises, and

(e) give a copy of the notice to the people who live on the premises and to any person who does not live there but was informed (under section 76(6)) that the notice was going to be issued.

(3) If the constable or local authority representative reasonably believes, at the time of serving the notice, that there are persons occupying another part of the building or other structure in which the premises are situated whose access to that part will be impeded if a closure order is made under section 80, the constable or representative must also if possible serve the notice on those persons.

(4) The constable or local authority representative may enter any premises, using reasonable force if necessary, for the purposes of complying with subsection (2)(a).

(5) In this section "representative", in relation to a local authority, means—

(a) an employee of the authority, or

(b) a person, or employee or a person, acting on behalf of the authority.

Closure orders

80 Power of court to make closure orders

(1) Whenever a closure notice is issued an application must be made to a magistrates' court for a closure order (unless the notice has been cancelled under section 78).

(2) An application for a closure order must be made—

(a) by a constable, if the closure notice was issued by a police officer;

(b) by the authority that issued the closure notice, if the notice was issued by a local authority.

(3) The application must be heard by the magistrates' court not later than 48 hours after service of the closure notice.

(4) In calculating when the period of 48 hours ends, Christmas Day is to be disregarded.

(5) The court may make a closure order if it is satisfied—

(a) that a person has engaged, or (if the order is not made) is likely to engage, in disorderly, offensive or criminal behaviour on the premises, or

(b) that the use of the premises has resulted, or (if the order is not made) is likely to result, in serious nuisance to members of the public, or

(c) that there has been, or (if the order is not made) is likely to be, disorder near those premises associated with the use of those premises,

and that the order is necessary to prevent the behaviour, nuisance or disorder from continuing, recurring or occurring.

(6) A closure order is an order prohibiting access to the premises for a period specified in the order.

The period may not exceed 3 months.

(7) A closure order may prohibit access—

(a) by all persons, or by all persons except those specified, or by all persons except those of a specified description;

(b) at all times, or at all times except those specified;

(c) in all circumstances, or in all circumstances except those specified.

(8) A closure order—

(a) may be made in respect of the whole or any part of the premises;

(b) may include provision about access to a part of the building or structure of which the premises form part.

(9) The court must notify the relevant licensing authority if it makes a closure order in relation to premises in respect of which a premises licence is in force.

81 Temporary orders

(1) This section applies where an application has been made to a magistrates' court under section 80 for a closure order.

(2) If the court does not make a closure order it may nevertheless order that the closure notice continues in force for a specified further period of not more than 48 hours, if satisfied—

(a) that the use of particular premises has resulted, or (if the notice is not continued) is likely soon to result, in nuisance to members of the public, or

(b) that there has been, or (if the notice is not continued) is likely soon to be, disorder near those premises associated with the use of those premises,

and that the continuation of the notice is necessary to prevent the nuisance or disorder from continuing, recurring or occurring.

(3) The court may adjourn the hearing of the application for a period of not more than 14 days to enable—

(a) the occupier of the premises,

(b) the person with control of or responsibility for the premises, or

(c) any other person with an interest in the premises,

to show why a closure order should not be made.

(4) If the court adjourns the hearing under subsection (3) it may order that the closure notice continues in force until the end of the period of the adjournment.

82 Extension of closure orders

(1) At any time before the expiry of a closure order, an application may be made to a justice of the peace, by complaint, for an extension (or further extension) of the period for which the order is in force.

(2) Those entitled to make an application under this section are—

(a) where the closure order was made on the application of a constable, a police officer of at least the rank of inspector;

(b) where the closure order was made on the application of a local authority, that authority.

(3) A police officer or local authority may make an application under this section only if satisfied on reasonable grounds that it is necessary for the period of the order to be extended to prevent the occurrence, recurrence or continuance of—

(a) disorderly, offensive or criminal behaviour on the premises,

(b) serious nuisance to members of the public resulting from the use of the premises, or

(c) disorder near the premises associated with the use of the premises,

and also satisfied that the appropriate consultee has been consulted about the intention to make the application.

(4) In subsection (3) "the appropriate consultee" means—

(a) the local authority, in the case of an application by a police officer;

(b) the chief officer of police for the area in which the premises are situated, in the case of an application by a local authority.

(5) Where an application is made under this section, the justice of the peace may issue a summons directed to—

(a) any person on whom the closure notice was served under section 79, or

(b) any other person who appears to the justice to have an interest in the premises but on whom the closure notice was not served,

requiring the person to appear before the magistrates' court to respond to the application.

(6) If a summons is issued under subsection (5), a notice stating the date, time and place of the hearing of the application must be served on the persons to whom the summons is directed.

(7) If the magistrates' court is satisfied as mentioned in subsection (3)(a), (b) or (c), it may make an order extending (or further extending) the period of the closure order by a period not exceeding 3 months.

(8) The period of a closure order may not be extended so that the order lasts for more than 6 months.

83 Discharge of closure orders

(1) At any time before the expiry of a closure order, an application may be made to a justice of the peace, by complaint, for the order to be discharged.

(2) Those entitled to make an application under this section are—
- (a) a constable, where the closure order was made on the application of a constable;
- (b) the authority that applied for the closure order, where the order was made on the application of a local authority;
- (c) a person on whom the closure notice was served under section 79;
- (d) anyone else who has an interest in the premises but on whom the closure notice was not served.

(3) Where a person other than a constable makes an application under this section for the discharge of an order that was made on the application of a constable, the justice may issue a summons directed to a constable considered appropriate by the justice requiring him or her to appear before the magistrates' court to respond to the application.

(4) If a summons is issued under subsection (3), a notice stating the date, time and place of the hearing of the application must be served on—
- (a) the constable to whom the summons is directed;
- (b) the persons mentioned in subsection (2)(c) and (d) (other than the complainant).

(5) Where—
- (a) the order in question was made on the application of a local authority, and
- (b) a person other than that authority makes an application under this section for the discharge of the order,

the justice may issue a summons directed to that authority requiring it to appear before the magistrates' court to respond to the application.

(6) If a summons is issued under subsection (5), a notice stating the date, time and place of the hearing of the application must be served on—
- (a) the authority mentioned in that subsection;
- (b) the persons mentioned in subsection (2)(c) and (d) (other than the complainant).

(7) The magistrates' court may not make an order discharging the closure order unless satisfied that the closure order is no longer necessary to prevent the occurrence, recurrence or continuance of—
- (a) disorderly, offensive or criminal behaviour on the premises,
- (b) serious nuisance to members of the public resulting from the use of the premises, or
- (c) disorder near the premises associated with the use of the premises.

Appeals

84 Appeals

(1) An appeal against a decision to make or extend a closure order may be made by—
- (a) a person on whom the closure notice was served under section 79;

(b) anyone else who has an interest in the premises but on whom the closure notice was not served.

(2) A constable may appeal against—

(a) a decision not to make a closure order applied for by a constable;

(b) a decision not to extend a closure order made on the application of a constable;

(c) a decision (under section 81) not to order the continuation in force of a closure notice issued by a constable.

(3) A local authority may appeal against—

(a) a decision not to make a closure order applied for by that authority;

(b) a decision not to extend a closure order made on the application of that authority;

(c) a decision (under section 81) not to order the continuation in force of a closure notice issued by that authority.

(4) An appeal under this section is to the Crown Court.

(5) An appeal under this section must be made within the period of 21 days beginning with the date of the decision to which it relates.

(6) On an appeal under this section the Crown Court may make whatever order it thinks appropriate.

(7) The Crown Court must notify the relevant licensing authority if it makes a closure order in relation to premises in respect of which a premises licence is in force.

Enforcement

85 Enforcement of closure orders

(1) An authorised person may—

(a) enter premises in respect of which a closure order is in force;

(b) do anything necessary to secure the premises against entry.

(2) In this section "authorised person"—

(a) in relation to a closure order made on the application of a constable, means a constable or a person authorised by the chief officer of police for the area in which the premises are situated;

(b) in relation to a closure order made on the application of a local authority, means a person authorised by that authority.

(3) A person acting under subsection (1) may use reasonable force.

(4) A person seeking to enter premises under subsection (1) must, if required to do so by or on behalf of the owner, occupier or other person in charge of the premises, produce evidence of his or her identity and authority before entering the premises.

(5) An authorised person may also enter premises in respect of which a closure order is in force to carry out essential maintenance or repairs to the premises.

86 Offences

(1) A person who without reasonable excuse remains on or enters premises in contravention of a closure notice (including a notice continued in force under section 81) commits an offence.

(2) A person who without reasonable excuse remains on or enters premises in contravention of a closure order commits an offence.

(3) A person who without reasonable excuse obstructs a person acting under section 79 or 85(1) commits an offence.

(4) A person guilty of an offence under subsection (1) or (3) is liable on summary conviction—

- (a) to imprisonment for a period not exceeding 3 months, or
- (b) to a fine,

or to both.

(5) A person guilty of an offence under subsection (2) is liable on summary conviction—

- (a) to imprisonment for a period not exceeding 51 weeks, or
- (b) to a fine,

or to both.

(6) In relation to an offence committed before the commencement of section 281(5) of the Criminal Justice Act 2003, the reference in subsection (5)(a) to 51 weeks is to be read as a reference to 6 months.

Supplemental

87 Access to other premises

(1) Where—

- (a) access to premises is prohibited or restricted by, or as a result of, an order under section 80, 81, 82 or 84,
- (b) those premises are part of a building or structure, and
- (c) there is another part of that building or structure that is not subject to the prohibition or restriction,

an occupier or owner of that other part may apply to the appropriate court for an order under this section.

(2) The appropriate court is—

- (a) the magistrates' court, in the case of an order under section 80, 81 or 82;
- (b) the Crown Court, in the case of an order under section 84.

(3) Notice of an application under this section must be given to—

- (a) whatever constable the court thinks appropriate;
- (b) the local authority;
- (c) a person on whom the closure notice was served under section 79;
- (d) anyone else who has an interest in the premises but on whom the closure notice was not served.

(4) On an application under this section the court may make whatever order it thinks appropriate in relation to access to any part of the building or structure mentioned in subsection (1).

It does not matter whether provision has been made under section 80(8)(b).

88 Reimbursement of costs

(1) A local policing body or a local authority that incurs expenditure for the purpose of clearing, securing or maintaining premises in respect of which a closure order is in force may apply to the court that made the order for an order under this section.

(2) On an application under this section the court may make whatever order it thinks appropriate for the reimbursement (in full or in part) by the owner or occupier of the premises of the expenditure mentioned in subsection (1).

(3) An application for an order under this section may not be heard unless it is made before the end of the period of 3 months starting with the day on which the closure order ceases to have effect.

(4) An order under this section may be made only against a person who has been served with the application for the order.

(5) An application under this section must also be served on—

(a) the local policing body for the area in which the premises are situated, if the application is made by a local authority;

(b) the local authority, if the application is made by a local policing body.

89 Exemption from liability

(1) A police officer, or the chief officer of police under whose direction or control he or she acts, is not liable for damages in proceedings for—

(a) judicial review, or

(b) the tort of negligence or misfeasance in public office,

arising out of anything done or omitted to be done by the police officer in the exercise or purported exercise of a power under this Chapter.

(2) A local authority is not liable for damages in proceedings for—

(a) judicial review, or

(b) the tort of negligence or misfeasance in public office,

arising out of anything done or omitted to be done by the authority in the exercise or purported exercise of a power under this Chapter.

(3) Subsections (1) and (2) do not apply to an act or omission shown to have been in bad faith.

(4) Subsections (1) and (2) do not apply so as to prevent an award of damages made in respect of an act or omission on the ground that the act or omission was unlawful by virtue of section 6(1) of the Human Rights Act 1998.

(5) This section does not affect any other exemption from liability (whether at common law or otherwise).

90 Compensation

(1) A person who claims to have incurred financial loss in consequence of a closure notice or a closure order may apply to the appropriate court for compensation.

(2) The appropriate court is—
- (a) the magistrates' court that considered the application for a closure order (except where paragraph (b) applies);
- (b) the Crown Court, in the case of a closure order that was made or extended by an order of that Court on an appeal under section 84.

(3) An application under this section may not be heard unless it is made before the end of the period of 3 months starting with whichever of the following is applicable—
- (a) the day on which the closure notice was cancelled under section 78;
- (b) the day on which a closure order was refused;
- (c) the day on which the closure order ceased to have effect.

(4) For the purposes of subsection (3)(b) the day on which a closure order was refused is—
- (a) the day on which the magistrates' court decided not to make a closure order (except where paragraph (b) applies);
- (b) the day on which the Crown Court dismissed an appeal against a decision not to make a closure order.

(5) On an application under this section the court may order the payment of compensation out of central funds if it is satisfied—
- (a) that the applicant is not associated with the use of the premises, or the behaviour on the premises, on the basis of which the closure notice was issued or the closure order made,
- (b) if the applicant is the owner or occupier of the premises, that the applicant took reasonable steps to prevent that use or behaviour,
- (c) that the applicant has incurred financial loss in consequence of the notice or order, and
- (d) that having regard to all the circumstances it is appropriate to order payment of compensation in respect of that loss.

(6) In this section "central funds" has the same meaning as in enactments providing for the payment of costs.

91 Guidance

(1) The Secretary of State may issue—
- (a) guidance to chief officers of police about the exercise, by officers under their direction or control, of those officers' functions under this Chapter;
- (b) guidance to local authorities about the exercise of their functions under this Chapter and those of their representatives (within the meaning of section 79).

(2) The Secretary of State may revise any guidance issued under this section.

(3) The Secretary of State must arrange for any guidance issued or revised under this section to be published.

92 Interpretation of Chapter 3

(1) In this Chapter—

"cancellation notice" has the meaning given by section 78(2);

"criminal behaviour" means behaviour that constitutes a criminal offence;

"extension notice" has the meaning given by section 77(5);

"local authority" means—

(a) in relation to England, a district council, a county council for an area for which there is no district council, a London borough council, the Common Council of the City of London or the Council of the Isles of Scilly;

(b) in relation to Wales, a county council or a county borough council;

"offensive behaviour" means behaviour by a person that causes or is likely to cause harassment, alarm or distress to one or more other persons not of the same household as that person;

"owner", in relation to premises, means—

(a) a person (other than a mortgagee not in possession) entitled to dispose of the fee simple of the premises, whether in possession or in reversion;

(b) a person who holds or is entitled to the rents and profits of the premises under a lease that (when granted) was for a term of not less then 3 years;

"premises" includes—

(a) any land or other place (whether enclosed or not);

(b) any outbuildings that are, or are used as, part of premises;

"premises licence" has the meaning given by section 11 of the Licensing Act 2003;

"relevant licensing authority" has the meaning given by section 12 of that Act;

"variation notice" has the meaning given by section 78(3).

(2) A reference in this Chapter to "the local authority", in relation to any premises or a notice or order relating to any premises, is a reference to the local authority (or, as the case may be, any of the local authorities) within whose area the premises are situated.

(3) A reference in this Chapter to "the premises", in relation to a closure notice or a closure order, is a reference to the premises to which the notice or order relates.

93 Saving and transitional provision

(1) The repeal or amendment by this Act of provisions about any of the notices specified in subsection (2) or orders specified in subsection (3) does not apply in relation to—

(a) any such notice issued or order made before the commencement day;

(b) anything done in connection with any such notice or order.

(2) The notices are—

(a) a notice issued under section 1 of the Anti-social Behaviour Act 2003;

(b) a notice issued under section 11A of that Act.

(3) The orders are—

(a) an order made under section 2 of the Anti-social Behaviour Act 2003;

(b) an order made under section 11B of that Act;

(c) an order made under section 40 of that Act;
(d) an order made under section 161 of the Licensing Act 2003;
(e) an order made under section 165(2)(b), (c) or (d) of that Act.

(4) A person deciding whether to issue a closure notice may take into account things that—
(a) happened before the commencement day, and
(b) would have given rise to the power to issue one of the notices specified in subsection (2) or to make an order specified in subsection (3)(c) or (d).

(5) A court deciding whether to make a closure order may take into account things that—
(a) happened before the commencement day, and
(b) would have given rise to the power to make an order specified in subsection (3)(a), (b) or (e).

(6) Subsections (4) and (5) apply only during the period of 3 months beginning with the commencement day.

(7) In this section "commencement day" means the day on which this Chapter comes into force.

PART 5

RECOVERY OF POSSESSION OF DWELLING-HOUSES: ANTI-SOCIAL BEHAVIOUR GROUNDS

Absolute ground for possession: secure tenancies

94 New ground for serious offences or breach of prohibitions etc

(1) After section 84 of the Housing Act 1985 (secure tenancies: grounds and orders for possession) there is inserted—

"84A Absolute ground for possession for anti-social behaviour

(1) If the court is satisfied that any of the following conditions is met, it must make an order for the possession of a dwelling-house let under a secure tenancy.

This is subject to subsection (2) (and to any available defence based on the tenant's Convention rights, within the meaning of the Human Rights Act 1998).

(2) Subsection (1) applies only where the landlord has complied with any obligations it has under section 85ZA (review of decision to seek possession).

(3) Condition 1 is that—
(a) the tenant, or a person residing in or visiting the dwelling-house, has been convicted of a serious offence, and
(b) the serious offence—
(i) was committed (wholly or partly) in, or in the locality of, the dwelling-house,

(ii) was committed elsewhere against a person with a right (of whatever description) to reside in, or occupy housing accommodation in the locality of, the dwelling-house, or

(iii) was committed elsewhere against the landlord of the dwelling-house, or a person employed (whether or not by the landlord) in connection with the exercise of the landlord's housing management functions, and directly or indirectly related to or affected those functions.

(4) Condition 2 is that a court has found in relevant proceedings that the tenant, or a person residing in or visiting the dwelling-house, has breached a provision of an injunction under section 1 of the Anti-social Behaviour, Crime and Policing Act 2014, other than a provision requiring a person to participate in a particular activity, and—

(a) the breach occurred in, or in the locality of, the dwelling-house, or

(b) the breach occurred elsewhere and the provision breached was a provision intended to prevent—

(i) conduct that is capable of causing nuisance or annoyance to a person with a right (of whatever description) to reside in, or occupy housing accommodation in the locality of, the dwelling-house, or

(ii) conduct that is capable of causing nuisance or annoyance to the landlord of the dwelling-house, or a person employed (whether or not by the landlord) in connection with the exercise of the landlord's housing management functions, and that is directly or indirectly related to or affects those functions.

(5) Condition 3 is that the tenant, or a person residing in or visiting the dwelling-house, has been convicted of an offence under section 30 of the Anti-social Behaviour, Crime and Policing Act 2014 consisting of a breach of a provision of a criminal behaviour order prohibiting a person from doing anything described in the order, and the offence involved—

(a) a breach that occurred in, or in the locality of, the dwelling-house, or

(b) a breach that occurred elsewhere of a provision intended to prevent—

(i) behaviour that causes or is likely to cause harassment, alarm or distress to a person with a right (of whatever description) to reside in, or occupy housing accommodation in the locality of, the dwelling-house, or

(ii) behaviour that causes or is likely to cause harassment, alarm or distress to the landlord of the dwelling-house, or a person employed (whether or not by the landlord) in connection with the exercise of the landlord's housing management functions, and that is directly or indirectly related to or affects those functions.

(6) Condition 4 is that—

(a) the dwelling-house is or has been subject to a closure order under section 80 of the Anti-social Behaviour, Crime and Policing Act 2014, and

(b) access to the dwelling-house has been prohibited (under the closure order or under a closure notice issued under section 76 of that Act) for a continuous period of more than 48 hours.

(7) Condition 5 is that—

(a) the tenant, or a person residing in or visiting the dwelling-house, has been convicted of an offence under—

(i) section 80(4) of the Environmental Protection Act 1990 (breach of abatement notice in relation to statutory nuisance), or

(ii) section 82(8) of that Act (breach of court order to abate statutory nuisance etc.), and

(b) the nuisance concerned was noise emitted from the dwelling-house which was a statutory nuisance for the purposes of Part 3 of that Act by virtue of section 79(1)(g) of that Act (noise emitted from premises so as to be prejudicial to health or a nuisance).

(8) Condition 1, 2, 3, 4 or 5 is not met if—

(a) there is an appeal against the conviction, finding or order concerned which has not been finally determined, abandoned or withdrawn, or

(b) the final determination of the appeal results in the conviction, finding or order being overturned.

(9) In this section—

"relevant proceedings" means proceedings for contempt of court or proceedings under Schedule 2 to the Anti-social Behaviour, Crime and Policing Act 2014;

"serious offence" means an offence which—

(a) was committed on or after the day on which subsection (3) comes into force,

(b) is specified, or falls within a description specified, in Schedule 2A at the time the offence was committed and at the time the court is considering the matter, and

(c) is not an offence that is triable only summarily by virtue of section 22 of the Magistrates' Courts Act 1980 (either-way offences where value involved is small).

(10) The Secretary of State may by order amend Schedule 2A as it applies in relation to dwelling-houses in England by—

(a) adding an indictable offence;

(b) removing an offence.

(11) The Welsh Ministers may by order amend Schedule 2A as it applies in relation to dwelling-houses in Wales by—

(a) adding an indictable offence;

(b) removing an offence.

(12) An order under subsection (10) or (11)—

(a) is to be made by statutory instrument;

(b) may make different provision for different purposes;

(c) may include incidental, supplementary, consequential, transitional or saving provision.

(13) A statutory instrument containing an order under subsection (10) or (11) may not be made unless a draft of the instrument has been laid before and approved by a resolution of—

(a) each House of Parliament (in the case of an order of the Secretary of State), or

(b) the National Assembly for Wales (in the case of an order of the Welsh Ministers)."

(2) After Schedule 2 to that Act there is inserted the Schedule set out in Schedule 3 to this Act.

95 Notice requirements for new ground

After section 83 of the Housing Act 1985 (proceedings for possession or termination: notice requirements) there is inserted—

"83ZA Notice requirements in relation to proceedings for possession on absolute ground for anti-social behaviour

(1) This section applies in relation to proceedings for possession of a dwelling-house under section 84A (absolute ground for possession for anti-social behaviour), including proceedings where possession is also sought on one or more of the grounds set out in Schedule 2.

(2) The court must not entertain the proceedings unless the landlord has served on the tenant a notice under this section.

(3) The notice must—

(a) state that the court will be asked to make an order under section 84A for the possession of the dwelling-house,

(b) set out the reasons for the landlord's decision to apply for the order (including the condition or conditions in section 84A on which the landlord proposes to rely), and

(c) inform the tenant of any right that the tenant may have under section 85ZA to request a review of the landlord's decision and of the time within which the request must be made.

(4) In a case where possession is also sought on one or more of the grounds set out in Schedule 2, the notice must also—

(a) specify the ground on which the court will be asked to make the order, and

(b) give particulars of that ground.

(5) A notice which states that the landlord proposes to rely upon condition 1, 3 or 5 in section 84A—

(a) must also state the conviction on which the landlord proposes to rely, and

(b) must be served on the tenant within—

(i) the period of 12 months beginning with the day of the conviction, or

(ii) if there is an appeal against the conviction, the period of 12 months beginning with the day on which the appeal is finally determined or abandoned.

(6) A notice which states that the landlord proposes to rely upon condition 2 in section 84A—

(a) must also state the finding on which the landlord proposes to rely, and

(b) must be served on the tenant within—

(i) the period of 12 months beginning with the day on which the court has made the finding, or

(ii) if there is an appeal against the finding, the period of 12 months beginning with the day on which the appeal is finally determined, abandoned or withdrawn.

(7) A notice which states that the landlord proposes to rely upon condition 4 in section 84A—

(a) must also state the closure order concerned, and

(b) must be served on the tenant within—

(i) the period of 3 months beginning with the day on which the closure order was made, or

(ii) if there is an appeal against the making of the order, the period of 3 months beginning with the day on which the appeal is finally determined, abandoned or withdrawn.

(8) A notice under this section must also inform the tenant that, if the tenant needs help or advice about the notice and what to do about it, the tenant should take it immediately to a Citizens' Advice Bureau, a housing aid centre, a law centre or a solicitor.

(9) The notice—

(a) must also specify the date after which proceedings for the possession of the dwelling-house may be begun, and

(b) ceases to be in force 12 months after the date so specified.

(10) The date specified in accordance with subsection (9)(a) must not be earlier than—

(a) in the case of a periodic tenancy, the date on which the tenancy could, apart from this Part, be brought to an end by notice to quit given by the landlord on the same day as the notice under this section;

(b) in the case of a secure tenancy for a term certain, one month after the date of the service of the notice.

(11) Where a notice under this section is served with respect to a secure tenancy for a term certain, it has effect also with respect to any periodic tenancy arising on the termination of that tenancy by virtue of section 86; and subsection (10)(a) does not apply to the notice."

96 Review requirements for new ground

After section 85 of the Housing Act 1985 (extended discretion of court in certain proceedings for possession) there is inserted—

"85ZA Review of decision to seek possession on absolute ground for anti-social behaviour

(1) A tenant may request a review of a landlord's decision to seek an order for possession of a dwelling-house under section 84A if the interest of the landlord belongs to—

(a) a local housing authority, or

(b) a housing action trust.

(2) Such a request must be made in writing before the end of the period of 7 days beginning with the day on which the notice under section 83ZA is served.

(3) On a request being duly made to it, the landlord must review its decision.

(4) The landlord must notify the tenant in writing of the decision on the review.

(5) If the decision is to confirm the original decision, the landlord must also notify the tenant of the reasons for the decision.

(6) The review must be carried out, and the tenant notified, before the day specified in the notice under section 83ZA as the day after which proceedings for the possession of the dwelling-house may be begun.

(7) The Secretary of State may by regulations make provision about the procedure to be followed in connection with a review under this section that relates to an order for possession of a dwelling-house in England.

(8) The Welsh Ministers may by regulations make provision about the procedure to be followed in connection with a review under this section that relates to an order for possession of a dwelling-house in Wales.

(9) Regulations under subsections (7) and (8) may, in particular, make provision—

(a) requiring the decision on review to be made by a person of appropriate seniority who was not involved in the original decision, and

(b) as to the circumstances in which the person concerned is entitled to an oral hearing, and whether and by whom the person may be represented at such a hearing.

(10) Regulations under this section—

(a) may contain transitional or saving provision;

(b) are to be made by statutory instrument which—

(i) in the case of regulations made by the Secretary of State, is subject to annulment in pursuance of a resolution of either House of Parliament;

(ii) in the case of regulations made by the Welsh Ministers, is subject to annulment in pursuance of a resolution of the National Assembly for Wales."

Absolute ground for possession: assured tenancies

97 Corresponding new ground and notice requirements for assured tenancies

(1) In Part 1 of Schedule 2 to the Housing Act 1988 (assured tenancies: grounds on which court must order possession), after ground 7 there is inserted—

"Ground 7A

Any of the following conditions is met.

Condition 1 is that—

(a) the tenant, or a person residing in or visiting the dwelling-house, has been convicted of a serious offence, and

(b) the serious offence—

(i) was committed (wholly or partly) in, or in the locality of, the dwelling-house,

(ii) was committed elsewhere against a person with a right (of whatever description) to reside in, or occupy housing accommodation in the locality of, the dwelling-house, or

(iii) was committed elsewhere against the landlord of the dwelling-house, or a person employed (whether or not by the landlord) in connection with the exercise of the landlord's housing management functions, and directly or indirectly related to or affected those functions.

Condition 2 is that a court has found in relevant proceedings that the tenant, or a person residing in or visiting the dwelling-house, has breached a provision of an injunction under section 1 of the Anti-social Behaviour, Crime and Policing Act 2014, other than a provision requiring a person to participate in a particular activity, and—

(a) the breach occurred in, or in the locality of, the dwelling-house, or

(b) the breach occurred elsewhere and the provision breached was a provision intended to prevent—

(i) conduct that is capable of causing nuisance or annoyance to a person with a right (of whatever description) to reside in, or occupy housing accommodation in the locality of, the dwelling-house, or

(ii) conduct that is capable of causing nuisance or annoyance to the landlord of the dwelling-house, or a person employed (whether or not by the landlord) in connection with the exercise of the landlord's housing management functions, and that is directly or indirectly related to or affects those functions.

Condition 3 is that the tenant, or a person residing in or visiting the dwelling-house, has been convicted of an offence under section 30 of the Anti-social Behaviour, Crime and Policing Act 2014 consisting of a breach of a provision of a criminal behaviour order prohibiting a person from doing anything described in the order, and the offence involved—

(a) a breach that occurred in, or in the locality of, the dwelling-house, or

(b) a breach that occurred elsewhere of a provision intended to prevent—

(i) behaviour that causes or is likely to cause harassment, alarm or distress to a person with a right (of whatever description) to reside in, or occupy housing accommodation in the locality of, the dwelling-house, or

(ii) behaviour that causes or is likely to cause harassment, alarm or distress to the landlord of the dwelling-house, or a person employed (whether or not by the landlord) in connection with the exercise of the landlord's housing management functions, and that is directly or indirectly related to or affects those functions.

Condition 4 is that—

(a) the dwelling-house is or has been subject to a closure order under section 80 of the Anti-social Behaviour, Crime and Policing Act 2014, and

(b) access to the dwelling-house has been prohibited (under the closure order or under a closure notice issued under section 76 of that Act) for a continuous period of more than 48 hours.

Condition 5 is that—

(a) the tenant, or a person residing in or visiting the dwelling-house, has been convicted of an offence under—

(i) section 80(4) of the Environmental Protection Act 1990 (breach of abatement notice in relation to statutory nuisance), or

(ii) section 82(8) of that Act (breach of court order to abate statutory nuisance etc.), and

(b) the nuisance concerned was noise emitted from the dwelling-house which was a statutory nuisance for the purposes of Part 3 of that Act by virtue of section 79(1)(g) of that Act (noise emitted from premises so as to be prejudicial to health or a nuisance).

Condition 1, 2, 3, 4 or 5 is not met if—

(a) there is an appeal against the conviction, finding or order concerned which has not been finally determined, abandoned or withdrawn, or

(b) the final determination of the appeal results in the conviction, finding or order being overturned.

In this ground—

"relevant proceedings" means proceedings for contempt of court or proceedings under Schedule 2 to the Anti-social Behaviour, Crime and Policing Act 2014;

"serious offence" means an offence which—

(a) was committed on or after the day on which this ground comes into force,

(b) is specified, or falls within a description specified, in Schedule 2A to the Housing Act 1985 at the time the offence was committed and at the time the court is considering the matter, and

(c) is not an offence that is triable only summarily by virtue of section 22 of the Magistrates' Courts Act 1980 (either-way offences where value involved is small)."

(2) In section 8 of that Act (notice of proceedings for possession)—

(a) in subsection (3)(b), for "subsections (4)" there is substituted "subsections (3A)";

(b) after subsection (3) there is inserted—

"(3A) If a notice under this section specifies in accordance with subsection (3)(a) Ground 7A in Schedule 2 to this Act (whether with or without other grounds), the date specified in the notice as mentioned in subsection (3)(b) is not to be earlier than—

(a) in the case of a periodic tenancy, the earliest date on which, apart from section 5(1), the tenancy could be brought to an end by a notice to quit given by the landlord on the same date as the date of service of the notice under this section;

(b) in the case of a fixed term tenancy, one month after the date on which the notice was served.";

(c) in subsection (4), for "(whether with or without other grounds)" there is substituted "(whether without other grounds or with any ground other than Ground 7A)";

(d) in subsection (4A), after "other than Ground" there is inserted "7A or";

(e) after subsection (4B) there is inserted—

"(4C) A notice under this section that specifies in accordance with subsection (3)(a) Ground 7A in Schedule 2 to this Act (whether with or without other grounds) must be served on the tenant within the time period specified in subsection (4D), (4E) or (4F).

(4D) Where the landlord proposes to rely on condition 1, 3 or 5 in Ground 7A, the notice must be served on the tenant within—

(a) the period of 12 months beginning with the day of the conviction, or

(b) if there is an appeal against the conviction, the period of 12 months beginning with the day on which the appeal is finally determined or abandoned.

(4E) Where the landlord proposes to rely on condition 2 in Ground 7A, the notice must be served on the tenant within—

(a) the period of 12 months beginning with the day on which the court has made the finding, or

(b) if there is an appeal against the finding, the period of 12 months beginning with the day on which the appeal is finally determined, abandoned or withdrawn.

(4F) Where the landlord proposes to rely on condition 4 in Ground 7A, the notice must be served on the tenant within—

(a) the period of 3 months beginning with the day on which the closure order was made, or

(b) if there is an appeal against the making of the order, the period of 3 months beginning with the day on which the appeal is finally determined, abandoned or withdrawn.";

(f) in subsection (5), after "Ground" there is inserted "7A or".

Discretionary grounds: secure and assured tenancies

98 Conduct causing nuisance to landlord etc

(1) In Part 1 of Schedule 2 to the Housing Act 1985 (grounds on which court may order possession in relation to secure tenancies if it considers it reasonable), in Ground 2, at the end of paragraph (a) (but before the "or") there is inserted—

"(aa) has been guilty of conduct causing or likely to cause a nuisance or annoyance to the landlord of the dwelling-house, or a person employed (whether or not by the landlord) in connection with the exercise of the landlord's housing management functions, and that is directly or indirectly related to or affects those functions,".

(2) In Part 2 of Schedule 2 to the Housing Act 1988 (grounds on which court may order possession in relation to assured tenancies if it considers it reasonable), in Ground 14, at the end of paragraph (a) (but before the "or") there is inserted—

"(aa) has been guilty of conduct causing or likely to cause a nuisance or annoyance to the landlord of the dwelling-house, or a person employed (whether or not by the landlord) in connection with the exercise of the landlord's housing management functions, and that is directly or indirectly related to or affects those functions,".

99 Offences connected with riot

(1) In Part 1 of Schedule 2 to the Housing Act 1985 (grounds on which court may order possession in relation to secure tenancies if it considers it reasonable), after Ground 2 there is inserted—

"Ground 2ZA

The tenant or an adult residing in the dwelling-house has been convicted of an indictable offence which took place during, and at the scene of, a riot in the United Kingdom.

In this Ground—

"adult" means a person aged 18 or over;

"indictable offence" does not include an offence that is triable only summarily by virtue of section 22 of the Magistrates' Courts Act 1980 (either way offences where value involved is small);

"riot" is to be construed in accordance with section 1 of the Public Order Act 1986.

This Ground applies only in relation to dwelling-houses in England."

(2) In Part 2 of Schedule 2 to the Housing Act 1988 (grounds on which court may order possession in relation to assured tenancies if it considers it reasonable), after Ground 14 there is inserted—

"Ground 14ZA

The tenant or an adult residing in the dwelling-house has been convicted of an indictable offence which took place during, and at the scene of, a riot in the United Kingdom.

In this Ground—

"adult" means a person aged 18 or over;

"indictable offence" does not include an offence that is triable only summarily by virtue of section 22 of the Magistrates' Courts Act 1980 (either way offences where value involved is small);

"riot" is to be construed in accordance with section 1 of the Public Order Act 1986.

This Ground applies only in relation to dwelling-houses in England."

Supplemental

100 Restrictions where new possession proceedings in progress etc

(1) In section 138 of the Housing Act 1985 (right to buy: suspension of duty of landlord to convey freehold or grant lease)—

(a) in subsection (2A)(a), for "or Ground 2 possession order" there is substituted ", Ground 2 or 2ZA possession order or section 84A possession order";

(b) in subsection (2B)(a), for "or an operative Ground 2 possession order" there is substituted ", an operative Ground 2 or 2ZA possession order or an operative section 84A possession order";

(c) in subsection (2C), for the definition of "Ground 2 possession order" there is substituted—

"""Ground 2 or 2ZA possession order" means an order for possession under Ground 2 or Ground 2ZA in Schedule 2;";

(d) for the definition of "operative Ground 2 possession order" there is substituted—

"""operative Ground 2 or 2ZA possession order" means an order made under Ground 2 or Ground 2ZA in Schedule 2 which requires possession of the dwelling-house to be given up on a date specified in the order;";

(e) after that definition there is inserted—

"""operative section 84A possession order" means an order under section 84A which requires possession of the dwelling-house to be given up on a date specified in the order;

"section 84A possession order" means an order for possession under section 84A;".

(2) In Schedule 3 to that Act (grounds for withholding consent to assignment of secure tenancy by way of exchange), after Ground 2 there is inserted—

"Ground 2ZA

Proceedings have been begun for possession of the dwelling-house, of which the tenant or the proposed assignee is the secure tenant, under section 84A (absolute ground for possession for anti-social behaviour), or there has been served on the tenant or the proposed assignee a notice under section 83ZA (notice requirements in relation to proceedings for possession on absolute ground for anti-social behaviour) which is still in force."

(3) In Schedule 14 to the Localism Act 2011 (grounds on which landlord may refuse to surrender and grant tenancies in pursuance of a request under section 158 of that Act) —

(a) after Ground 4 there is inserted—

"4A Ground 4A

4A (1) This ground is that either of the following conditions is met.

(2) The first condition is that—

(a) proceedings have begun for possession of a dwelling-house let on an existing tenancy which is a secure tenancy, and

(b) possession is sought under section 84A of the Housing Act 1985 (absolute ground for possession for anti-social behaviour).

(3) The second condition is that—

(a) a notice has been served on a relevant tenant under section 83ZA of that Act (notice requirements in relation to proceedings for possession on absolute ground for anti-social behaviour), and

(b) the notice is still in force.";

(b) after Ground 5 there is inserted—

"5A Ground 5A

5A (1) This ground is that either of the following conditions is met.

(2) The first condition is that—

(a) proceedings have begun for possession of a dwelling-house let on an existing tenancy which is an assured tenancy, and

(b) possession is sought on ground 7A in Part 1 of Schedule 2 to the Housing Act 1988 (absolute ground for possession for anti-social behaviour).

(3) The second condition is that—

(a) a notice has been served on a relevant tenant under section 8 of that Act (notice of proceedings for possession), and

(b) the notice specifies ground 7A and is still in force."

PART 6

LOCAL INVOLVEMENT AND ACCOUNTABILITY

Community remedies

101 The community remedy document

(1) Each local policing body must prepare a community remedy document for its area, and may revise it at any time.

(2) A community remedy document is a list of actions any of which might, in the opinion of the local policing body, be appropriate in a particular case to be carried out by a person who—

(a) has engaged in anti-social behaviour or has committed an offence, and

(b) is to be dealt with for that behaviour or offence without court proceedings.

(3) For the purposes of subsection (2), an action is appropriate to be carried out by a person only if it has one or more of the following objects—

(a) assisting in the person's rehabilitation;

(b) ensuring that the person makes reparation for the behaviour or offence in question;

(c) punishing the person.

(4) In preparing or revising the community remedy document for its area a local policing body must—

(a) have regard to the need to promote public confidence in the out-of-court disposal process;

(b) have regard to any guidance issued by the Secretary of State about how local policing bodies are to discharge their functions under this section;

(c) carry out the necessary consultation and take account of all views expressed by those consulted.

(5) In subsection (4)(c) "the necessary consultation" means—

(a) consultation with the chief officer of police for the area,

(b) consultation with the local authority for any part of the area,

(c) consultation with whatever community representatives the local policing body thinks it appropriate to consult, and

(d) whatever other public consultation the local policing body thinks appropriate.

(6) A local policing body must agree the community remedy document for its area, and any revised document, with the chief officer of police for the area.

(7) Once the community remedy document, or a revised document, has been agreed with the chief officer of police, the local policing body must publish it in whatever way it thinks appropriate.

(8) The Secretary of State must publish any guidance issued under subsection (4)(b).

(9) In this section—

"anti-social behaviour" has the meaning given by section 2 (ignoring subsection (2) of that section);

"community representative", in relation to a police area, means any individual or body appearing to the local policing body to represent the views of people who live in, work in or visit the area;

"local authority" means—

(a) in relation to England, a district council, a county council for an area for which there is no district council, a London borough council, the Common Council of the City of London or the Council of the Isles of Scilly;

(b) in relation to Wales, a county council or a county borough council;

"“out-of-court disposal process” means the process by which a person is dealt with under section 102 or by means of a conditional caution or youth conditional caution.

102 Anti-social behaviour etc: out-of-court disposals

(1) This section applies where—

(a) a person (P) within subsection (2) has evidence that an individual (A) has engaged in anti-social behaviour or committed an offence,

(b) A admits to P that he or she has done so,

(c) P thinks that the evidence is enough for taking proceedings against A for an injunction under section 1, or taking other court proceedings, but decides that it would be appropriate for A to carry out action of some sort instead, and

(d) if the evidence is that A has committed an offence, P does not think that it would be more appropriate for A to be given a caution or a fixed penalty notice.

(2) The persons within this subsection are—

(a) a constable;

(b) an investigating officer;

(c) a person authorised by a relevant prosecutor for the purposes of section 22 of the Criminal Justice Act 2003 (conditional cautions) or section 66A of the Crime and Disorder Act 1998 (youth conditional cautions).

(3) Before deciding what action to invite A to carry out, P must make reasonable efforts to obtain the views of the victim (if any) of the anti-social behaviour or the offence, and in particular the victim's views as to whether A should carry out any of the actions listed in the community remedy document.

(4) If the victim expresses the view that A should carry out a particular action listed in the community remedy document, P must invite A to carry out that action unless it seems to P that it would be inappropriate to do so.

(5) Where—

(a) there is more than one victim and they express different views, or

(b) for any other reason subsection (4) does not apply,

P must nevertheless take account of any views expressed by the victim (or victims) in deciding what action to invite A to carry out.

(6) In this section—

“action” includes the making of a payment to the victim (but does not include the payment of a fixed penalty);

“anti-social behaviour” has the meaning given by section 2 (ignoring subsection (2) of that section);

“community remedy document” means the community remedy document (as revised from time to time) published under section 101 for the police area in which A's anti-social behaviour or offence took place;

“caution”—

(a) in the case of a person aged 18 or over, includes a conditional caution within the meaning of Part 3 of the Criminal Justice Act 2003;

(b) in the case of a person under that age, means a youth caution or youth conditional caution within the meaning of Chapter 1 of Part 4 of the Crime and Disorder Act 1998;

"investigating officer" and "relevant prosecutor" have the same meaning as in Part 3 of the Criminal Justice Act 2003 (see section 27 of that Act);

"victim" means the particular person who seems to P to have been affected, or principally affected, by A's anti-social behaviour or offence.

103 Criminal behaviour: conditional cautions

(1) In Part 3 of the Criminal Justice Act 2003 (conditional cautions), after section 23 there is inserted—

"23ZA Duty to consult victims

(1) Before deciding what conditions to attach to a conditional caution, a relevant prosecutor or the authorised person must make reasonable efforts to obtain the views of the victim (if any) of the offence, and in particular the victim's views as to whether the offender should carry out any of the actions listed in the community remedy document.

(2) If the victim expresses the view that the offender should carry out a particular action listed in the community remedy document, the prosecutor or authorised person must attach that as a condition unless it seems to the prosecutor or authorised person that it would be inappropriate to do so.

(3) Where—

(a) there is more than one victim and they express different views, or

(b) for any other reason subsection (2) does not apply,

the prosecutor or authorised person must nevertheless take account of any views expressed by the victim (or victims) in deciding what conditions to attach to the conditional caution.

(4) In this section—

"community remedy document" means the community remedy document (as revised from time to time) published under section 101 of the Anti-social Behaviour, Crime and Policing Act 2014 for the police area in which the offence was committed;

"victim" means the particular person who seems to the relevant prosecutor or authorised person to have been affected, or principally affected, by the offence."

(2) After section 66B of the Crime and Disorder Act 1998 (requirements for youth conditional cautions) there is inserted—

"66BA Duty to consult victims

(1) Before deciding what conditions to attach to a youth conditional caution, a relevant prosecutor or the authorised person must make reasonable efforts to obtain the views of the victim (if any) of the offence, and in particular the victim's views as to whether the offender should carry out any of the actions listed in the community remedy document.

(2) If the victim expresses the view that the offender should carry out a particular action listed in the community remedy document, the prosecutor or authorised person must attach that as a condition unless it seems to the prosecutor or authorised person that it would be inappropriate to do so.

(3) Where—

(a) there is more than one victim and they express different views, or

(b) for any other reason subsection (2) does not apply,

the prosecutor or authorised person must nevertheless take account of any views expressed by the victim (or victims) in deciding what conditions to attach to the conditional caution.

(4) In this section—

"community remedy document" means the community remedy document (as revised from time to time) published under section 101 of the Anti-social Behaviour, Crime and Policing Act 2014 for the police area in which the offence was committed;

"victim" means the particular person who seems to the relevant prosecutor or authorised person to have been affected, or principally affected, by the offence."

Response to complaints about anti-social behaviour

104 Review of response to complaints

(1) In a case where a person has made a complaint about anti-social behaviour in a particular local government area, the relevant bodies in that area must carry out a review of the response to that behaviour (an "ASB case review)" if—

(a) that person, or any other person, makes an application for such a review, and

(b) the relevant bodies decide that the threshold for a review is met.

(2) The relevant bodies in each local government area must—

(a) make arrangements about the carrying out of ASB case reviews by those bodies ("review procedures"), and

(b) ensure that the current review procedures are published.

(3) The review procedures must include provision about the making of applications for ASB case reviews; and, in particular, must—

(a) specify the point of contact for making applications, and

(b) ensure that applications made to that point of contact are passed on to all the relevant bodies in the local government area.

(4) In a situation where—

(a) an application for an ASB case review is made, and

(b) at least three (or, if a different number is specified in the review procedures, at least that number of) qualifying complaints have been made about the anti-social behaviour to which the application relates,

the relevant bodies must decide that the threshold for a review is met.

(5) In any other situation where an application for an ASB case review is made, the question whether the threshold for a review is met must be decided by the

relevant bodies in accordance with the review procedures; and the procedures may, in particular, include provision for this purpose which is framed by reference to any of these matters—

(a) the persistence of the anti-social behaviour about which the original complaint was made;

(b) the harm caused, or the potential for harm to be caused, by that behaviour;

(c) the adequacy of the response to that behaviour.

(6) After the relevant bodies have decided whether or not the threshold for a review is met, they must inform the applicant of their decision.

(7) The relevant bodies who carry out an ASB case review may make recommendations to a person who exercises public functions (including recommendations to a relevant body) in respect of any matters arising from the review; and the person must have regard to the recommendations in exercising public functions.

(8) The relevant bodies who carry out an ASB case review must inform the applicant of—

(a) the outcome of the review, and

(b) any recommendations made in accordance with subsection (7).

(9) As soon as practicable after the end of a reporting period, the relevant bodies in a local government area must publish information about the following matters which relates to that period—

(a) the number of applications for ASB case reviews made to those bodies;

(b) the number of times those bodies decided that the threshold for a review was not met;

(c) the number of ASB case reviews those bodies have carried out;

(d) the number of ASB case reviews carried out by those bodies that have resulted in recommendations being made.

(10) The question whether a complaint made about anti-social behaviour is a "qualifying complaint" for the purposes of subsection (4) is to be determined in accordance with subsections (11) and (12).

(11) A complaint about anti-social behaviour is a qualifying complaint if—

(a) the complaint is made within the period of one month (or, if a different period is specified in the review procedures, that period) beginning with the date on which the behaviour is alleged to have occurred; and

(b) the application for the ASB case review is made within the period of six months (or, if a different period is specified in the review procedures, that period) beginning with the date on which the complaint is made.

(12) But where a person makes two or more complaints about anti-social behaviour which meet the requirements in subsection (11), the question of which complaint is, or which complaints are, qualifying complaints is to be decided by the relevant bodies in accordance with the review procedures.

The procedures may, in particular, include provision for this purpose which is framed by reference to whether different complaints relate to different aspects of particular anti-social behaviour (including different incidents comprised in particular anti-social behaviour).

(13) Schedule 4 (ASB case reviews: supplementary provision) has effect.

105 ASB case reviews: interpretation

(1) This section applies for the purposes of section 104, this section and Schedule 4.

(2) In relation to England—

"local government area" means an area for which there is—

(a) a relevant district council, or

(b) a unitary authority;

"relevant district council" means the council of a district so far as it is not a unitary authority;

"unitary authority" means—

(a) the council of a county so far as it is the council for an area for which there are no district councils,

(b) the council of any district comprised in an area for which there is no county council,

(c) a London borough council,

(d) the Common Council of the City of London in its capacity as a local authority, or

(e) the Council of the Isles of Scilly;

and, in relation to a local government area in England—

"local provider of social housing" means a private registered provider of social housing that—

(a) grants tenancies of dwelling-houses in that area, or

(b) manages any house or other property in that area;

"relevant bodies" means—

(a) the relevant district council or the unitary authority,

(b) the chief officer of police for the police area which that local government area is within,

(c) each clinical commissioning group established under section 14V of the National Health Service Act 2006 whose area is wholly or partly within that local government area, and

(d) any local providers of social housing who are among the relevant bodies by virtue of the co-option arrangements made in relation to that local government area.

(3) In relation to Wales—

"local government area" means—

(a) a county, or

(b) a county borough;

and, in relation to a local government area in Wales—

"local provider of social housing" means a body registered as a social landlord under section 3 of the Housing Act 1996 that—

(a) grants tenancies of dwelling-houses in that area, or

(b) manages any house or other property in that area;

"relevant bodies" means—

(a) the council for the area,

(b) the chief officer of police for the police area which that local government area is within,

(c) each Local Health Board whose area is wholly or partly within that local government area, and

(d) any local providers of social housing who are among the relevant bodies by virtue of the co-option arrangements made in relation to that local government area.

(4) These expressions have the meanings given—

"anti-social behaviour" means behaviour causing harassment, alarm or distress to members or any member of the public;

"applicant" means a person who makes an application for an ASB case review;

"ASB case review" has the meaning given in section 104(1);

"dwelling-house" has the same meaning as in the Housing Act 1985;

"co-option arrangements" has the meaning given in paragraph 5 of Schedule 4;

"reporting period", in relation to the publication of information by the relevant bodies in a local government area, means a period, not exceeding 12 months, determined by those bodies.

PART 7

DANGEROUS DOGS

106 Keeping dogs under proper control

(1) The Dangerous Dogs Act 1991 is amended as follows.

(2) In section 3 (keeping dogs under proper control)—

(a) in subsection (1)—

(i) for "a public place" there is substituted "any place in England or Wales (whether or not a public place)";

(ii) after "injures any person" there is inserted "or assistance dog";

(b) after subsection (1) there is inserted—

"(1A) A person ("D") is not guilty of an offence under subsection (1) in a case which is a householder case.

(1B) For the purposes of subsection (1A) "a householder case" is a case where—

(a) the dog is dangerously out of control while in or partly in a building, or part of a building, that is a dwelling or is forces accommodation (or is both), and

(b) at that time—

(i) the person in relation to whom the dog is dangerously out of control ("V") is in, or is entering, the building or part as a trespasser, or

(ii) D (if present at that time) believed V to be in, or entering, the building or part as a trespasser.

Section 76(8B) to (8F) of the Criminal Justice and Immigration Act 2008 (use of force at place of residence) apply for the purposes of this subsection as they apply for the purposes of subsection (8A) of that section (and for those purposes the reference in section 76(8D) to subsection (8A)(d) is to be read as if it were a reference to paragraph (b)(ii) of this subsection).";

(c) subsection (3) is repealed;

(d) in subsection (4)—

(i) the words "or (3)" are omitted;

(ii) for "either of those subsections" there is substituted "that subsection";

(iii) in paragraph (b), for "two years" there is substituted "the relevant maximum specified in subsection (4A)";

(e) after subsection (4) there is inserted—

"(4A) For the purposes of subsection (4)(b), the relevant maximum is—

(a) 14 years if a person dies as a result of being injured;

(b) 5 years in any other case where a person is injured;

(c) 3 years in any case where an assistance dog is injured (whether or not it dies)."

(3) In section 4 (destruction and disqualification orders), the words "or (3)" are omitted in both places where they occur in subsection (1).

(4) In section 4A (contingent destruction orders)—

(a) in subsection (1)(a) the words "or (3)" are omitted;

(b) in subsection (4) the words "or (3)" are omitted.

(5) In section 5 (seizure, entry of premises and evidence)—

(a) in subsection (1)(c), for "one" there is substituted "a dog";

(b) after subsection (1) there is inserted—

"(1A) A constable or an officer of a local authority authorised by it to exercise the powers conferred by this subsection may seize any dog in a place in England or Wales which is not a public place, if the dog appears to the constable or officer to be dangerously out of control."

(6) In section 10 (interpretation)—

(a) in subsection (2), after the definition of "advertisement" there is inserted—

""assistance dog" has the meaning given by section 173(1) of the Equality Act 2010;";

(b) in subsection (3)—

(i) after "injure any person" there is inserted "or assistance dog";

(ii) after "injuring a person" there is inserted "or assistance dog".

107 Whether a dog is a danger to public safety

(1) The Dangerous Dogs Act 1991 is amended as follows.

(2) In section 1 (dogs bred for fighting) after subsection (6) there is inserted—

"(6A) A scheme under subsection (3) or (5) may in particular include provision requiring a court to consider whether a person is a fit and proper person to be in charge of a dog."

(3) In section 4 (destruction and disqualification orders) after subsection (1A) there is inserted—

"(1B) For the purposes of subsection (1A)(a), when deciding whether a dog would constitute a danger to public safety, the court—

(a) must consider—

(i) the temperament of the dog and its past behaviour, and

(ii) whether the owner of the dog, or the person for the time being in charge of it, is a fit and proper person to be in charge of the dog, and

(b) may consider any other relevant circumstances."

(4) Section 4B (destruction orders otherwise than on a conviction) is amended as follows—

(a) in subsection (1), after "section 5(1) or (2) below" there is inserted "or in exercise of a power of seizure conferred by any other enactment";

(b) after subsection (2) there is inserted—

"(2A) For the purposes of subsection (2)(a), when deciding whether a dog would constitute a danger to public safety, the justice or sheriff—

(a) must consider—

(i) the temperament of the dog and its past behaviour, and

(ii) whether the owner of the dog, or the person for the time being in charge of it, is a fit and proper person to be in charge of the dog, and

(b) may consider any other relevant circumstances."

PART 8

FIREARMS

108 Offence of possessing firearm for supply etc

(1) The Firearms Act 1968 is amended as set out in subsections (2) to (8).

(2) In section 5 (which includes, in subsections (1) and (1A), offences of unauthorised possession etc of prohibited weapons and ammunition)—

(a) in subsection (1) the words ", or manufactures, sells or transfers" are omitted;

(b) in subsection (1A) the words "or sells or transfers" are omitted.

(3) After subsection (2) of that section there is inserted—

"(2A) A person commits an offence if without authority—

(a) he manufactures any weapon or ammunition specified in subsection (1) of this section,

(b) he sells or transfers any prohibited weapon or prohibited ammunition,

(c) he has in his possession for sale or transfer any prohibited weapon or prohibited ammunition, or

(d) he purchases or acquires for sale or transfer any prohibited weapon or prohibited ammunition."

(4) For subsection (3) of that section there is substituted—

"(3) In this section "authority" means an authority given in writing by—

(a) the Secretary of State (in or as regards England and Wales), or

(b) the Scottish Ministers (in or as regards Scotland)."

(5) In section 5A (exemptions from requirement of authority under section 5)—

(a) in subsections (1), (3), (4), (5), (6) and (7), the words "subsection (1A) of" are omitted;

(b) in subsections (1) and (3), for "any prohibited weapon or ammunition" there is substituted "any weapon, ammunition or missile specified in subsection (1A) of that section".

(6) In section 51A (minimum sentences for certain offences), in subsection (1A), before paragraph (a) there is inserted—

"(za) section 5(2A) (manufacture, sale or transfer of firearm, or possession etc for sale or transfer);".

(7) In Schedule 6 (prosecution and punishment of offences), in Part 1 (table of punishments) the words "or distributing" are omitted in the entries for—

(a) section 5(1)(a), (ab), (aba), (ac), (ad), (ae), (af) or (c),

(b) section 5(1)(b),

(c) section 5(1A)(a), and

(d) section 5(1A)(b), (c), (d), (e), (f) or (g).

(8) In Part 1 of that Schedule, after the entry for section 5(1A)(b), (c), (d), (e), (f) or (g) there is inserted—

"Section 5(2A)	Manufacturing or distributing, or possessing for distribution, prohibited weapons or ammunition	On indictment	Imprisonment for life."

(9) In section 1 of the Firearms (Amendment) Act 1997 (extension of section 5 of the 1968 Act to prohibit certain small firearms etc), after subsection (7) there is inserted—

"(7A) In sections 2 to 7 below any reference to subsection (1)(aba) of section 5 of the 1968 Act shall include a reference to subsection (2A) of that section as it applies in relation to a firearm specified in subsection (1)(aba) of that section.

(7B) In section 8 below the reference to subsection (1)(aba), (b) or (c) of section 5 of the 1968 Act shall include a reference to subsection (2A) of that section as it applies in relation to any weapon or ammunition specified in subsection (1)(aba), (b) or (c) of that section."

109 Functions of Scottish Ministers under Firearms Acts

(1) In section 5 of the Firearms Act 1968 (weapons subject to general prohibition)—

(a) in subsections (1) and (1A), for the words between "commits an offence if," and ", he has in his possession" there is substituted "without authority";

(b) in subsection (4), for the words from the beginning to "the Scottish Ministers" there is substituted "An authority shall be subject to conditions specified in it, including such as the Secretary of State or the Scottish Ministers (as appropriate)";

(c) in subsection (6), for the words before "revoke an authority" there is substituted "The Secretary of State or the Scottish Ministers (as appropriate) may at any time, if they think fit,".

(2) In section 5A of that Act (exemptions from requirement of authority under section 5) —

(a) in subsections (1), (2)(a), (2)(b), (3), (4), (5), (6) and (7), for "or the Scottish Ministers (by virtue of provision made under section 63 of the Scotland Act 1998)" there is substituted "or the Scottish Ministers";

(b) in subsection (6), for the words after "without the authority of the Secretary of State" there is substituted "or the Scottish Ministers (as appropriate)".

(3) In the Firearms (Amendment) Act 1997—

(a) in sections 2, 3, 4, 5, 6, 7(1) and 8 (exemptions from prohibition on small firearms etc), for "The authority of the Secretary of State or the Scottish Ministers (by virtue of provision made under section 63 of the Scotland Act 1998)" there is substituted "The authority of the Secretary of State or the Scottish Ministers";

(b) in section 7(3), for the words "or the Scottish Ministers (by virtue of provision made under section 63 of the Scotland Act 1998)", in the first place where they occur, there is substituted "or the Scottish Ministers".

(4) In the Scotland Act 1998 (Transfer of Functions to the Scottish Ministers etc.) Order 1999 (S.I. 1999/1750)—

(a) in Schedule 1, in the entry for the Firearms Act 1968, the words "5 and" are omitted;

(b) in Schedule 5, paragraph 3 and paragraph 18(2) to (6), (7)(a) and (8) are omitted.

110 Possession of firearms by persons previously convicted of crime

(1) In section 21 of the Firearms Act 1968 (possession of firearms by persons previously convicted of crime), before subsection (3) there is inserted—

"(2C) Where—

(a) a person has been sentenced to imprisonment for a term of three months or more, and

(b) the sentence is suspended under section 189 of the Criminal Justice Act 2003,

the person shall not have a firearm or ammunition in his possession at any time during the period of five years beginning with the second day after the date on which the sentence is passed."

(2) In section 58(2) of that Act (saving for antique firearms), for "Nothing in this Act" there is substituted

"Apart from—

(a) section 21 and Schedule 3, and

(b) any other provision of this Act so far as it applies in relation to an offence under section 21,

nothing in this Act".

(3) Where—

(a) a person is in possession of a firearm or ammunition immediately before the day on which subsection (1) comes into force,

(b) by reason of a sentence imposed before that day, subsection (1) would (but for this subsection) make the person's possession of the firearm or ammunition subject to a prohibition under section 21 of the Firearms Act 1968, and

(c) the person's possession of the firearm or ammunition immediately before that day is authorised by a certificate within the meaning given in section 57(4) of that Act,

the prohibition does not apply while the certificate remains in force.

111 Increased penalty for improper importation of firearms etc

(1) The Customs and Excise Management Act 1979 is amended as follows.

(2) In section 50 (penalty for improper importation of goods), in subsection (5A) (firearms and counterfeit currency etc), for the words after "shall have effect" there is substituted "as if for the words "imprisonment for a term not exceeding 7 years" there were substituted the words "imprisonment for life"".

(3) In that section—

(a) in subsection (4), after "(5A)," there is inserted "(5AA),";

(b) at the end of paragraph (a) of subsection (5A) there is inserted "or";

(c) paragraph (c) of that subsection and the word "or" before it are omitted;

(d) after that subsection there is inserted—

"(5AA) In the case of an offence under subsection (2) or (3) above committed in connection with the prohibition contained in section 20 of the Forgery and Counterfeiting Act 1981, subsection (4)(b) above shall have effect as if for the words "7 years" there were substituted the words "10 years"."

(4) In section 170 (penalty for fraudulent evasion of duty or prohibition, etc), in subsection (4A) (firearms and counterfeit currency etc)—

(a) in paragraph (a), for "subsection (2) or (3)" there is substituted "subsection (1) or (2)";

(b) for the words after "shall have effect" there is substituted "as if for the words "imprisonment for a term not exceeding 7 years" there were substituted the words "imprisonment for life"".

(5) In that section—

(a) in subsection (3), after "(4A)," there is inserted "(4AA),";

(b) at the end of paragraph (a) of subsection (4A) there is inserted "or";

(c) paragraph (c) of that subsection and the word "or" before it are omitted;

(d) after that subsection there is inserted—

"(4AA) In the case of an offence under subsection (1) or (2) above committed in connection with the prohibitions contained in sections 20 and 21 of the Forgery and Counterfeiting Act 1981, subsection (3)(b) above shall have effect as if for the words "7 years" there were substituted the words "10 years"."

(6) In section 68 (offences in relation to exportation of prohibited or restricted goods), in subsection (4A) (firearms and counterfeit currency etc)—

(a) in paragraph (a) the words "or (3)" are omitted";

(b) for the words after "shall have effect" there is substituted "as if for the words "imprisonment for a term not exceeding 7 years" there were substituted the words "imprisonment for life"".

(7) In that section—

(a) in subsection (3), after "(4A)" there is inserted ", (4AA)";

(b) at the end of paragraph (a) of subsection (4A) there is inserted "or";

(c) paragraph (c) of that subsection and the word "or" before it are omitted;

(d) after that subsection there is inserted—

"(4AA) In the case of an offence under subsection (2) above committed in connection with the prohibition contained in section 21 of the Forgery and Counterfeiting Act 1981, subsection (3)(b) above shall have effect as if for the words "7 years" there were substituted the words "10 years"."

112 British Transport Police: Crown status under Firearms Act 1968

(1) In section 54 of the Firearms Act 1968 (application to Crown servants), in subsection (3), at the end of paragraph (d) there is inserted ", or

(e) a member of the British Transport Police Force, or

(f) a person employed by the British Transport Police Authority who is under the direction and control of the Chief Constable of the British Transport Police Force."

(2) The following are repealed—

(a) subsections (3A) and (3B) of section 54 of the Firearms Act 1968, and

(b) paragraph 9 of Schedule 7 to the Anti-terrorism, Crime and Security Act 2001 (which inserted those subsections).

PART 9

PROTECTION FROM SEXUAL HARM AND VIOLENCE

Protection from sexual harm

113 Sexual harm prevention orders and sexual risk orders, etc

(1) Schedule 5 (amendments of Parts 2 and 3 of the Sexual Offences Act 2003) has effect.

(2) In section 142 of the Sexual Offences Act 2003 (extent etc)—

(a) in subsection (2) (provisions that extend to Northern Ireland, as well as England and Wales), for paragraph (c) there is substituted—

"(c) sections 80 to 85, 86 to 88, 89 to 91, 92 to 96, 96B to 103, 122F and 130 to 136ZD;

(ca) Part 2A;";

(b) after that subsection there is inserted—

"(2A) Sections 85A, 96A, 96AA, 110, 117A, 119 and 123 to 129 and Schedule 3A extend only to Northern Ireland."

(c) In subsection (3) (provisions that extend to Scotland, as well as England and Wales) for paragraph (a) there is substituted—

"(a) sections 80 to 85, 86 to 88, 89 to 91, 92, 94 to 96, 97 to 103, 122F, 130 to 132 and 133 to 136ZB;";

(d) after that subsection there is inserted—

"(3A) Sections 88A to 88I, 96A, 111A, 117B, 120 and 121 extend only to Scotland.

(3B) Sections 104 to 109, 111, 112 to 117, 118 and 122 extend to Northern Ireland and Scotland but not to England and Wales.

(3C) The references to section 96A in subsections (2A) and (3A) are references respectively to—

(a) the section 96A inserted by the Criminal Justice Act (Northern Ireland) 2013, and

(b) the section 96A inserted by the Police, Public Order and Criminal Justice (Scotland) Act 2006."

114 Saving and transitional provision

(1) In this section—

"the 2003 Act" means the Sexual Offences Act 2003;

"existing order" means—

(a) a sexual offences prevention order under section 104 of the 2003 Act;

(b) a foreign travel order under section 114 of that Act;

(c) a risk of sexual harm order under section 123 of that Act;

"new order" means—

(a) a sexual harm prevention order (made under section 103A of the 2003 Act, inserted by Schedule 5);

(b) a sexual risk order (made under section 122A of that Act, inserted by that Schedule);

"old order" means—

(a) a restraining order under section 5A of the Sex Offenders Act 1997;

(b) a sex offender order under section 2 of the Crime and Disorder Act 1998.

(2) The repeal or amendment by this Act of sections 104 to 122 or sections 123 to 129 of the 2003 Act does not apply in relation to—

(a) an application made before the commencement day for an existing order;

(b) an existing order (whether made before or after that day) applied for before that day;

(c) anything done in connection with such an application or order.

(3) The following sections of the 2003 Act inserted by Schedule 5 apply (as appropriate) to an old order as they apply to a new order—

(a) section 103E (variation, renewal and discharge of sexual harm prevention order);

(b) section 103I (offence of breach of sexual harm prevention order);

(c) section 122D (variation, renewal and discharge of sexual risk order);

(d) section 122H (offence of breach of sexual risk order).

(4) As from the commencement day there may be no variation of an existing order or an old order that extends the period of the order or of any of its provisions.

(5) At the end of the period of 5 years beginning with the commencement day—

(a) in relation to any existing order or old order that is still in force, sections 103E and 103I of the 2003 Act or sections 122D and 122H of that Act (as appropriate) have effect, with any necessary modifications (and with any modifications specified in an order under section 185(7) of this Act), as if the provisions of the order were provisions of a new order;

(b) subsections (2) and (3) cease to have effect.

(6) In this section "commencement day" means the day on which this section comes into force.

115 Use of premises for child sex offences

(1) Schedule 6 (amendments of Part 2A of the Sexual Offences Act 2003) has effect.

(2) For the purposes of sections 136BA and 136D(7A) of the Sexual Offences Act 2003 (inserted by that Schedule), it does not matter whether the offence or offences in question were committed before, or on or after, the date on which this section comes into force.

Child sexual exploitation at hotels

116 Information about guests at hotels believed to be used for child sexual exploitation

(1) A police officer of at least the rank of inspector may issue a notice under this section to the owner, operator or manager of a hotel that the officer reasonably believes has been or will be used for the purposes of—

(a) child sexual exploitation, or

(b) conduct that is preparatory to, or otherwise connected with, child sexual exploitation.

(2) A notice under this section must be in writing and must—

(a) specify the hotel to which it relates;

(b) specify the date on which it comes into effect and the date on which it expires;

(c) explain the effect of subsections (4) and (5) and sections 117 and 118.

(3) The date on which the notice expires must not be more than 6 months after the date on which it comes into effect.

(4) A constable may require a person issued with a notice under this section to provide the constable with information about guests at the hotel.

(5) The only information that a constable may require under subsection (4) is—

(a) guests' names and addresses;

(b) other information about guests that—

(i) is specified in regulations made by the Secretary of State, and

(ii) can be readily obtained from one or more of the guests themselves.

(6) A requirement under subsection (4)—

(a) must be in writing;

(b) must specify the period to which the requirement relates;

(c) must specify the date or dates on or by which the required information is to be provided.

The period specified under paragraph (b) must begin no earlier than the time when the requirement is imposed and must end no later than the expiry of the notice under this section.

(7) In this section—

"child sexual exploitation" means conduct that constitutes an offence listed in subsection (8)(a) or (b), or an offence listed in subsection (8)(c) against a person under 18;

"guest" means a person who, for a charge payable by that person or another, has the use of a guest room at the hotel in question;

"hotel" includes any guest house or other establishment of a similar kind at which accommodation is provided for a charge.

(8) The offences are—

(a) an offence under any of the following sections of the Sexual Offences Act 2003—

sections 5 to 8 (rape and other offences against children under 13);

sections 9 to 13 (child sex offences);

sections 16 to 19 (abuse of position of trust);

sections 25 and 26 (familial child sex offences);

sections 47 to 50 (abuse of children through prostitution and pornography);

(b) an offence under section 1 of the Protection of Children Act 1978 (indecent photographs of children);

(c) an offence under any of the following sections of the Sexual Offences Act 2003—

sections 1 to 4 (rape, assault and causing sexual activity without consent);

sections 30 to 41 (persons with a mental disorder impeding choice, inducements etc to persons with a mental disorder, and care workers for persons with a mental disorder);

section 59A (trafficking people for sexual exploitation);

section 61 (administering a substance with intent);

sections 66 and 67 (exposure and voyeurism).

117 Appeals against notices under section 116

(1) A person issued with a notice under section 116 may appeal against it to a magistrates' court.

(2) An appeal must be made within the period of 21 days beginning with the day on which the person is issued with the notice.

(3) Where there is an appeal against a notice under section 116, then until the appeal is finally determined or withdrawn—

(a) no requirement may be imposed under subsection (4) of that section in relation to the premises in question;

(b) any such requirement already imposed is of no effect.

(4) A magistrates' court hearing an appeal against a notice under section 116 must—

(a) quash the notice,

(b) modify the notice, or

(c) dismiss the appeal.

118 Offences

(1) An offence is committed by a person who fails without reasonable excuse to comply with a requirement imposed on the person under section 116(4).

(2) An offence is committed by a person who, in response to a requirement imposed on the person under section 116(4), provides incorrect information which the person—

(a) did not take reasonable steps to verify or to have verified, or

(b) knows to be incorrect.

(3) A person does not commit an offence under subsection (2)(a) if there were no steps that the person could reasonably have taken to verify the information or to have it verified.

(4) A person guilty of an offence under this section is liable on summary conviction to a fine not exceeding level 4 on the standard scale.

Violent offending

119 Violent offender orders

(1) In section 98 of the Criminal Justice and Immigration Act 2008 (violent offender orders), after subsection (5) there is inserted—

"(6) The Secretary of State may by order—

(a) amend subsection (3);

(b) make consequential amendments to subsection (4)."

(2) In section 147(5) of that Act (orders etc subject to affirmative resolution procedure), after paragraph (d) there is inserted—

"(da) an order under section 98(6),".

(3) In section 99 of that Act (qualifying offenders), in paragraph (b) of subsection (5) (meaning of "relevant offence") after "a specified offence" there is inserted ", or the offence of murder,".

PART 10

FORCED MARRIAGE

120 Offence of breaching forced marriage protection order

(1) The Family Law Act 1996 is amended as follows.

(2) After section 63C there is inserted—

"63CA Offence of breaching order

(1) A person who without reasonable excuse does anything that the person is prohibited from doing by a forced marriage protection order is guilty of an offence.

(2) In the case of a forced marriage protection order made by virtue of section 63D(1), a person can be guilty of an offence under this section only in respect of conduct engaged in at a time when the person was aware of the existence of the order.

(3) Where a person is convicted of an offence under this section in respect of any conduct, that conduct is not punishable as a contempt of court.

(4) A person cannot be convicted of an offence under this section in respect of any conduct which has been punished as a contempt of court.

(5) A person guilty of an offence under this section is liable—

(a) on conviction on indictment, to imprisonment for a term not exceeding five years, or a fine, or both;

(b) on summary conviction, to imprisonment for a term not exceeding 12 months, or a fine, or both.

(6) A reference in any enactment to proceedings under this Part, or to an order under this Part, does not include a reference to proceedings for an offence under this section or to an order made in proceedings for such an offence.

(7) "Enactment" includes an enactment contained in subordinate legislation within the meaning of the Interpretation Act 1978."

(3) For subsections (1) to (3) of section 63E there is substituted—

"(1) In any case where the court has power to make a forced marriage protection order, the court may accept an undertaking from the respondent instead of making the order.

(2) But a court may not accept an undertaking under subsection (1) if it appears to the court—

(a) that the respondent has used or threatened violence against the person to be protected, and

(b) that, for the person's protection, it is necessary to make a forced marriage protection order so that any breach of it by the respondent may be punishable under section 63CA."

(4) In section 63J(2), for "the order" there is substituted "a forced marriage protection order".

(5) The following are repealed—
- (a) section 63G(6) and (7);
- (b) section 63H;
- (c) section 63I;
- (d) section 63J(1);
- (e) in section 63K(1) the words "under section 63I(3) or";
- (f) section 63L(4)(a).

(6) This section applies only in relation to conduct occurring on or after the day on which it comes into force.

(7) In relation to an offence committed before the commencement of section 154(1) of the Criminal Justice Act 2003, the reference to 12 months in section 63CA(5)(b) of the Family Law Act 1996 (inserted by subsection (2) above) is to be read as a reference to six months.

121 Offence of forced marriage: England and Wales

(1) A person commits an offence under the law of England and Wales if he or she—
- (a) uses violence, threats or any other form of coercion for the purpose of causing another person to enter into a marriage, and
- (b) believes, or ought reasonably to believe, that the conduct may cause the other person to enter into the marriage without free and full consent.

(2) In relation to a victim who lacks capacity to consent to marriage, the offence under subsection (1) is capable of being committed by any conduct carried out for the purpose of causing the victim to enter into a marriage (whether or not the conduct amounts to violence, threats or any other form coercion).

(3) A person commits an offence under the law of England and Wales if he or she—
- (a) practises any form of deception with the intention of causing another person to leave the United Kingdom, and
- (b) intends the other person to be subjected to conduct outside the United Kingdom that is an offence under subsection (1) or would be an offence under that subsection if the victim were in England or Wales.

(4) "Marriage" means any religious or civil ceremony of marriage (whether or not legally binding).

(5) "Lacks capacity" means lacks capacity within the meaning of the Mental Capacity Act 2005.

(6) It is irrelevant whether the conduct mentioned in paragraph (a) of subsection (1) is directed at the victim of the offence under that subsection or another person.

(7) A person commits an offence under subsection (1) or (3) only if, at the time of the conduct or deception—
- (a) the person or the victim or both of them are in England or Wales,
- (b) neither the person nor the victim is in England or Wales but at least one of them is habitually resident in England and Wales, or

(c) neither the person nor the victim is in the United Kingdom but at least one of them is a UK national.

(8) "UK national" means an individual who is—

(a) a British citizen, a British overseas territories citizen, a British National (Overseas) or a British Overseas citizen;

(b) a person who under the British Nationality Act 1981 is a British subject; or

(c) a British protected person within the meaning of that Act.

(9) A person guilty of an offence under this section is liable—

(a) on summary conviction, to imprisonment for a term not exceeding 12 months or to a fine or both;

(b) on conviction on indictment, to imprisonment for a term not exceeding 7 years.

(10) In relation to an offence committed before the commencement of section 154(1) of the Criminal Justice Act 2003, the reference to 12 months in subsection (9)(a) is to be read as a reference to six months.

122 Offence of forced marriage: Scotland

(1) A person commits an offence under the law of Scotland if he or she—

(a) uses violence, threats or any other form of coercion for the purpose of causing another person to enter into a marriage, and

(b) believes, or ought reasonably to believe, that the conduct may cause the other person to enter into the marriage without free and full consent.

(2) In relation to a victim who is incapable of consenting to marriage by reason of mental disorder, the offence under subsection (1) is capable of being committed by any conduct carried out for the purpose of causing the victim to enter into a marriage (whether or not the conduct amounts to violence, threats or any other form coercion).

(3) A person commits an offence under the law of Scotland if he or she—

(a) practises any form of deception with the intention of causing another person to leave the United Kingdom, and

(b) intends the other person to be subjected to conduct outside the United Kingdom that is an offence under subsection (1) or would be an offence under that subsection if the victim were in Scotland.

(4) "Marriage" means any religious or civil ceremony of marriage (whether or not legally binding).

(5) "Mental disorder" has the meaning given by section 328 of the Mental Health (Care and Treatment) (Scotland) Act 2003.

(6) It is irrelevant whether the conduct mentioned in paragraph (a) of subsection (1) is directed at the victim of the offence under that subsection or another person.

(7) A person commits an offence under subsection (1) or (3) only if, at the time of the conduct or deception—

(a) the person or the victim or both of them are in Scotland,

(b) neither the person nor the victim is in Scotland but at least one of them is habitually resident in Scotland, or

(c) neither the person nor the victim is in the United Kingdom but at least one of them is a UK national.

(8) "UK national" means an individual who is—

(a) a British citizen, a British overseas territories citizen, a British National (Overseas) or a British Overseas citizen;

(b) a person who under the British Nationality Act 1981 is a British subject; or

(c) a British protected person within the meaning of that Act.

(9) A person guilty of an offence under this section is liable—

(a) on summary conviction, to imprisonment for a term not exceeding 12 months or to a fine not exceeding the statutory maximum or both;

(b) on conviction on indictment, to imprisonment for a term not exceeding 7 years or to a fine or both.

PART 11

POLICING ETC

College of Policing

123 Regulations to be prepared or approved by the College

(1) In section 50 of the Police Act 1996 (regulations for police forces), after subsection (2ZA) there is inserted—

"(2ZB) If the College of Policing submits to the Secretary of State draft regulations with respect to any of the matters mentioned in subsection (2)(a), (b), (c) or (g), the Secretary of State shall make regulations in terms of the draft unless the Secretary of State considers that—

(a) doing so would impair the efficiency or effectiveness of the police, or

(b) it would be unlawful to do so, or

(c) it would for some other reason be wrong to do so.

(2ZC) The Secretary of State may not make regulations with respect to any of the matters mentioned in subsection (2)(a), (b), (c) or (g) unless the text of the regulations has been prepared or approved by the College of Policing."

(2) In section 51 of that Act (regulations for special constables), after subsection (2ZA) there is inserted—

"(2ZB) If the College of Policing submits to the Secretary of State draft regulations with respect to—

(a) the ranks to be held by special constables,

(b) the qualifications for appointment and promotion of special constables,

(c) periods of service on probation, or

(d) maintenance of personal records of special constables,

the Secretary of State shall make regulations in terms of the draft.

(2ZC) The duty in subsection (2ZB) does not apply if the Secretary of State considers that—

(a) making regulations in terms of the draft would impair the efficiency or effectiveness of the police, or

(b) it would be unlawful to make regulations in those terms, or

(c) it would for some other reason be wrong to make regulations in those terms.

(2ZD) The Secretary of State may not make regulations with respect to the matters mentioned in subsection (2ZB) unless the text of the regulations has been prepared or approved by the College of Policing."

(3) In section 53A of that Act (regulation of procedures and practices)—

(a) after subsection (1) there is inserted—

"(1A) If the College of Policing, having consulted the National Crime Agency, submits to the Secretary of State a draft of regulations under this section, the Secretary of State shall make regulations in terms of the draft unless the Secretary of State considers that—

(a) doing so would impair the efficiency or effectiveness of the police, or

(b) it would be unlawful to do so, or

(c) it would for some other reason be wrong to do so.

(1B) The Secretary of State may not make regulations under this section unless the text of the regulations has been prepared or approved by the College of Policing.";

(b) subsections (2), (3), (4), (6), (7) and (10) are repealed;

(c) in subsection (9), for "the first regulations to be made" there is substituted "regulations".

(4) In section 63 of that Act (Police Advisory Board for England and Wales, etc), in subsection (3)(a), before "with respect to" there is inserted "to which section 50(2ZC) applies or regulations".

(5) In section 97 of the Criminal Justice and Police Act 2001 (regulations about police training etc)—

(a) after subsection (1) there is inserted—

"(1A) If the College of Policing submits to the Secretary of State a draft of regulations under this section, the Secretary of State shall make regulations in terms of the draft unless the Secretary of State considers that—

(a) doing so would impair the efficiency or effectiveness of the police, or

(b) it would be unlawful to do so, or

(c) it would for some other reason be wrong to do so.

(1B) The Secretary of State may not make regulations under this section unless the text of the regulations has been prepared or approved by the College of Policing.";

(b) subsection (4) is repealed.

124 Codes of practice issued by the College

(1) Section 39A of the Police Act 1996 (codes of practice for chief officers) is amended as follows.

(2) For subsection (1) there is substituted—

"(1) The College of Policing may, with the approval of the Secretary of State, issue codes of practice relating to the discharge of their functions by chief officers of police if the College considers that—

(a) it is necessary to do so in order to promote the efficiency and effectiveness of police forces generally,

(b) it is necessary to do so in order to facilitate the carrying out by members of any two or more police forces of joint or co-ordinated operations, or

(c) it is for any other reason in the national interest to do so."

(3) In subsection (2), for "The Secretary of State may" there is substituted "The College of Policing may, with the approval of the Secretary of State,".

(4) For subsection (4) there is substituted—

"(4) The College of Policing shall consult with the National Crime Agency before issuing or revising a code of practice under this section."

(5) In subsection (5), for "him" there is substituted "the College of Policing".

125 Guidance by the College about employment of civilian staff

After section 53D of the Police Act 1996 there is inserted—

"Civilian staff

53E Guidance about civilian staff employed by local policing bodies and chief officers

(1) In this section "relevant civilian staff" means individuals, other than constables, who—

(a) are employed by a local policing body or a chief officer of police, or

(b) provide services to a local policing body or a chief officer of police, in pursuance of contractual arrangements but without being employed by the body or officer, and can be expected to have frequent contact with members of the public in the course of doing so.

(2) The College of Policing may issue guidance to local policing bodies and chief officers of police with regard to—

(a) the experience or qualifications to be expected of relevant civilian staff;

(b) the training to be undertaken by such staff.

(3) The College may from time to time revise the whole or any part of any guidance issued under this section.

(4) The College shall publish any guidance issued under this section and any revision of it.

(5) In discharging any function to which guidance under this section relates, a local policing body or chief officer of police shall have regard to the guidance."

126 Power to give directions to the College

After section 40B of the Police Act 1996 there is inserted—

"40C Power to give directions to College of Policing

(1) The Secretary of State may give a direction to the College of Policing requiring it to exercise any particular function that is conferred on the College by this Act or any other enactment.

(2) The College of Policing shall carry out such other duties for the purpose of furthering the efficiency, effectiveness or integrity of the police as the Secretary of State may from time to time direct."

127 Charging of fees by the College

After section 95 of the Police Act 1996 there is inserted—

"95A Charging of fees by College of Policing

(1) The College of Policing may charge fees for providing services of a public nature only if—

(a) the services are of a specified description and are provided with a view to promoting the efficiency, effectiveness or professionalism of the police, and

(b) the fees are of a specified amount or are determined in a specified manner.

(2) In this section "specified" means specified in an order made by the Secretary of State.

(3) A statutory instrument containing an order under this section shall be subject to annulment in pursuance of a resolution of either House of Parliament."

128 Appointment of senior police officers as staff of the College

After section 100 of the Police Act 1996 there is inserted—

"100A Appointment of senior police officers as staff of College of Policing

(1) This section applies where a person who—

(a) holds the office of constable with a rank above that of chief superintendent, or

(b) hold that office and is eligible to be appointed to a rank above that of chief superintendent,

is appointed as a member of the staff of the College of Policing.

(2) The person continues to hold the office of constable while a member of the staff of the College.

(3) On appointment—

(a) a person within subsection (1)(a) holds that office with the same rank that the person held immediately before appointment, or with whatever higher rank the College decides;

(b) a person within subsection (1)(b) holds that office with whatever rank, above that of chief superintendent, the College decides."

129 Disclosure of information to the College

After section 100A of the Police Act 1996 (inserted by section 128 above) there is inserted—

"100B Disclosure of information to College of Policing

A person who, apart from this section, would not have power to disclose information to the College of Policing has power to do so where the disclosure is made for the purposes of the exercise by the College of any of its functions."

130 The College and the IPCC

In Part 2 of the Police Reform Act 2002 (complaints and misconduct), before section 26C (inserted by section 11 of the Crime and Courts Act 2013) there is inserted—

"26BA College of Policing

(1) The Commission and the College of Policing must enter into an agreement for the establishment, in relation to members of the College's staff, of procedures corresponding or similar to those provided for by or under this Part.

(2) An agreement under this section—

(a) must not be made or varied except with the approval of the Secretary of State; and

(b) must not be terminated unless—

(i) it is replaced by another such agreement, and

(ii) the Secretary of State approves.

(3) An agreement under this section may contain provision for enabling the Commission to bring and conduct, or otherwise participate or intervene in, any proceedings that are identified by the agreement as disciplinary hearings in relation to members of the College's staff.

(4) Procedures established in accordance with an agreement under this section shall have no effect in relation to anything done outside England and Wales by any member of the College's staff."

Review bodies for police remuneration etc

131 Abolition of Police Negotiating Board for the United Kingdom

(1) The Police Negotiating Board for the United Kingdom is abolished.

(2) Sections 61 and 62 of the Police Act 1996 (the Police Negotiating Board for the United Kingdom, and its functions with respect to regulations) are repealed.

(3) The Secretary of State may secure the reimbursement of payments made under section 61(5) or (7) of the Police Act 1996 (payment by Scottish Ministers or Department of Justice in Northern Ireland towards expenses incurred by the Police Negotiating Board for the United Kingdom) to the extent that, by reason of the abolition of the Board, the payments are not needed.

132 Establishment of Police Remuneration Review Body

(1) After Part 3 of the Police Act 1996 there is inserted—

"PART 3A

THE POLICE REMUNERATION REVIEW BODY

64A The Police Remuneration Review Body

(1) There shall be a body called the Police Remuneration Review Body.

(2) It shall consist of—

(a) a chair appointed by the Prime Minister, and

(b) five or more other members appointed by the Secretary of State, one of whom the Secretary of State may appoint as deputy chair.

(3) Before making an appointment, the Prime Minister or the Secretary of State shall consult the Department of Justice in Northern Ireland.

(4) The Secretary of State may by order—

(a) change the name of the body established by this section, and

(b) make consequential amendments to any provision contained in or made under this or any other Act.

(5) A statutory instrument containing an order under subsection (4) shall be subject to annulment in pursuance of a resolution of either House of Parliament.

(6) Schedule 4B shall have effect in relation to the Police Remuneration Review Body.

64B Reports by the Police Remuneration Review Body

(1) The Police Remuneration Review Body shall consider and report on any matter referred to it by the Secretary of State that relates to—

(a) hours of duty,

(b) leave,

(c) pay and allowances, or

(d) the issue, use and return of police clothing, personal equipment and accoutrements, as regards members of police forces of or below the rank of chief superintendent or police cadets appointed under section 28.

(2) A report under subsection (1) shall be submitted to—

(a) the Secretary of State, and

(b) the Prime Minister,

and the Secretary of State shall arrange for it to be published.

(3) The Police Remuneration Review Body shall also consider and report on any matter referred to it by the Department of Justice in Northern Ireland that relates to—

(a) hours of duty,

(b) leave,

(c) pay and allowances, or

(d) the issue, use and return of equipment,

as regards members of the Police Service of Northern Ireland of or below the rank of chief superintendent, police trainees appointed under section 39 of the Police (Northern Ireland) Act 2000 or police cadets appointed under section 42 of that Act.

(4) A report under subsection (3) shall be submitted to the Department of Justice, and that Department shall arrange for it to be published.

(5) When referring a matter to the Police Remuneration Review Body, the Secretary of State or Department of Justice may give directions to that body about—

(a) the time within which it must report;

(b) considerations to which it must have particular regard;

(c) the evidence that it must obtain;

(d) matters on which it is to make recommendations.

(6) The Police Remuneration Review Body may include in a report under this section any recommendations it considers appropriate arising out of matters referred to it under this section (whether or not it is required to do so by a direction under subsection (5)).

(7) A reference or direction under this section may be varied or revoked."

(2) After Schedule 4A to that Act there is inserted the Schedule set out in Schedule 7 to this Act.

(3) An order under section 185(7) may include provision requiring the first members of the Police Remuneration Review Body to be, or to include, persons of a particular description.

133 Consultation about regulations: England and Wales

(1) After section 52 of the Police Act 1996 there is inserted—

"52A Regulations about hours, leave or pay: consultation etc

(1) This section applies where the Secretary of State is proposing to make regulations under section 50 or 52 on a matter that relates to—

(a) hours of duty,

(b) leave,

(c) pay and allowances, or

(d) the issue, use and return of police clothing, personal equipment and accoutrements.

(2) In the case of regulations under section 50 concerning members of police forces of or below the rank of chief superintendent, or regulations under section 52, before making the regulations the Secretary of State shall (subject to subsection (5))—

(a) refer the matter to the Police Remuneration Review Body under section 64B(1), and

(b) consider that body's report on the matter.

(3) In the case of regulations under section 50 concerning members of police forces above the rank of chief superintendent, before making the regulations the Secretary of State shall (subject to subsection (5))—

(a) consider advice on the matter from the Senior Salaries Review Body, or

(b) where subsection (4) applies, refer the matter to the Police Remuneration Review Body under section 64B(1) and consider that body's report on the matter.

(4) This subsection applies where—

(a) the regulations would affect members of police forces who are not above the rank of chief superintendent as well as those who are, and

(b) the Secretary of State thinks that it would be preferable for the matter to be considered by the same body.

(5) The duty to consider advice from the Senior Salaries Review Body or to refer the matter to the Police Remuneration Review Body does not apply if the Secretary of State considers that—

(a) there is not enough time to do so because the need to make the regulations is so urgent, or

(b) it is unnecessary to do so by reason of the nature of the proposed regulations.

(6) In all cases, before making the regulations the Secretary of State shall supply a draft of them to, and consider any representations made by, persons whom the Secretary of State considers to represent the interests of—

(a) the persons and bodies who between them maintain police forces;

(b) chief officers of police;

(c) members of police forces;

(d) police cadets appointed under section 28.

(7) The Secretary of State may by order amend this section in consequence of a change in the name or functions of the body for the time being specified in subsection (3)(a).

(8) A statutory instrument containing an order under subsection (7) shall be subject to annulment in pursuance of a resolution of either House of Parliament."

(2) In section 63 of that Act (Police Advisory Board for England and Wales, etc), in subsection (3)(a), for "regulations with respect to any of the matters mentioned in section 61(1)" there is substituted "regulations of a kind referred to in section 52A(1)".

(3) In section 1 of the Police Pensions Act 1976 (police pensions regulations)—

(a) in subsection (1), for "the Police Negotiating Board for the United Kingdom" there is substituted "the appropriate advisory or negotiating body";

(b) after that subsection there is inserted—

"(1ZA) In subsection (1) above, "the appropriate advisory or negotiating body" means—

(a) as regards England and Wales, the Police Advisory Board for England and Wales;

(b) as regards Scotland, the Police Negotiating Board for Scotland.

(1ZB) When carrying out consultation under subsection (1) above as regards England and Wales, the Secretary of State shall also invite the views of the Northern Ireland Policing Board and the Police Association for Northern Ireland."

(4) In section 52 of the Police Act 1996 (regulations for police cadets), at the end there is inserted—

"(3) Before making regulations under this section relating to pensions the Secretary of State shall consult with the Police Advisory Board for England and Wales and shall also invite the views of the Northern Ireland Policing Board and the Police Association for Northern Ireland."

(5) In Schedule 3 to the Police and Justice Act 2006 (power to merge police pension schemes), in paragraph 3, for sub-paragraph (3) there is substituted—

"(3) The Secretary of State shall—

(a) consult with the Police Advisory Board for England and Wales before exercising the power as regards England and Wales;

(b) consult with the Police Negotiating Board for Scotland before exercising the power as regards Scotland;

(c) consult with the Northern Ireland Policing Board and the Police Association for Northern Ireland before exercising the power as regards Northern Ireland."

134 Consultation about regulations: Northern Ireland

(1) In section 25 of the Police (Northern Ireland) Act 1998 (regulations for the Police Service of Northern Ireland)—

(a) in subsection (8), the words ", other than regulations made by virtue of subsection (2)(j), (k) or (l)" are omitted;

(b) after that subsection there is inserted—

"(9) Subsection (8) does not apply to—

(a) regulations made by virtue of subsection (2)(k), as to which the Department of Justice shall invite the views of the Police Advisory Board for England and Wales, or

(b) regulations made by virtue of subsection (2)(j) or (l), as to which section 25A applies."

(2) After that section there is inserted—

"25A Regulations about hours, leave, pay or equipment: consultation etc

(1) This section applies where the Department of Justice is proposing to make regulations under section 25 by virtue of subsection (2)(j) or (l) of that section.

(2) In the case of regulations concerning officers of or below the rank of chief superintendent, before making the regulations the Department of Justice shall (subject to subsection (5))—

(a) refer the matter to the Police Remuneration Review Body under section 64B(3) of the Police Act 1996, and

(b) consider that body's report on the matter.

(3) In the case of regulations concerning officers above the rank of chief superintendent, before making the regulations the Department of Justice shall (subject to subsection (5))—

(a) consider advice on the matter from the Senior Salaries Review Body, or

(b) where subsection (4) applies, refer the matter to the Police Remuneration Review Body under section 64B(3) of the Police Act 1996 and consider that body's report on the matter.

(4) This subsection applies where—

(a) the regulations would affect officers who are not above the rank of chief superintendent as well as those who are, and

(b) the Department of Justice thinks that it would be preferable for the matter to be considered by the same body.

(5) The duty to consider advice from the Senior Salaries Review Body or to refer the matter to the Police Remuneration Review Body does not apply if Department of Justice considers that—

(a) there is not enough time to do so because the need to make the regulations is so urgent, or

(b) it is unnecessary to do so by reason of the nature of the proposed regulations.

(6) In all cases, before making the regulations the Department of Justice shall supply a draft of them to, and consider any representations made by—

(a) the Board,

(b) the Police Association, and

(c) the Chief Constable of the Police Service of Northern Ireland.

(7) The Department of Justice may by order amend this section in consequence of a change in the name or functions of the body for the time being specified in subsection (3)(a)."

(3) In section 41 of the Police (Northern Ireland) Act 2000 (police trainees and police reserve trainees)—

(a) at the end of subsection (6) there is inserted ", other than regulations to which subsection (8) applies";

(b) after that subsection there is inserted—

"(7) Subsection (8) applies to regulations under subsection (3), concerning police trainees, on a matter that relates to—

(a) hours of duty,

(b) leave,

(c) pay and allowances, or

(d) the issue, use and return of equipment.

(8) Before making any such regulations the Department of Justice shall—

(a) (subject to subsection (9)) refer the matter to the Police Remuneration Review Body under section 64B(3) of the Police Act 1996 and consider that body's report on the matter, and

(b) supply a draft of the regulations to, and consider any representations made by—

(i) the Board,

(ii) the Police Association, and

(iii) the Chief Constable of the Police Service of Northern Ireland.

(9) The duty in subsection (8)(a) does not apply if the Department of Justice considers that—

(a) there is not enough time to refer to the matter to the Police Remuneration Review Body because the need to make the regulations is so urgent, or

(b) it is unnecessary to do so by reason of the nature of the proposed regulations."

Independent Police Complaints Commission

135 Application of IPCC provisions to contractors

In section 12 of the Police Reform Act 2002 (complaints, matters and persons to which Part 2 applies), at the end there is inserted—

"(8) The Secretary of State may make regulations providing that, for the purposes of this Part and of any regulations made under this Part—

(a) a contractor,

(b) a sub-contractor of a contractor, or

(c) an employee of a contractor or a sub-contractor,

is to be treated as a person serving with the police.

(9) Regulations under subsection (8) may make modifications to this Part, and to any regulations made under this Part, in its application to those persons.

(10) In subsection (8) "contractor" means a person who has entered into a contract with a local policing body or a chief officer to provide services to a chief officer."

136 Application to IPCC of provisions about investigation of offences

(1) In Schedule 3 to the Police Reform Act 2002 (handling of complaints and conduct matters etc), paragraph 19 (investigations by the Independent Police Complaints Commission itself) is amended as follows.

(2) In sub-paragraph (6), for the words from "provide that such provisions" to "shall apply" there is substituted "provide that—

(a) such provisions of the 1984 Act relating to investigations of offences conducted by police officers as may be specified in the order, and

(b) such provisions of a code of practice under section 60, 60A or 66 of that Act as may be so specified,

shall apply".

(3) After sub-paragraph (6) there is inserted—

"(6A) An order under sub-paragraph (6) may, in particular, provide that where a provision applied by the order allows a power to be exercised only if an authorisation is given by a police officer of or above a particular rank, the authorisation may be given by a member of the Commission's staff of or above a specified grade."

137 Provision of information to IPCC

After paragraph 19 of Schedule 3 to the Police Reform Act 2002 there is inserted—

"19ZA Investigations by the Commission: power to serve information notice

19ZA (1) The Commission may serve upon any person an information notice requiring the person to provide it with information that it reasonably requires for the purposes of an investigation in accordance with paragraph 19.

(2) But an information notice must not require a person—

(a) to provide information that might incriminate the person;

(b) to provide an item subject to legal privilege within the meaning of the Police and Criminal Evidence Act 1984 (see section 10 of that Act);

(c) to make a disclosure that would be prohibited by Part 1 of the Regulation of Investigatory Powers Act 2000;

(d) to provide information that was provided to the person by, or by an agency of, the government of a country or territory outside the United Kingdom where that government does not consent to the disclosure of the information.

(3) Neither must an information notice require a postal or telecommunications operator (within the meaning of Chapter 2 of Part 1 of the Regulation of Investigatory Powers Act 2000) to provide communications data (within the meaning of that Chapter).

(4) An information notice must—

(a) specify or describe the information that is required by the Commission and the form in which it must be provided;

(b) specify the period within which the information must be provided;

(c) give details of the right of appeal against the information notice under paragraph 19ZC.

(5) The period specified under sub-paragraph (4)(b) must not end before the end of the period within which an appeal can be brought against the notice and, if such an appeal is brought, the information need not be provided pending the determination or withdrawal of the appeal.

(6) The Commission may cancel an information notice by written notice to the person on whom it was served.

19ZB Failure to comply with information notice

19ZB (1) If a person who has received an information notice—

(a) fails or refuses to provide the information required by the notice, or

(b) knowingly or recklessly provides information in response to the notice that is false in a material respect,

the Commission may certify in writing to the High Court that the person has failed to comply with the information notice.

(2) The High Court may then inquire into the matter and, after hearing any witness who may be produced against or on behalf of the person, and after hearing any statement offered in defence, deal with the person as if the person had committed a contempt of court.

19ZC Appeals against information notices

19ZC (1) A person on whom an information notice is served may appeal against the notice to the First-tier Tribunal on the ground that the notice is not in accordance with the law.

(2) If the Tribunal considers that the notice is not in accordance with the law—

(a) it must quash the notice, and

(b) it may give directions to the Commission in relation to the service of a further information notice.

19ZD Sensitive information: restriction on further disclosure

19ZD (1) Where the Commission receives information within sub-paragraph (2) under an information notice, it must not disclose (whether under section 11, 20 or 21 or otherwise) the information, or the fact that it has received it, unless the relevant authority consents to the disclosure.

(2) The information is—

(a) intelligence service information,

(b) intercept information, or

(c) information obtained (directly or indirectly) from a government department which, at the time it is provided to the Commission, is identified by the department as information the disclosure of which may, in the opinion of the relevant authority, cause damage to—

(i) national security or international relations, or

(ii) the economic interests of the United Kingdom or any part of the United Kingdom.

(3) Where the Commission discloses to another person information within sub-paragraph (2), or the fact that it has received it, that person must not disclose that information or that fact unless the relevant authority consents to the disclosure.

(4) In this paragraph—

"government department" means a department of Her Majesty's Government but does not include—

(a) the Security Service,

(b) the Secret Intelligence Service, or

(c) the Government Communications Headquarters ("GCHQ");

"intelligence service information" means information which was obtained (directly or indirectly) from an intelligence service or which relates to an intelligence service;

"intelligence service" means—

(a) the Security Service,

(b) the Secret Intelligence Service,

(c) GCHQ, or

(d) any part of Her Majesty's forces (within the meaning of the Armed Forces Act 2006), or of the Ministry of Defence, which engages in intelligence activities;

"intercept information" means information relating to any of the matters mentioned in section 19(3) of the Regulation of Investigatory Powers Act 2000;

"Minister of the Crown" includes the Treasury;

"relevant authority" means—

(a) in the case of intelligence service information obtained from the Security Service, the Director-General of the Security Service;

(b) in the case of intelligence service information obtained from the Secret Intelligence Service, the Chief of the Secret Intelligence Service;

(c) in the case of intelligence service information obtained from GCHQ, the Director of GCHQ;

(d) in the case of intelligence service information obtained from Her Majesty's forces or the Ministry of Defence, the Secretary of State;

(e) in the case of intercept information, the person to whom the relevant interception warrant is or was addressed;

(f) in the case of information within sub-paragraph (2)(c)—

(i) the Secretary of State, or

(ii) the Minister of the Crown in charge of the government department from which the information was obtained (if that Minister is not a Secretary of State);

"relevant interception warrant" means the interception warrant issued under section 5 of the Regulation of Investigatory Powers Act 2000 that relates to the intercept information."

138 Unsatisfactory performance procedures following investigation of death or serious injury matter

(1) In paragraph 24C of Schedule 3 to the Police Reform Act 2002 (cases of death or serious injury where Independent Police Complaints Commission determines that disciplinary proceedings not justified), at the end there is inserted—

"(3) The Commission may notify the appropriate authority that it must, in accordance with regulations under section 50 or 51 of the 1996 Act, determine—

(a) whether or not the performance of a person serving with the police is unsatisfactory, and

(b) what action (if any) the authority will take in respect of any such person's performance.

(4) On receipt of a notification under sub-paragraph (3) the appropriate authority shall make those determinations and submit a memorandum to the Commission setting out the determinations the authority has made.

(5) On receipt of a memorandum under sub-paragraph (4), the Commission shall—

(a) consider the memorandum and whether the appropriate authority has made the determinations under sub-paragraph (4) that the Commission considers appropriate;

(b) determine whether or not to make recommendations under paragraph 27;

(c) make such recommendations (if any) under that paragraph as it thinks fit."

(2) Paragraph 27 of that Schedule (duties with respect to disciplinary proceedings) is amended as follows.

(3) In sub-paragraph (1), at the end there is inserted "; or

(c) has submitted, or is required to submit, a memorandum to the Commission under paragraph 24C(4)."

(4) After sub-paragraph (3) there is inserted—

"(3A) Where this paragraph applies by virtue of sub-paragraph (1)(c), the Commission may make a recommendation to the appropriate authority—

(a) that the performance of a person serving with the police is, or is not, satisfactory;

(b) that action of the form specified in the recommendation is taken in respect of the person's performance;

and it shall be the duty of the appropriate authority to notify the Commission whether it accepts the recommendation and (if it does) to set out in the notification the steps that it is proposing to take to give effect to it."

139 Recommendations by IPCC and requirement to respond

After paragraph 28 of Schedule 3 to the Police Reform Act 2002 there is inserted—

"28A Recommendations by the Commission

28A (1) This paragraph applies where the Commission has received a report under—

(a) paragraph 22(3) (report on completion of investigation of complaint or conduct matter supervised or managed by Commission),

(b) paragraph 22(5) (report on completion of investigation of complaint or conduct matter by Commission itself), or

(c) paragraph 24A(2) (report on completion of investigation of DSI matter that is not also conduct matter).

(2) This paragraph also applies where the Commission has made a determination on an appeal under—

(a) paragraph 8A (appeal relating to complaint dealt with other than by investigation), or

(b) paragraph 25 (appeal with respect to an investigation).

(3) The Commission may make a recommendation in relation to a matter dealt with in the report or appeal.

(4) A recommendation under this paragraph may be made to any person if it is made—

(a) following the receipt of a report relating to—

(i) a DSI matter,

(ii) a conduct matter of a type specified in regulations, or

(iii) a complaint of a type specified in regulations; or

(b) following a determination on an appeal relating to a complaint of a type specified in regulations.

(5) In any other case, a recommendation under this paragraph may be made only to—

(a) a person serving with the police, or

(b) a local policing body.

(6) Where the Commission makes a recommendation under this paragraph, it must also—

(a) publish the recommendation, and

(b) send a copy of it—

(i) in a case where the recommendation is made to a local policing body, to the chief officer of the police force maintained by that body;

(ii) in a case where the recommendation is made to a chief officer of a police force, to the local policing body that maintains the police force;

(iii) in a case where the recommendation is made to a contractor (within the meaning of section 12(10)), to the chief officer of a police force to whom the contractor is providing services, and the local policing body that maintains the police force;

(iv) in a case where the recommendation is made to a sub-contractor or an employee of a contractor, to the contractor and the persons to whom a copy must be sent under paragraph (iii);

(v) in a case where the recommendation is made to an employee of a sub-contractor, to the sub-contractor, the contractor and the persons to whom a copy must be sent under sub-paragraph (iii);

(vi) in any other case, to any person to whom the Commission thinks a copy should be sent.

(7) Nothing in this paragraph affects the power of the Commission to make recommendations or give advice under section 10(1)(e) (whether arising under this Schedule or otherwise).

28B Response to recommendation

28B (1) A person to whom a recommendation under paragraph 28A is made must provide to the Commission a response in writing stating—

(a) what action the person has taken or proposes to take in response to the recommendation, or

(b) why the person has not taken, or does not propose to take, any action in response.

(2) The person must provide the response to the Commission before the end of the period of 56 days beginning with the day on which the recommendation was made, unless sub-paragraph (3) applies.

(3) The Commission may extend the period of 56 days following an application received before the end of the period; and if the Commission grants an extension, the person must provide the response before the end of the extended period.

(4) But if proceedings for judicial review of the Commission's decision to make a recommendation are started during the period allowed by sub-paragraph (2) or (3), that period is extended by however many days the proceedings are in progress.

(5) On receiving a response, the Commission must, within the period of 21 days beginning with the day on which the Commission received it—

(a) publish the response, and

(b) send a copy of it to any person who was sent a copy of the recommendation under paragraph 28A(6)(b),

unless the person giving the response has made representations under sub-paragraph (6).

(6) The person giving the response may, at the time of providing it to the Commission, make representations to the Commission asserting that the requirements of publication and disclosure under sub-paragraph (5) should not apply to the response, or to particular parts of it.

(7) On receiving such representations, the Commission may decide—

(a) that the response should not be published, or that only parts of it should be published;

(b) that the response should not be disclosed, or that only parts of the response should be disclosed.

(8) Where, following a decision on representations, the Commission decides to publish or disclose a response (in whole or in part), it must do so only after the person giving the response has been informed of the Commission's decision, and—

(a) in a case where the Commission has decided to accept all of the representations, it must do so within the period of 21 days beginning with the day on which it received the response;

(b) in a case where the Commission has decided to reject any of the representations, it must do so—

(i) within the period of 21 days beginning with the day on which the person was informed of the Commission's decision on the representations, but

(ii) not before the end of the period of 7 days beginning with that day.

(9) But if proceedings for judicial review of the Commission's decision to reject a representation are started during the period of 7 days referred to in sub-paragraph (8)(b)(ii)—

(a) the Commission must not publish or disclose the response while the proceedings are in progress;

(b) if the court upholds the Commission's decision to reject a representation, the Commission must publish and disclose the response (in whole or in part, as appropriate) before the end of the period of 7 days beginning with the day on which the proceedings are no longer in progress.

(10) Where a local policing body or a chief officer makes a response under this paragraph, the body or officer must, at the time the Commission publishes the response, also publish the response (to the same extent as published by the Commission) and the recommendation under paragraph 28A.

(11) For the purposes of this paragraph—

(a) "disclosing" a response means sending a copy of it as mentioned in sub-paragraph (5)(b);

(b) the period during which judicial review proceedings are in progress includes any day on which an appeal is in progress or may be brought."

Chief officers of police and local policing bodies

140 Appointment of chief officers of police

(1) Paragraph 2 of Schedule 8 to the Police Reform and Social Responsibility Act 2011 (appointment of chief constables) is amended as follows.

(2) In sub-paragraph (1)(a), for "is, or has been, a constable in any part of the United Kingdom" there is substituted "is eligible for appointment".

(3) After sub-paragraph (1) there is inserted—

"(1A) A person is eligible for appointment if the person is or has been—

(a) a constable in any part of the United Kingdom, or

(b) a police officer in an approved overseas police force, of at least the approved rank.

(1B) An "approved overseas police force" is a police force which—

(a) is in a country or territory outside the United Kingdom designated by regulations made by the Secretary of State, and

(b) is designated in relation to that country or territory by the regulations.

(1C) The "approved rank" for an approved overseas police force is the rank which is designated as the approved rank for that police force by the regulations.

(1D) The College of Policing must recommend to the Secretary of State matters to be designated under this paragraph.

(1E) The Secretary of State may make regulations under this paragraph only if they give effect to a recommendation under sub-paragraph (1D)."

(4) Section 42 of that Act (appointment of Commissioner of Police of the Metropolis) is amended as follows.

(5) In subsection (3), for "is, or has been, a constable in any part of the United Kingdom" there is substituted "is eligible for appointment".

(6) After subsection (3) there is inserted—

"(3A) A person is eligible for appointment if the person is or has been—

(a) a constable in any part of the United Kingdom, or

(b) a police officer in an approved overseas police force, of at least the approved rank.

(3B) An "approved overseas police force" is a police force which—

(a) is in a country or territory outside the United Kingdom designated by regulations made by the Secretary of State, and

(b) is designated in relation to that country or territory by the regulations.

(3C) The "approved rank" for an approved overseas police force is the rank which is designated as the approved rank for that police force by the regulations.

(3D) The College of Policing must recommend to the Secretary of State matters to be designated under this section.

(3E) The Secretary of State may make regulations under this section only if they give effect to a recommendation under subsection (3D)."

141 Financial arrangements etc for chief officers of police

(1) In Schedule 2 to the Police Reform and Social Responsibility Act 2011 (chief constables), after paragraph 7 there is inserted—

"7A Financial arrangements etc

7A (1) A chief constable may, by way of temporary loan or overdraft from a bank or otherwise, borrow sums temporarily required by the chief constable, but only—

(a) for the purpose of meeting expenses pending the receipt of revenues receivable by the chief constable in respect of the period of account in which the expenses are chargeable,

(b) in sterling, and

(c) with the consent of the relevant police and crime commissioner.

(2) A chief constable—

(a) may not borrow money except as permitted by sub-paragraph (1);

(b) may not enter into a credit arrangement.

(3) A chief constable may invest—

(a) for any purpose relevant to the chief constable's functions under any enactment, or

(b) for the purpose of the prudent management of the chief constable's financial affairs,

but only with the consent of the relevant police and crime commissioner.

(4) The following provisions of Part 1 of the Local Government Act 2003 (capital finance etc and accounts) apply in relation to a chief constable as they apply in relation to a local authority—

(a) section 6 (protection of lenders);

(b) section 7 (meaning of "credit arrangements");

(c) sections 9 to 11 (capital receipts), except for section 11(2)(b) and (3) to (6);

(d) section 13 (security for money borrowed etc);

(e) section 14 (information);

(f) section 15 (guidance);

(g) section 16 (meaning of "capital expenditure");

(h) section 17 (external funds);

(i) section 18 (companies etc), ignoring any reference to a Passenger Transport Executive;

(j) section 20 (directions);

(k) sections 21 and 22 (accounts);

(l) section 24(1) and (2)(b) (application to Wales).

(5) Regulations made by the Secretary of State under any of the provisions listed in sub-paragraph (4) apply in relation to the chief constable of a police force in England as they apply in relation to a local authority in England.

(6) Regulations made by the Welsh Ministers under any of those provisions apply in relation to the chief constable of a police force in Wales as they apply in relation to a local authority in Wales.

(7) Any of those provisions, or regulations made under them, that apply for the purposes of Chapter 1 of Part 1 of the Local Government Act 2003 apply also (so far as relevant) for the purposes of sub-paragraphs (1) to (3).

(8) An order under section 217 or 218 of the Local Government and Public Involvement in Health Act 2007, as it has effect for the purposes of section 18(2)(b) of the Local Government Act 2003 as applied by sub-paragraph (4)(i), applies—

- (a) with the substitution of a reference to a chief constable for a reference to a local authority, and
- (b) with any other necessary modifications."

(2) In Schedule 4 to that Act (Commissioner of Police of the Metropolis), after paragraph 4 there is inserted—

"4A Financial arrangements etc

4A (1) The Commissioner of Police of the Metropolis may, by way of temporary loan or overdraft from a bank or otherwise, borrow sums temporarily required by the Commissioner, but only—

- (a) for the purpose of meeting expenses pending the receipt of revenues receivable by the Commissioner in respect of the period of account in which the expenses are chargeable,
- (b) in sterling, and
- (c) with the consent of the Mayor's Office for Policing and Crime.

(2) The Commissioner of Police of the Metropolis—

- (a) may not borrow money except as permitted by sub-paragraph (1);
- (b) may not enter into a credit arrangement.

(3) The Commissioner of Police of the Metropolis may invest—

- (a) for any purpose relevant to the Commissioner's functions under any enactment, or
- (b) for the purpose of the prudent management of the Commissioner's financial affairs,

but only with the consent of the Mayor's Office for Policing and Crime.

(4) The following provisions of Part 1 of the Local Government Act 2003 (capital finance etc and accounts), and any regulations made under them by the Secretary of State, apply in relation to the Commissioner of Police of the Metropolis as they apply in relation to a local authority in England—

- (a) section 6 (protection of lenders);
- (b) section 7 (meaning of "credit arrangements");
- (c) sections 9 to 11 (capital receipts), except for section 11(2)(b) and (3) to (6);
- (d) section 13 (security for money borrowed etc);
- (e) section 14 (information);
- (f) section 15 (guidance);
- (g) section 16 (meaning of "capital expenditure");
- (h) section 17 (external funds);

(i) section 18 (companies etc), ignoring any reference to a Passenger Transport Executive;

(j) section 20 (directions);

(k) sections 21 and 22 (accounts).

(5) Any of those provisions, or regulations made under them by the Secretary of State, that apply for the purposes of Chapter 1 of Part 1 of the Local Government Act 2003 apply also (so far as relevant) for the purposes of sub-paragraphs (1) to (3).

(6) An order under section 217 of the Local Government and Public Involvement in Health Act 2007, as it has effect for the purposes of section 18(2)(b) of the Local Government Act 2003 as applied by sub-paragraph (4)(i), applies—

(a) with the substitution of a reference to the Commissioner of Police of the Metropolis for a reference to a local authority, and

(b) with any other necessary modifications."

142 Grants to local policing bodies

(1) In section 46 of the Police Act 1996 (police grant), in subsection (1), for the words from "for each financial year" to the end of paragraph (b) there is substituted "for each financial year—

(a) make grants to police and crime commissioners for the purposes of their functions,

(b) make grants to the Common Council for the purposes of its functions as police authority, and

(c) make grants to the Greater London Authority for the purposes of the functions of the Mayor's Office for Policing and Crime;".

(2) The words "for police purposes" are omitted—

(a) in subsection (1) of section 47 of the Police Act 1996 (grants for capital expenditure);

(b) in subsection (2) of section 92 of that Act (grants by local authorities).

143 Powers of local policing bodies to provide or commission services

(1) A local policing body may provide or arrange for the provision of—

(a) services that in the opinion of the local policing body will secure, or contribute to securing, crime and disorder reduction in the body's area;

(b) services that are intended by the local policing body to help victims or witnesses of, or other persons affected by, offences and anti-social behaviour;

(c) services of a description specified in an order made by the Secretary of State.

(2) An order under subsection (1)(c) may make different provision for different areas.

(3) A local policing body arranging for the provision of services under this section may make grants in connection with the arrangements.

A grant may be subject to any conditions (including conditions as to repayment) that the local policing body thinks appropriate.

(4) In this section—

"anti-social behaviour" means behaviour by a person that causes or is likely to cause harassment, alarm or distress to one or more other persons not of the same household as that person;

"crime and disorder reduction" means reduction in levels of—

(a) crime and disorder (including anti-social behaviour and other behaviour adversely affecting the local environment),

(b) the misuse of drugs, alcohol and other substances, and

(c) re-offending.

Personal samples and DNA profiles

144 Power to take further fingerprints or non-intimate samples

(1) In section 61 of the Police and Criminal Evidence Act 1984 (fingerprinting)—

(a) in subsections (5A) and (5B), for the words after "investigation" in paragraph (b) there is substituted "but

(i) subsection (3A)(a) or (b) above applies, or

(ii) subsection (5C) below applies.";

(b) after subsection (5B) there is inserted—

"(5C) This subsection applies where—

(a) the investigation was discontinued but subsequently resumed, and

(b) before the resumption of the investigation the fingerprints were destroyed pursuant to section 63D(3) below."

(2) In section 63 of that Act (non-intimate samples)—

(a) at the end of subsection (3ZA)(b) there is inserted ", or

"(iii) subsection (3AA) below applies.";

(b) in subsection (3A)(b), for "insufficient; or" there is substituted "insufficient, or

(iii) subsection (3AA) below applies; or";

(c) after subsection (3A) there is inserted—

"(3AA) This subsection applies where the investigation was discontinued but subsequently resumed, and before the resumption of the investigation—

(a) any DNA profile derived from the sample was destroyed pursuant to section 63D(3) below, and

(b) the sample itself was destroyed pursuant to section 63R(4), (5) or (12) below."

145 Power to retain fingerprints or DNA profile in connection with different offence

(1) For section 63P of the Police and Criminal Evidence Act 1984 (section 63D material obtained for one purpose and used for another) there is substituted—

"63P Retention of 63D material in connection with different offence

(1) Subsection (2) applies if—

(a) section 63D material is taken (or, in the case of a DNA profile, derived from a sample taken) from a person in connection with the investigation of an offence, and

(b) the person is subsequently arrested for or charged with a different offence, or convicted of or given a penalty notice for a different offence.

(2) Sections 63E to 63O and sections 63Q and 63T have effect in relation to the material as if the material were also taken (or, in the case of a DNA profile, derived from a sample taken)—

(a) in connection with the investigation of the offence mentioned in subsection (1)(b),

(b) on the date on which the person was arrested for that offence (or charged with it or given a penalty notice for it, if the person was not arrested)."

(2) The amendment made by subsection (1) applies even where the event referred to in subsection (1)(b) of the substituted section 63P occurs before the day on which this section comes into force.

146 Retention of personal samples that are or may be disclosable

(1) In section 63U of the Police and Criminal Evidence Act 1984 (fingerprints and samples etc: exclusions from destruction rules)—

(a) in subsection (5) (material that is or may become disclosable to the defence), for "Sections 63D to 63Q, 63S and 63T" there is substituted "Sections 63D to 63T";

(b) after that subsection there is inserted—

"(5A) A sample that—

(a) falls within subsection (5), and

(b) but for that subsection would be required to be destroyed under section 63R,

must not be used other than for the purposes of any proceedings for the offence in connection with which the sample was taken.

(5B) A sample that once fell within subsection (5) but no longer does, and so becomes a sample to which section 63R applies, must be destroyed immediately if the time specified for its destruction under that section has already passed."

(2) In Schedule 8 to the Terrorism Act 2000 (detention of terrorist suspects etc), in paragraph 20I (substituted by paragraph 1 of Schedule 1 to the Protection of Freedoms Act 2012) (fingerprints and samples etc: exclusion from destruction rules of material that is or may become disclosable to the defence)—

(a) for "Paragraphs 20A to 20F and 20H do not apply to paragraph 20A material" there is substituted "Paragraphs 20A to 20H do not apply to material";

(b) at the end of that paragraph (which becomes sub-paragraph (1)) there is inserted—

"(2) A sample that—

(a) falls within sub-paragraph (1), and

(b) but for that sub-paragraph would be required to be destroyed under paragraph 20G,

must not be used other than for the purposes of any proceedings for the offence in connection with which the sample was taken.

(3) A sample that once fell within sub-paragraph (1) but no longer does, and so becomes a sample to which paragraph 20G applies, must be destroyed immediately if the time specified for its destruction under that paragraph has already passed."

Miscellaneous

147 Powers to seize invalid passports etc

Schedule 8 (powers to seize invalid passports etc) has effect.

148 Port and border controls

Schedule 9 (amendments of or relating to Schedules 7 and 8 to the Terrorism Act 2000) has effect.

149 Inspection of Serious Fraud Office

(1) In section 2 of the Crown Prosecution Service Inspectorate Act 2000 (functions of the Chief Inspector of the Crown Prosecution Service), after subsection (3) there is inserted—

"(3A) This section applies to the Serious Fraud Office as it applies to the Crown Prosecution Service."

(2) In section 3 of the Criminal Justice Act 1987 (disclosure of information by Serious Fraud Office)—

(a) the word "and" before paragraph (c) of subsection (1) is omitted;

(b) after that paragraph there is inserted "; and

(d) in order to comply with a requirement imposed under paragraph 7 of the Schedule to the Crown Prosecution Service Inspectorate Act 2000,";

(c) in subsection (3), for the words from "by a member of the Serious Fraud Office" to "or elsewhere and" there is substituted "by a member of the Serious Fraud Office—

(a) for the purposes of any prosecution in England and Wales, Northern Ireland or elsewhere, or

(b) in order to comply with a requirement imposed under paragraph 7 of the Schedule to the Crown Prosecution Service Inspectorate Act 2000,

and".

150 Jurisdiction of Investigatory Powers Tribunal over Surveillance Commissioners

(1) Section 91 of the Police Act 1997 (Surveillance Commissioners) is amended as follows.

(2) In subsection (10), for "sections 104 and 106" there is substituted "section 104".

(3) After subsection (10) there is inserted—

"(11) Subsection (10) is not to be read as affecting the jurisdiction of the Tribunal conferred by section 65 of the Regulation of Investigatory Powers Act 2000 or section 23 of the Regulation of Investigatory Powers (Scotland) Act 2000."

151 Fees for criminal record certificates etc

In Part 5 of the Police Act 1997 (criminal record certificates etc), in section 125 (regulations), after subsection (1) there is inserted—

"(1A) In prescribing the amount of a fee that—

(a) is payable in relation to applications under a particular provision of this Part, but

(b) is not payable in relation to applications made by volunteers,

the Secretary of State may take into account not only the costs associated with applications in relation to which the fee is payable but also the costs associated with applications under that provision made by volunteers."

152 Powers of community support officers

Schedule 10 (which amends Part 1 of Schedule 4 to the Police Reform Act 2002) has effect.

153 Use of amplified noise equipment in vicinity of the Palace of Westminster

(1) The Police Reform and Social Responsibility Act 2011 is amended as follows.

(2) After section 142 there is inserted—

"142A Other controlled areas in vicinity of the Palace of Westminster

(1) For the purposes of this Part, the "Palace of Westminster controlled area" means the area of land in the City of Westminster that is comprised in—

(a) the highways in the postal district SW1 known as—

(i) Bridge Street,

(ii) St Margaret's Street, and

(iii) Abingdon Street,

(b) so much of the highway in the postal district SW1 known as Great College Street as immediately adjoins Abingdon Street Garden,

(c) Old Palace Yard,

(d) Abingdon Street Garden (and its pathways), and

(e) Victoria Tower Gardens.

(2) In subsection (1)—

"Abingdon Street Garden" means the garden constructed on the sites of properties formerly known as 18 to 28 (both inclusive) Abingdon Street, London, SW1, together with the garden surrounding the adjoining Jewel Tower and the lawn surrounding the King George V Memorial;

"highway" has the same meaning as in the Highways Act 1980 (see section 328 of that Act);

"Old Palace Yard" includes the King George V Memorial."

(3) In section 143 (prohibited activities in controlled area of Parliament Square)—

(a) in the heading, at the end there is inserted "**or in Palace of Westminster controlled area**";

(b) in subsection (2)(a), after "Parliament Square" there is inserted "or in the Palace of Westminster controlled area".

(4) In section 144 (directions under section 143: further provision), in subsection (5), after "Parliament Square" there is inserted ", or the Palace of Westminster controlled area,".

(5) In section 145 (power to seize property)—

(a) in subsection (1), at the end there is inserted "in that area";

(b) after that subsection there is inserted—

"(1A) A constable or authorised officer may seize and retain a prohibited item that is on any land in the Palace of Westminster controlled area if it appears to that constable or officer that the item is being, or has been, used in connection with the commission of an offence under section 143 in that area.";

(c) in subsection (2), at the end there is inserted "in that area";

(d) after that subsection there is inserted—

"(2A) A constable may seize and retain a prohibited item that is on any land outside of the Palace of Westminster controlled area if it appears to the constable that the item has been used in connection with the commission of an offence under section 143 in that area.";

(e) in subsection (8), for "subsections (1) and (2)" there is substituted "this section".

(6) In section 146 (power of court on conviction)—

(a) in subsection (1)(b), for "the controlled area of Parliament Square" there is substituted "a relevant area";

(b) in subsection (2), for "the controlled area of Parliament Square" there is substituted "a relevant area";

(c) after that subsection there is inserted—

"(2A) In this section "relevant area" means an area consisting of either or both of the following areas—

(a) the controlled area of Parliament Square, and

(b) the Palace of Westminster controlled area."

(7) In section 147 (authorisation for operation of amplified noise equipment), in subsection (1)—

(a) after "Parliament Square" there is inserted "or the Palace of Westminster controlled area";

(b) after "that land" there is inserted "(or any part of it)".

(8) In section 148 (meaning of "authorised officer" and "responsible authority")—

(a) in subsection (2), after "Parliament Square" there is inserted ", or in relation to any land in the Palace of Westminster controlled area other than Royal Park land,";

(b) after subsection (3) there is inserted—

"(4) Responsible authority", in relation to any land in the Palace of Westminster controlled area, means—

(a) the Secretary of State, for any land comprised in Royal Park land;

(b) Westminster City Council, for any other land.

(5) In this section "Royal Park land" means any land of a description specified in Schedule 1 to the Royal Parks and Other Open Spaces Regulations 1997 (S.I. 1997/1639), as that Schedule has effect on the day on which the Anti-social Behaviour, Crime and Policing Act 2014 is passed."

(9) In section 149 (effect of Part on byelaws), in subsection (3), after "Parliament Square" there is inserted "or the Palace of Westminster controlled area".

(10) In the italic cross-heading before section 142, for "*Garden and adjoining pavements*" there is substituted "*etc*".

(11) In the heading of Part 3, for "GARDEN AND SURROUNDING AREA" there is substituted "ETC".

154 Littering from vehicles

(1) The Environmental Protection Act 1990 is amended as follows.

(2) After section 88 (fixed penalty notices for leaving litter) there is inserted—

"88A Littering from vehicles: civil penalty regime

(1) The Secretary of State may make regulations under which the keeper of a vehicle may be required to pay a fixed penalty to a litter authority where there is reason to believe that a littering offence in England has been committed in respect of the vehicle.

(2) A littering offence is committed in respect of a vehicle if an offence under section 87(1) occurs as a result of litter being thrown, dropped or otherwise deposited from the vehicle (whether or not by the vehicle's keeper).

(3) Regulations under this section must make provision—

(a) setting the amount of fixed penalties or specifying how the amount is to be determined;

(b) about the period within which fixed penalties must be paid;

(c) for payment within that period of a fixed penalty imposed for a littering offence committed in respect of a vehicle to discharge any liability for conviction for the offence (whether on the part of the keeper or anybody else);

(d) for a fixed penalty to be payable by the keeper of a vehicle only if a written notice is given to the keeper ("a penalty notice");
(e) about the persons authorised to give penalty notices;
(f) about the procedure to be followed in giving penalty notices;
(g) about the form and content of penalty notices;
(h) conferring rights to make representations about, and to bring appeals against, penalty notices.

(4) Provision under subsection (3)(e) may authorise a person to give a penalty notice for a littering offence committed in respect of a vehicle only if—
(a) the person is under a duty under section 89(1) in respect of the land where the offence is committed (and that person is a "litter authority" in relation to a fixed penalty payable under the regulations), or
(b) the person is an authorised officer of a litter authority,

and regulations under this section may include provision about the meaning of "authorised officer".

(5) Regulations under this section may include provision—
(a) for the enforcement of penalty notices (and such provision may in particular authorise an unpaid fixed penalty to be recovered summarily as a civil debt or as if payable under an order of a court if the court so orders);
(b) about the application of sums paid under penalty notices (and such provision may in particular authorise sums paid to a litter authority to be applied for the purposes of such functions of the authority as the regulations may specify);
(c) about the application of the regulations to keepers of vehicles in the public service of the Crown.

(6) Regulations under this section may, in consequence of any provision contained in the regulations, amend—
(a) this Part, or
(b) Part 2 of the London Local Authorities Act 2007.

(7) Regulations under this section may—
(a) make provision corresponding or similar to any provision made by or under section 88;
(b) make provision subject to exceptions;
(c) include saving, transitional, transitory, supplementary or consequential provision.

(8) Provision of the kind mentioned in subsection (7)(a) may include provision—
(a) conferring a discretion on a litter authority, subject to such constraints or limitations as the regulations may specify (whether or not of a corresponding or similar kind to those mentioned in section 97A(2));
(b) creating an offence of the kind mentioned in section 88(8B) and (8C),

but may not include provision conferring power on a person to make orders or regulations.

(9) In this section—

"keeper", in relation to a vehicle, means the person by whom the vehicle is kept at the time when the littering offence in question occurs, which in the case of a registered vehicle is to be presumed, unless the contrary is proved, to be the registered keeper;

"litter authority" has the meaning given in subsection (4)(a);

"registered keeper", in relation to a registered vehicle, means the person in whose name the vehicle is registered;

"registered vehicle" means a vehicle which is for the time being registered under the Vehicle Excise and Registration Act 1994;

"vehicle" means a mechanically-propelled vehicle or a vehicle designed or adapted for towing by a mechanically-propelled vehicle."

(3) In section 161 (regulations, orders and directions), after subsection (2ZA) there is inserted—

"(2ZB) Subsection (2) does not apply to a statutory instrument containing regulations under section 88A if the regulations—

(a) are the first set of regulations to be made under that section, or

(b) include provision falling within subsection (3)(a) or (6) of that section.

(2ZC) A statutory instrument to which subsection (2) does not apply by virtue of subsection (2ZB) may not be made unless a draft of the instrument has been laid before, and approved by a resolution of, each House of Parliament."

PART 12

EXTRADITION

Amendments of the Extradition Act 2003

155 Date of extradition hearing

In section 8 of the Extradition Act 2003 (date of extradition hearing etc: extradition to category 1 territory) after subsection (4) there is inserted—

"(4A) But if proceedings in respect of the extradition are adjourned under section 8A or 8B, the permitted period is extended by the number of days for which the proceedings are so adjourned."

156 Extradition barred if no prosecution decision in requesting territory

(1) In section 11 of the Extradition Act 2003 (bars to extradition), after paragraph (a) of subsection (1) there is inserted—

"(aa) absence of prosecution decision;".

(2) After section 12 of that Act there is inserted—

"12A Absence of prosecution decision

(1) A person's extradition to a category 1 territory is barred by reason of absence of prosecution decision if (and only if)—

(a) it appears to the appropriate judge that there are reasonable grounds for believing that—

(i) the competent authorities in the category 1 territory have not made a decision to charge or have not made a decision to try (or have made neither of those decisions), and

(ii) the person's absence from the category 1 territory is not the sole reason for that failure,

and

(b) those representing the category 1 territory do not prove that—

(i) the competent authorities in the category 1 territory have made a decision to charge and a decision to try, or

(ii) in a case where one of those decisions has not been made (or neither of them has been made), the person's absence from the category 1 territory is the sole reason for that failure.

(2) In this section "to charge" and "to try", in relation to a person and an extradition offence, mean—

(a) to charge the person with the offence in the category 1 territory, and

(b) to try the person for the offence in the category 1 territory."

(3) In a case where the Part 1 warrant (within the meaning of the Extradition Act 2003) has been issued before the time when the amendments made by this section come into force, those amendments apply to the extradition concerned only if, at that time, the judge has not yet decided all of the questions in section 11(1) of that Act.

157 Proportionality

(1) In section 11 of the Extradition Act 2003 (bars to extradition), in subsection (5), for "21" there is substituted "21A".

(2) After section 21 of that Act there is inserted—

"21A Person not convicted: human rights and proportionality

(1) If the judge is required to proceed under this section (by virtue of section 11), the judge must decide both of the following questions in respect of the extradition of the person ("D")—

(a) whether the extradition would be compatible with the Convention rights within the meaning of the Human Rights Act 1998;

(b) whether the extradition would be disproportionate.

(2) In deciding whether the extradition would be disproportionate, the judge must take into account the specified matters relating to proportionality (so far as the judge thinks it appropriate to do so); but the judge must not take any other matters into account.

(3) These are the specified matters relating to proportionality—

(a) the seriousness of the conduct alleged to constitute the extradition offence;

(b) the likely penalty that would be imposed if D was found guilty of the extradition offence;

(c) the possibility of the relevant foreign authorities taking measures that would be less coercive than the extradition of D.

(4) The judge must order D's discharge if the judge makes one or both of these decisions—

(a) that the extradition would not be compatible with the Convention rights;

(b) that the extradition would be disproportionate.

(5) The judge must order D to be extradited to the category 1 territory in which the warrant was issued if the judge makes both of these decisions—

(a) that the extradition would be compatible with the Convention rights;

(b) that the extradition would not be disproportionate.

(6) If the judge makes an order under subsection (5) he must remand the person in custody or on bail to wait for extradition to the category 1 territory.

(7) If the person is remanded in custody, the appropriate judge may later grant bail.

(8) In this section "relevant foreign authorities" means the authorities in the territory to which D would be extradited if the extradition went ahead."

(3) In section 2 of that Act (Part 1 warrant and certificate), after subsection (7) there is inserted—

"(7A) But in the case of a Part 1 warrant containing the statement referred to in subsection (3), the designated authority must not issue a certificate under this section if it is clear to the designated authority that a judge proceeding under section 21A would be required to order the person's discharge on the basis that extradition would be disproportionate.

In deciding that question, the designated authority must apply any general guidance issued for the purposes of this subsection.

(7B) Any guidance under subsection (7A) may be revised, withdrawn or replaced.

(7C) The function of issuing guidance under subsection (7A), or of revising, withdrawing or replacing any such guidance, is exercisable by the Lord Chief Justice of England and Wales with the concurrence of—

(a) the Lord Justice General of Scotland, and

(b) the Lord Chief Justice of Northern Ireland."

(4) In deciding any question whether section 21A of the Extradition Act 2003 is compatible with European Union law, regard must be had (in particular) to Article 1(3) of the framework decision of the Council of the European Union made on 13 June 2002 on the European arrest warrant and the surrender procedures between member states (2002/584/JHA) (which provides that that decision shall not have the effect of modifying the obligation to respect fundamental rights and fundamental legal principles as enshrined in Article 6 of the Treaty on European Union).

(5) In a case where the Part 1 warrant (within the meaning of the Extradition Act 2003) has been issued before the time when the amendments made by this section come into force, those amendments apply to the extradition concerned only if, at that time, the judge has not yet decided all of the questions in section 11(1) of that Act.

158 Hostage-taking considerations

(1) Section 16 of the Extradition Act 2003 (extradition to category 1 territory barred by reason of hostage-taking considerations) is repealed.

(2) In section 11 of that Act (bars to extradition), paragraph (e) of subsection (1) is omitted.

(3) In a case where the Part 1 warrant (within the meaning of the Extradition Act 2003) has been issued before the time when the amendments made by this section come into force, those amendments apply to the extradition concerned only if, at that time, the judge has not yet decided all of the questions in section 11(1) of that Act.

159 Request for temporary transfer etc

Before section 22 of the Extradition Act 2003 there is inserted—

"21B Request for temporary transfer etc

(1) This section applies if—

(a) a Part 1 warrant is issued which contains the statement referred to in section 2(3) (warrant issued for purposes of prosecution for offence in category 1 territory), and

(b) at any time before or in the extradition hearing, the appropriate judge is informed that a request under subsection (2) or (3) has been made.

(2) A request under this subsection is a request by a judicial authority of the category 1 territory in which the warrant is issued ("the requesting territory")—

(a) that the person in respect of whom the warrant is issued be temporarily transferred to the requesting territory, or

(b) that arrangements be made to enable the person to speak with representatives of an authority in the requesting territory responsible for investigating, prosecuting or trying the offence specified in the warrant.

(3) A request under this subsection is a request by the person in respect of whom the warrant is issued—

(a) to be temporarily transferred to the requesting territory, or

(b) that arrangements be made to enable the person to speak with representatives of an authority in the requesting territory responsible for investigating, prosecuting or trying the offence specified in the warrant.

(4) The judge must order further proceedings in respect of the extradition to be adjourned if the judge thinks it necessary to do so to enable the person (in the case of a request under subsection (2)) or the authority by which the warrant is issued (in the case of a request under subsection (3)) to consider whether to consent to the request.

An adjournment under this subsection must not be for more than 7 days.

(5) If the person or authority consents to the request, the judge must—

(a) make whatever orders and directions seem appropriate for giving effect to the request;

(b) order further proceedings in respect of the extradition to be adjourned for however long seems necessary to enable the orders and directions to be carried out.

(6) If the request, or consent to the request, is withdrawn before effect (or full effect) has been given to it—

(a) no steps (or further steps) may be taken to give effect to the request;

(b) the judge may make whatever further orders and directions seem appropriate (including an order superseding one made under subsection (5)(b)).

(7) A person may not make a request under paragraph (a) or (b) of subsection (3) in respect of a warrant if the person has already given consent to a request under the corresponding paragraph of subsection (2) in respect of that warrant (even if that consent has been withdrawn).

(8) A person may not make a further request under paragraph (a) or (b) of subsection (3) in respect of a warrant if the person has already made a request under that paragraph in respect of that warrant (even if that request has been withdrawn).

(9) If—

(a) a request under subsection (2) or (3) is made before a date has been fixed on which the extradition hearing is to begin, and

(b) the proceedings are adjourned under this section,

the permitted period for the purposes of fixing that date (see section 8(4)) is extended by the number of days for which the proceedings are so adjourned."

160 Appeals

(1) In section 26 of the Extradition Act 2003 (appeal against extradition order: category 1 territory)—

(a) in subsection (3), for "section may" there is substituted "section—

(a) may";

(b) at the end of that subsection there is inserted ", but

(b) lies only with the leave of the High Court.";

(c) after subsection (4) there is inserted—

"(5) But where a person gives notice of application for leave to appeal after the end of the permitted period, the High Court must not for that reason refuse to entertain the application if the person did everything reasonably possible to ensure that the notice was given as soon as it could be given."

(2) In section 28 of that Act (appeal against discharge at extradition hearing: category 1 territory)—

(a) in subsection (4), for "section may" there is substituted "section—

(a) may";

(b) at the end of that subsection there is inserted ", but

(b) lies only with the leave of the High Court."

(3) In section 103 of that Act (appeal where case sent to Secretary of State)—

(a) in subsection (4), for "section may" there is substituted "section—

(a) may";

(b) at the end of that subsection there is inserted ", but

(b) lies only with the leave of the High Court.";

(c) after subsection (9) there is inserted—

"(10) But where a person gives notice of application for leave to appeal after the end of the permitted period, the High Court must not for that reason refuse to entertain the application if the person did everything reasonably possible to ensure that the notice was given as soon as it could be given."

(4) In section 105 of that Act (appeal against discharge at extradition hearing: category 2 territory)—

(a) in subsection (4), for "section may" there is substituted "section—

(a) may";

(b) at the end of that subsection there is inserted ", but

(b) lies only with the leave of the High Court."

(5) In section 108 of that Act (appeal against extradition order: category 2 territory)—

(a) in subsection (3), for "section may" there is substituted "section—

(a) may";

(b) at the end of that subsection there is inserted ", but

(b) lies only with the leave of the High Court.";

(c) after subsection (7) there is inserted—

"(7A) Where a person gives notice of application for leave to appeal after the end of the permitted period (whether or not the application is for leave to appeal on human rights grounds), the High Court must not for that reason refuse to entertain the application if the person did everything reasonably possible to ensure that the notice was given as soon as it could be given."

(6) In section 110 of that Act (appeal against discharge by Secretary of State)—

(a) in subsection (4), for "section may" there is substituted "section—

(a) may";

(b) at the end of that subsection there is inserted ", but

(b) lies only with the leave of the High Court."

161 Judge informed after extradition hearing or order that person is charged with offence or serving sentence in United Kingdom

(1) After section 36A of the Extradition Act 2003 there is inserted—

"36B Judge informed after extradition hearing that person is charged with offence in United Kingdom

(1) This section applies if—

(a) an order has been made for the extradition of the person in respect of whom the Part 1 warrant is issued, and

(b) before the extradition order is carried out the appropriate judge is informed that the person is charged with an offence in the United Kingdom.

(2) The appropriate judge must order the extradition order not to be carried out until one of these occurs—

(a) the charge is disposed of;

(b) the charge is withdrawn;

(c) proceedings in respect of the charge are discontinued;

(d) an order is made for the charge to lie on the file, or in relation to Scotland, the diet is deserted *pro loco et tempore*.

(3) If a sentence of imprisonment or another form of detention is imposed in respect of the offence charged, the appropriate judge may order the extradition order not to be carried out until the person is released from detention pursuant to the sentence (whether on licence or otherwise).

(4) Rules of court may provide that where there is an appeal against the extradition order —

(a) a reference in this section to the appropriate judge has effect, in prescribed circumstances, as if it were a reference to the court hearing the appeal, and

(b) this section has effect with any other prescribed modifications.

36C Judge informed after extradition hearing that person is serving sentence in United Kingdom

(1) This section applies if—

(a) an order has been made for the extradition of the person in respect of whom the Part 1 warrant is issued, and

(b) before the extradition order is carried out the appropriate judge is informed that the person is serving a sentence of imprisonment or another form of detention in the United Kingdom.

(2) The appropriate judge may order the extradition order not to be carried out until the person is released from detention pursuant to the sentence (whether on licence or otherwise).

(3) Rules of court may provide that where there is an appeal against the extradition order —

(a) a reference in this section to the appropriate judge has effect, in prescribed circumstances, as if it were a reference to the court hearing the appeal, and

(b) this section has effect with any other prescribed modifications."

(2) After section 118B of that Act there is inserted—

"118C Judge informed after extradition order that person is charged with offence in United Kingdom

(1) This section applies if—

(a) the Secretary of State has made an order for a person's extradition under this Part, and

(b) before the extradition order is carried out the appropriate judge is informed that the person is charged with an offence in the United Kingdom.

(2) The appropriate judge must order the extradition order not to be carried out until one of these occurs—

(a) the charge is disposed of;

(b) the charge is withdrawn;

(c) proceedings in respect of the charge are discontinued;

(d) an order is made for the charge to lie on the file, or in relation to Scotland, the diet is deserted *pro loco et tempore*.

(3) If a sentence of imprisonment or another form of detention is imposed in respect of the offence charged, the appropriate judge may order the extradition order not to be carried out until the person is released from detention pursuant to the sentence (whether on licence or otherwise).

(4) Rules of court may provide that where there is an appeal against the extradition order —

(a) a reference in this section to the appropriate judge has effect, in prescribed circumstances, as if it were a reference to the court hearing the appeal, and

(b) this section has effect with any other prescribed modifications.

118D Judge informed after extradition order that person is serving sentence in United Kingdom

(1) This section applies if—

(a) the Secretary of State has made an order for a person's extradition under this Part, and

(b) before the extradition order is carried out the appropriate judge is informed that the person is serving a sentence of imprisonment or another form of detention in the United Kingdom.

(2) The appropriate judge may order the extradition order not to be carried out until the person is released from detention pursuant to the sentence (whether on licence or otherwise).

(3) Rules of court may provide that where there is an appeal against the extradition order—

(a) a reference in this section to the appropriate judge has effect, in prescribed circumstances, as if it were a reference to the court hearing the appeal, and

(b) this section has effect with any other prescribed modifications."

162 Asylum etc

(1) In section 39 of the Extradition Act 2003 (asylum claim: extradition to category 1 territory)—

(a) subsections (1) and (2) are repealed;

(b) in subsection (3), for "The person" there is substituted "If—

(a) an order is made under this Part for a person to be extradited in pursuance of a Part 1 warrant, and

(b) the person has made an asylum claim (whether before or after the issue of the warrant),

the person".

(2) In section 121 of that Act (asylum claim: extradition to category 2 territory)—

(a) subsections (1) and (2) are repealed;

(b) in subsection (3), for "The person" there is substituted "If—

(a) an order is made under this Part for a person to be extradited in pursuance of a request, and

(b) the person has made an asylum claim (whether before or after the making of the request),

the person".

(3) In section 93 of that Act (Secretary of State's consideration of case)—

(a) in subsection (4)(c), after "he orders the person's discharge" there is inserted "under subsection (6A) or";

(b) after subsection (6) there is inserted—

"(6A) The Secretary of State may order the person's discharge if the person—

(a) has been recorded by the Secretary of State as a refugee within the meaning of the Refugee Convention, or

(b) has been granted leave to enter or remain in the United Kingdom on the ground that it would be a breach of Article 2 or 3 of the Human Rights Convention to remove the person to the territory to which extradition is requested."

163 Consent to extradition not to be taken as waiver of speciality rights

In the Extradition Act 2003 the following provisions are repealed—

(a) section 45(3);

(b) section 128(5).

164 Definition of "extradition offence"

(1) For sections 64 and 65 of the Extradition Act 2003 there is substituted—

"64 Extradition offences: person not sentenced for offence

(1) This section sets out whether a person's conduct constitutes an "extradition offence" for the purposes of this Part in a case where the person—

(a) is accused in a category 1 territory of an offence constituted by the conduct, or

(b) has been convicted in that territory of an offence constituted by the conduct but not sentenced for it.

(2) The conduct constitutes an extradition offence in relation to the category 1 territory if the conditions in subsection (3), (4) or (5) are satisfied.

(3) The conditions in this subsection are that—

(a) the conduct occurs in the category 1 territory;

(b) the conduct would constitute an offence under the law of the relevant part of the United Kingdom if it occurred in that part of the United Kingdom;

(c) the conduct is punishable under the law of the category 1 territory with imprisonment or another form of detention for a term of 12 months or a greater punishment.

(4) The conditions in this subsection are that—

(a) the conduct occurs outside the category 1 territory;

(b) in corresponding circumstances equivalent conduct would constitute an extra-territorial offence under the law of the relevant part of the United Kingdom;

(c) the conduct is punishable under the law of the category 1 territory with imprisonment or another form of detention for a term of 12 months or a greater punishment.

(5) The conditions in this subsection are that—

(a) the conduct occurs in the category 1 territory;

(b) no part of the conduct occurs in the United Kingdom;

(c) a certificate issued by an appropriate authority of the category 1 territory shows that the conduct falls within the European framework list;

(d) the certificate shows that the conduct is punishable under the law of the category 1 territory with imprisonment or another form of detention for a term of 3 years or a greater punishment.

(6) For the purposes of subsections (3)(b) and (4)(b)—

(a) if the conduct relates to a tax or duty, it does not matter whether the law of the relevant part of the United Kingdom imposes the same kind of tax or duty or contains rules of the same kind as those of the law of the category 1 territory;

(b) if the conduct relates to customs or exchange, it does not matter whether the law of the relevant part of the United Kingdom contains rules of the same kind as those of the law of the category 1 territory.

65 Extradition offences: person sentenced for offence

(1) This section sets out whether a person's conduct constitutes an "extradition offence" for the purposes of this Part in a case where the person—

(a) has been convicted in a category 1 territory of an offence constituted by the conduct, and

(b) has been sentenced for the offence.

(2) The conduct constitutes an extradition offence in relation to the category 1 territory if the conditions in subsection (3), (4) or (5) are satisfied.

(3) The conditions in this subsection are that—

(a) the conduct occurs in the category 1 territory;

(b) the conduct would constitute an offence under the law of the relevant part of the United Kingdom if it occurred in that part of the United Kingdom;

(c) a sentence of imprisonment or another form of detention for a term of 4 months or a greater punishment has been imposed in the category 1 territory in respect of the conduct.

(4) The conditions in this subsection are that—

(a) the conduct occurs outside the category 1 territory;

(b) in corresponding circumstances equivalent conduct would constitute an extra-territorial offence under the law of the relevant part of the United Kingdom;

(c) a sentence of imprisonment or another form of detention for a term of 4 months or a greater punishment has been imposed in the category 1 territory in respect of the conduct.

(5) The conditions in this subsection are that—

(a) the conduct occurs in the category 1 territory;

(b) no part of the conduct occurs in the United Kingdom;

(c) a certificate issued by an appropriate authority of the category 1 territory shows that the conduct falls within the European framework list;

(d) the certificate shows that a sentence of imprisonment or another form of detention for a term of 4 months or a greater punishment has been imposed in the category 1 territory in respect of the conduct.

(6) For the purposes of subsections (3)(b) and (4)(b)—

(a) if the conduct relates to a tax or duty, it does not matter whether the law of the relevant part of the United Kingdom imposes the same kind of tax or duty or contains rules of the same kind as those of the law of the category 1 territory;

(b) if the conduct relates to customs or exchange, it does not matter whether the law of the relevant part of the United Kingdom contains rules of the same kind as those of the law of the category 1 territory."

(2) In section 66 (supplementary provision for the purposes of sections 64 and 65) after subsection (1) there is inserted—

"(1A) References to "conduct" (except in the expression "equivalent conduct") are to the conduct specified in the Part 1 warrant."

(3) In section 137 of that Act (definition of extradition offence for the purposes of Part 2 of the Act: person not sentenced for offence) for subsections (1) to (5) there is substituted—

"(1) This section sets out whether a person's conduct constitutes an "extradition offence" for the purposes of this Part in a case where the person—

(a) is accused in a category 2 territory of an offence constituted by the conduct, or

(b) has been convicted in that territory of an offence constituted by the conduct but not sentenced for it.

(2) The conduct constitutes an extradition offence in relation to the category 2 territory if the conditions in subsection (3), (4) or (5) are satisfied.

(3) The conditions in this subsection are that—

(a) the conduct occurs in the category 2 territory;

(b) the conduct would constitute an offence under the law of the relevant part of the United Kingdom punishable with imprisonment or another form of detention for a term of 12 months or a greater punishment if it occurred in that part of the United Kingdom;

(c) the conduct is so punishable under the law of the category 2 territory.

(4) The conditions in this subsection are that—

(a) the conduct occurs outside the category 2 territory;

(b) in corresponding circumstances equivalent conduct would constitute an extra-territorial offence under the law of the relevant part of the United Kingdom punishable with imprisonment or another form of detention for a term of 12 months or a greater punishment;

(c) the conduct is so punishable under the law of the category 2 territory.

(5) The conditions in this subsection are that—

(a) the conduct occurs outside the category 2 territory;

(b) no part of the conduct occurs in the United Kingdom;

(c) the conduct constitutes, or if committed in the United Kingdom would constitute, an offence mentioned in subsection (6);

(d) the conduct is punishable under the law of the category 2 territory with imprisonment or another form of detention for a term of 12 months or a greater punishment."

(4) After subsection (7) of that section there is inserted—

"(7A) References in this section to "conduct" (except in the expression "equivalent conduct") are to the conduct specified in the request for the person's extradition".

(5) In section 138 of that Act (definition of "extradition offence" for the purposes of Part 2 of the Act: person sentenced for offence) for subsections (1) to (5) there is substituted—

"(1) This section sets out whether a person's conduct constitutes an "extradition offence" for the purposes of this Part in a case where the person—

(a) has been convicted, in the category 2 territory to which extradition is requested, of an offence constituted by the conduct, and

(b) has been sentenced for the offence.

(2) The conduct constitutes an extradition offence in relation to the category 2 territory if the conditions in subsection (3), (4) or (5) are satisfied.

(3) The conditions in this subsection are that—

(a) the conduct occurs in the category 2 territory;

(b) the conduct would constitute an offence under the law of the relevant part of the United Kingdom punishable with imprisonment or another form of detention for a term of 12 months or a greater punishment if it occurred in that part of the United Kingdom;

(c) a sentence of imprisonment or another form of detention for a term of 4 months or a greater punishment has been imposed in the category 2 territory in respect of the conduct.

(4) The conditions in this subsection are that—

(a) the conduct occurs outside the category 2 territory;

(b) in corresponding circumstances equivalent conduct would constitute an extra-territorial offence under the relevant part of the United Kingdom punishable as mentioned in subsection (3)(b);

(c) a sentence of imprisonment or another form of detention for a term of 4 months or a greater punishment has been imposed in the category 2 territory in respect of the conduct.

(5) The conditions in this subsection are that—

(a) the conduct occurs outside the category 2 territory;

(b) no part of the conduct occurs in the United Kingdom;

(c) the conduct constitutes, or if committed in the United Kingdom would constitute, an offence mentioned in subsection (6);

(d) a sentence of imprisonment or another form of detention for a term of 4 months or a greater punishment has been imposed in the category 2 territory in respect of the conduct."

(6) After subsection (7) of that section there is inserted—

"(7A) References in this section to "conduct" (except in the expression "equivalent conduct") are to the conduct specified in the request for the person's extradition".

165 Extradition to the United Kingdom to be sentenced or to serve a sentence

In section 142 of the Extradition Act 2003 (issue of Part 3 warrant), for subsection (2A) there is substituted—

"(2A) The condition is that—

(a) the person has been convicted of an extradition offence by a court in the United Kingdom,

(b) his extradition is sought for the purpose of his being sentenced for the offence or of his serving a sentence of imprisonment or another form of detention imposed in respect of the offence, and

(c) either a domestic warrant has been issued in respect of the person or the person may be arrested without a warrant."

166 Detention of extradited person for trial in England and Wales for other offences

(1) In sections 150 and 151A of the Extradition Act 2003 (dealing with extradited person for other offences), at the end of subsection (2) there is inserted—

"This is subject to section 151B."

(2) After section 151A of that Act there is inserted—

"151B Detention of person for trial in England and Wales for other offences

(1) Section 150 or 151A does not prevent a person in whose case that section applies from being detained with a view to trial in England and Wales for an offence if the conditions in subsection (2) are satisfied.

(2) The conditions are that—

(a) the United Kingdom and the territory from which the person was extradited have each made a declaration under Article 14(3) of the Extradition Convention, and the declarations are still in force;

(b) the Secretary of State makes a request for the consent referred to in section 150(3)(c) or 151A(3)(c) in respect of the offence ("the consent request");

(c) the Secretary of State gives notification, which is explicitly acknowledged on behalf of the territory, of the date on which the detention is to begin ("the notified date").

(3) The Extradition Convention is the European Convention on Extradition done at Paris on 13 December 1957.

(4) This section applies only to detention during the period beginning with the notified date and ending with whichever of the following occurs first—

(a) if a notification of opposition to the detention is given on behalf of the territory, the date on which Secretary of State receives it;

(b) the date on which the Secretary of State receives notification given on behalf of the territory as to whether the consent request is granted or refused;

(c) the expiry of the period of 90 days beginning with the date on which the consent request is received."

167 Proceedings on deferred warrant or request etc

(1) In section 180 of the Extradition Act 2003 (proceedings on deferred warrant or request) —

(a) in subsection (1), at the end of paragraph (b) there is inserted "in the person's favour";

(b) after subsection (9) there is inserted—

"(10) An extradition claim made in respect of a person is disposed of in the person's favour if—

(a) in the case of a Part 1 warrant, the warrant is disposed of as mentioned in subsection (1)(a) or (b) of section 213;

(b) in the case of a request for extradition, the request is disposed of as mentioned in subsection (2)(a) or (b) of that section."

(2) In section 181 of that Act (proceedings where extradition deferred)—

(a) in subsection (1), at the end of paragraph (b) there is inserted "in the person's favour";

(b) after subsection (9) there is inserted—

"(10) An extradition claim made in respect of a person is disposed of in the person's favour if—

(a) in the case of a Part 1 warrant, the warrant is disposed of as mentioned in subsection (1)(a) or (b) of section 213;

(b) in the case of a request for extradition, the request is disposed of as mentioned in subsection (2)(a) or (b) of that section."

168 Non-UK extradition: transit through the United Kingdom

After section 189 of the Extradition Act 2003 there is inserted—

"Non-UK extradition: transit through the United Kingdom

189A Facilitating transit through the United Kingdom

(1) The relevant UK authority may issue a transit certificate in relation to the non-UK extradition of a person if that authority has been requested to facilitate the transit of the person through the United Kingdom for the purposes of the extradition.

(2) If the relevant UK authority issues a transit certificate in relation to the non-UK extradition of a person, an authorised officer may do any or all of the following—

(a) escort the person from, or to, any means of transport used for the purposes of the extradition;

(b) take the person into custody to facilitate the transit of the person through the United Kingdom for the purposes of the extradition;

(c) search the person, and any item in the possession of the person, for any item which the person might use to cause physical injury to that person or any other person;

(d) in a case where the person has been taken into custody under paragraph (b), search the person, and any item in the possession of the person, for any item which the person might use to escape from custody.

(3) An authorised officer searching a person in the exercise of a power conferred by subsection (2)(c) or (d) may seize any item found if the officer has reasonable grounds for believing that the person searched might use the item—

(a) to cause physical injury to that person or any other person; or
(b) in a case where the person has been taken into custody, to escape from custody.

(4) If no request is made under subsection (1) in relation to the non-UK extradition of a person, or if such a request is made but a transit certificate is not issued, that does not—
(a) prevent the transit of the person through the United Kingdom for the purposes of the extradition; or
(b) affect the powers which an authorised officer has (otherwise than under this section) in relation to the person while in the United Kingdom.

189B Unscheduled arrival in the United Kingdom

(1) This section applies in a case where—
(a) a person is being extradited,
(b) the extradition is a non-UK extradition, and
(c) the person makes an unscheduled arrival in the United Kingdom.

(2) An authorised officer may do any or all of the following—
(a) take the person into custody to facilitate the transit of the person through the United Kingdom for the purposes of the extradition;
(b) search the person, and any item in the possession of the person, for any item which the person might use to cause physical injury to that person or any other person;
(c) in a case where the person has been taken into custody under paragraph (a), search the person, and any item in the possession of the person, for any item which the person might use to escape from custody.

(3) Any power conferred by subsection (2) may be exercised—
(a) upon the unscheduled arrival, or
(b) at any later time when the person is still in the United Kingdom after the unscheduled arrival.

(4) A person taken into custody under this section may be kept in custody until the expiry of the period of 72 hours beginning with the time when the person is taken (or first taken) into custody under this section.

(5) But if a transit certificate is issued under section 189A in respect of the non-UK extradition of the person, the person must not be kept in custody under this section after the issue of the certificate.

(6) Subsection (5) does not prevent the person from being taken into custody under section 189A.

(7) An authorised officer searching a person in the exercise of a power conferred by subsection (2)(b) or (c) may seize any item found if the officer has reasonable grounds for believing that the person searched might use the item—
(a) to cause physical injury to that person or any other person; or
(b) in a case where the person has been taken into custody, to escape from custody.

189C Exercise of the extradition transit powers

(1) The extradition transit powers include power to use reasonable force when necessary.

(2) An authorised officer may not, when exercising a relevant search power, require a person to remove any clothing other than an outer coat, jacket, headgear or gloves.

(3) Any item seized from a person in the exercise of a relevant search power may be retained while the person is in transit through the United Kingdom.

189D Codes of practice

(1) The Secretary of State must issue a code of practice in connection with—
- (a) the exercise of extradition transit powers;
- (b) the retention, use and return of anything seized under a relevant search power.

(2) If the Secretary of State proposes to issue a code of practice under this section the Secretary of State must—
- (a) publish a draft of the code;
- (b) consider any representations made to the Secretary of State about the draft;
- (c) if the Secretary of State thinks it appropriate, modify the draft in the light of any such representations.

(3) The Secretary of State must lay the code before Parliament.

(4) After doing so the Secretary of State may bring the code into operation by order.

(5) The Secretary of State may revise the whole or any part of a code issued under this section and issue the code as revised; and subsections (2) to (4) apply to such a revised code as they apply to the original code.

(6) A failure by an authorised officer to comply with a provision of a code issued under this section does not of itself make the authorised officer liable to criminal or civil proceedings.

(7) A code issued under this section is admissible in evidence in any proceedings and must be taken into account by a court in determining any question to which it appears to the court to be relevant.

(8) If the Secretary of State publishes a draft code of practice in connection with a matter specified in subsection (1) before the date on which this section comes into force—
- (a) the draft is as effective as one published under subsection (2) on or after that date;
- (b) representations made to the Secretary of State about the draft before that date are as effective as such representations made after that date;
- (c) modifications made by the Secretary of State to the draft in the light of any such representations before that date are as effective as any such modifications made on or after that date.

189E Sections 189A to 189D: interpretation

(1) An "authorised officer" is—

(a) a constable, or

(b) a person who is of a description specified by the Secretary of State by order.

(2) A National Crime Agency officer, prison officer, or any other person who has the powers of a constable (but is not a constable)—

(a) does not have the extradition transit powers by virtue of having the powers of a constable; and

(b) accordingly, has the extradition transit powers only if the person is of a description specified under subsection (1)(b).

(3) These expressions have the meanings given—

"extradition transit powers" means the powers under—

(a) section 189A (except the power to issue transit certificates), and

(b) section 189B;

"foreign territory" means a territory outside the United Kingdom;

"non-UK extradition" means extradition from one foreign territory to another foreign territory;

"relevant search power" means a power of search under—

(a) section 189A(2)(c) or (d), or

(b) section 189B(2)(b) or (c);

"relevant UK authority" means—

(a) the National Crime Agency (in the case of a non-UK extradition to a category 1 territory), or

(b) the Secretary of State (in any other case).

(4) A reference to the transit of a person through the United Kingdom is a reference to the person arriving in, being in, and departing from the United Kingdom (whether or not the person travels within the United Kingdom between arrival and departure).

(5) This section applies for the purposes of section 189A to 189D (and this section)."

169 Extradition to a territory that is party to an international Convention

For section 193 of the Extradition Act 2003 there is substituted—

"193 Parties to international Conventions

(1) The Secretary of State may by order—

(a) designate an international Convention to which the United Kingdom is a party, and

(b) specify conduct to which the Convention applies.

(2) If the Secretary of State believes, in respect of a request for a person's extradition, that—

(a) the request is for extradition to a territory that is a party to a Convention designated under subsection (1)(a),

(b) the territory is not a category 1 territory or a category 2 territory, and

(c) the conduct specified in the request is conduct specified under subsection (1)(b),

the Secretary of State may certify that the conditions in paragraphs (a) to (c) are satisfied in relation to the extradition of the person.

(3) If the Secretary of State issues a certificate under subsection (2) this Act applies in respect of the person's extradition to the territory as if the territory were a category 2 territory.

(4) As applied by subsection (3), this Act has effect as if—

(a) sections 71(4), 73(5), 74(11)(b), 84(7), 86(7), 137 and 138 were omitted;

(b) the conduct that constituted an extradition offence for the purposes of Part 2 were the conduct specified under subsection (1)(b).

(5) A certificate under subsection (3) in relation to a person is conclusive evidence that the conditions in paragraphs (a) to (c) of subsection (2) are satisfied in relation to the person's extradition."

170 Electronic transmission of European arrest warrant etc

In section 204 of the Extradition Act 2003 (warrant issued by category 1 territory: transmission by electronic means), in subsection (5)—

(a) for "subsection (1), a" there is substituted "subsection (1)—

(a) a";

(b) at the end there is inserted—

"(b) information contained in the warrant is treated as being received by the designated authority in a form in which it is intelligible if the authority receives—

(i) a summary of that information in English, and

(ii) the text of the warrant itself,

in a form in which it is legible."

Time spent in custody awaiting extradition to the United Kingdom

171 Discount on sentence for time spent in custody awaiting extradition: England and Wales

In section 49 of the Prison Act 1952 (persons unlawfully at large), after subsection (3) there is inserted—

"(3A) Where—

(a) a person is extradited to the United Kingdom from a category 1 territory for the purpose of serving a term of imprisonment or another form of detention mentioned in subsection (2) of this section, and

(b) the person was for any time kept in custody in that territory with a view to the extradition (and not also for any other reason), the Secretary of State shall exercise the power under that subsection to direct that account shall be taken of that time in calculating the period for which the person is liable to be detained.

(3B) In subsection (3A) of this section "category 1 territory" means a territory designated under the Extradition Act 2003 for the purposes of Part 1 of that Act."

172 Discount on sentence for time spent in custody awaiting extradition: Scotland

(1) Section 210 of the Criminal Procedure (Scotland) Act 1995 (consideration of time spent in custody) is amended as follows.

(2) In subsection (1)—

(a) in paragraph (a), after "United Kingdom" there is inserted "otherwise than from a category 1 territory";

(b) in paragraph (c)(ii), for "for the purposes of this section" there is substituted "who was extradited to the United Kingdom otherwise than from a category 1 territory".

(3) After subsection (1) there is inserted—

"(1A) Subsection (1B) applies where—

(a) a court is passing a sentence of imprisonment or detention on a person for an offence, and

(b) the person is an extradited prisoner who was extradited to the United Kingdom from a category 1 territory.

(1B) The court shall specify—

(a) the period of time spent in custody awaiting extradition, and

(b) the date of commencement of the sentence in accordance with subsection (1C).

(1C) The date of commencement of the sentence is to be a date the relevant number of days earlier than the date the sentence would have commenced had the person not spent time in custody awaiting extradition.

(1D) In subsection (1C), "the relevant number of days" means the number of days in the period specified under subsection (1B)(a)."

(4) After subsection (2) there is inserted—

"(2A) In this section, "category 1 territory" means a territory designated under the Extradition Act 2003 for the purposes of Part 1 of that Act."

(5) Subsection (3) is repealed.

173 Discount on sentence for time spent in custody awaiting extradition: Northern Ireland

(1) In section 38 of the Prison Act (Northern Ireland) 1953 (arrest, etc, of persons unlawfully at large), for subsection (3) there is substituted—

"(3) The provisions of subsection (2) shall not apply to any period during which any such person—

(a) is detained in pursuance of any other sentence of any court in the United Kingdom in a prison or other institution, or

(b) is kept in custody in a category 1 territory before, and only for the purpose of, being extradited to the United Kingdom to serve the term of imprisonment or detention referred to in that subsection,

but shall apply in addition to any other provisions of this Act imposing any punishment for an escape.

(3A) In subsection (3) "category 1 territory" means a territory designated under the Extradition Act 2003 for the purposes of Part 1 of that Act."

(2) In section 26 of the Treatment of Offenders Act (Northern Ireland) 1968 (duration of sentence), at the end of subsection (2A) there is inserted "; or

(c) any period during which he was in custody in a category 1 territory with a view to his being extradited to the United Kingdom to be tried or sentenced for that offence (and not for any other reason).

In paragraph (c) "category 1 territory" means a territory designated under the Extradition Act 2003 for the purposes of Part 1 of that Act."

Procedure rules

174 Criminal Procedure Rules to apply to extradition proceedings etc

(1) In section 68 of the Courts Act 2003 (Criminal Procedure Rules: meaning of "criminal court"), at the end there is inserted—

"(c) the High Court in relation to its jurisdiction under the Extradition Act 2003."

(2) In section 1 of the Civil Procedure Act 1997 (Civil Procedure Rules), in subsection (1)(b), after "the High Court" there is inserted "except in relation to its jurisdiction under the Extradition Act 2003".

(3) In section 157 of the Extradition Act 2003 (production orders), after subsection (8) there is inserted—

"(9) Criminal Procedure Rules may make provision about applications under this section to a circuit judge."

(4) In section 160 of that Act (warrants: special procedure material and excluded material), after subsection (9) there is inserted—

"(10) Criminal Procedure Rules may make provision about applications under this section to a circuit judge."

PART 13

CRIMINAL JUSTICE AND COURT FEES

175 Compensation for miscarriages of justice

(1) In section 133 of the Criminal Justice Act 1988 (compensation for miscarriages of justice) after subsection (1) there is inserted—

"(1ZA) For the purposes of subsection (1), there has been a miscarriage of justice in relation to a person convicted of a criminal offence in England and Wales or, in a case where subsection (6H) applies, Northern Ireland, if and only if the new or newly discovered fact shows beyond reasonable doubt that the person did not commit the offence (and references in the rest of this Part to a miscarriage of justice are to be construed accordingly)."

(2) Subsection (1ZA) of section 133 of the Criminal Justice Act 1988 has effect in relation to—

(a) any application for compensation made under subsection (2) of that section on or after the day on which this section comes into force, and

(b) any application for compensation made before that day in relation to which the question whether there is a right to compensation has not been finally determined before that day by the Secretary of State under subsection (3) of that section.

176 Low-value shoplifting

(1) The Magistrates' Courts Act 1980 is amended as follows.

(2) In section 2 (trial of summary offences), in subsection (3)(a) for "22" there is substituted "22A".

(3) After section 22 there is inserted—

"22A Low-value shoplifting to be a summary offence

(1) Low-value shoplifting is triable only summarily.

(2) But where a person accused of low-value shoplifting is aged 18 or over, and appears or is brought before the court before the summary trial of the offence begins, the court must give the person the opportunity of electing to be tried by the Crown Court for the offence and, if the person elects to be so tried—

(a) subsection (1) does not apply, and

(b) the court must send the person to the Crown Court for trial for the offence.

(3) "Low-value shoplifting" means an offence under section 1 of the Theft Act 1968 in circumstances where—

(a) the value of the stolen goods does not exceed £200,

(b) the goods were being offered for sale in a shop or any other premises, stall, vehicle or place from which there is carried on a trade or business, and

(c) at the time of the offence, the person accused of low-value shoplifting was, or was purporting to be, a customer or potential customer of the person offering the goods for sale.

(4) For the purposes of subsection (3)(a)—

(a) the value of the stolen goods is the price at which they were being offered for sale at the time of the offence, and

(b) where the accused is charged on the same occasion with two or more offences of low-value shoplifting, the reference to the value involved has effect as if it were a reference to the aggregate of the values involved.

(5) A person guilty of low-value shoplifting is liable on summary conviction to—

(a) imprisonment for a period not exceeding 51 weeks (or 6 months, if the offence was committed before the commencement of section 281(4) and (5) of the Criminal Justice Act 2003),

(b) a fine, or

(c) both.

(6) A person convicted of low-value shoplifting by a magistrates' court may not appeal to the Crown Court against the conviction on the ground that the convicting court was mistaken as to whether the offence was one of low-value shoplifting.

(7) For the purposes of this section, any reference to low-value shoplifting includes aiding, abetting, counselling or procuring the commission of low-value shoplifting."

(4) In section 143 (power to alter sums specified in certain provisions)—

(a) after subsection (2)(a) there is inserted—

"(aza) section 22A(3)(a) above;";

(b) the word "or" after paragraph (a) of subsection (3) is omitted;

(c) after subsection (3)(a) there is inserted—

"(aa) in relation to section 22A(3)(a) above, the date of the coming into force of that section; or".

(5) The Criminal Attempts Act 1981 is amended as follows—

(a) in section 1 (attempting to commit an offence) after subsection (4) there is inserted—

"(5) This section also applies to low-value shoplifting (which is defined in, and is triable only summarily by virtue of, section 22A of the Magistrates' Courts Act 1980).";

(b) in section 4 (trial and penalties) in paragraph (c) of subsection (1), after "either way," there is inserted "or is low-value shoplifting (which is defined in, and is triable only summarily by virtue of, section 22A of the Magistrates' Courts Act 1980),".

(6) Any reference in the Police and Criminal Evidence Act 1984 to an "indictable offence" has effect as if it included a reference to low-value shoplifting (as defined in section 22A(3) of the Magistrates' Courts Act 1980).

(7) In section 84 of the Armed Forces Act 2006 (definitions), after subsection (2) there is inserted—

"(2A) In subsection (2)(a), the reference to an "indictable offence" has effect as if it included a reference to low-value shoplifting (as defined in section 22A(3) of the Magistrates' Courts Act 1980)."

(8) The amendments made by this section have effect in relation to—

(a) low-value shoplifting (which is defined in section 22A(3) of the 1980 Act) committed on or after the day on which this section comes into force, and

(b) low-value shoplifting committed before that day in respect of which proceedings have not yet been instituted.

177 Abolition of defence of marital coercion

(1) The defence of marital coercion is abolished.

(2) Accordingly, section 47 of the Criminal Justice Act 1925 (coercion of married woman by husband) is repealed.

(3) This section does not have effect in respect of an offence alleged to have been committed before the date on which it comes into force.

178 Protection arrangements for persons at risk

(1) The Serious Organised Crime and Police Act 2005 is amended as follows.

(2) In section 82 (protection of persons involved in investigations or proceedings)—

(a) in the heading, for "**of persons involved in investigations or proceedings**" there is substituted "**arrangements for persons at risk**";

(b) in subsection (1), for the words from "a person" to "United Kingdom" there is substituted "any person if he reasonably believes that the person's safety is at risk in view of the criminal conduct or possible criminal conduct of another person";

(c) after subsection (5) there is inserted—

"(5A) In subsection (1), "criminal conduct" means conduct which constitutes an offence in England and Wales or Scotland, or would do if it occurred there.

(5B) Nothing in this section prevents a protection provider from making arrangements under this section for the protection of a person where non-statutory arrangements have already been made in respect of that person.";

(d) subsection (6) is repealed.

(3) Sections 91 and 92 are repealed.

(4) In section 93, paragraph (b) of subsection (1) and the word "or" before it are repealed.

(5) In section 172, paragraph (e) of subsection (5) is repealed.

(6) Schedule 5 is repealed.

(7) Nothing in this section affects arrangements made before the commencement of this section for the purpose of protecting a person under section 82(1) of the 2005 Act.

179 Surcharges: imprisonment in default and remission of fines

(1) In section 82 of the Magistrates' Courts Act 1980 (restriction on power to impose imprisonment for default), after subsection (1) there is inserted—

"(1A) Subsection (1)(c) above does not apply in relation to a surcharge ordered to be paid under section 161A of the Criminal Justice Act 2003."

(2) In section 85 of that Act (power to remit fine), after subsection (3) there is inserted—

"(3A) Where—

(a) the court remits the whole or part of the fine, and

(b) the offender was ordered under section 161A of the Criminal Justice Act 2003 to pay a surcharge the amount of which was set by reference to the amount of the fine,

the court shall determine how much the surcharge would have been if the fine had not included the amount remitted, and remit the balance of the surcharge."

(3) In section 165 of the Criminal Justice Act 2003 (remission of fines), after subsection (4) there is inserted—

"(5) Where—

(a) under this section the court remits the whole or part of a fine, and

(b) the offender was ordered under section 161A to pay a surcharge the amount of which was set by reference to the amount of the fine,

the court must determine how much the surcharge would have been if the fine had not included the amount remitted, and remit the balance of the surcharge."

(4) Subsections (2) and (3) apply in any case where the fine, or part of it, is remitted on or after the day on which this section comes into force.

180 Court and tribunal fees

(1) In prescribing a fee under an enactment specified in subsection (2), the Lord Chancellor may with the consent of the Treasury prescribe a fee of an amount which is intended to exceed the cost of anything in respect of which the fee is charged.

(2) The enactments are—

(a) section 92 of the Courts Act 2003 (Senior Courts, county courts and magistrates' courts fees);

(b) section 54 of the Mental Capacity Act 2005 (Court of Protection fees);

(c) section 58(4)(b) of that Act (Public Guardian fees);

(d) section 42 of the Tribunals, Courts and Enforcement Act 2007 (tribunal fees).

(3) Before prescribing a fee by virtue of subsection (1) under an enactment specified in subsection (2)(a), (b) or (d), the Lord Chancellor must have regard to—

(a) the financial position of the courts and tribunals for which the Lord Chancellor is responsible, including in particular any costs incurred by those courts and tribunals that are not being met by current fee income, and

(b) the competitiveness of the legal services market.

(4) For the purposes of subsection (3)(a), the courts and tribunals for which the Lord Chancellor is responsible are the courts listed in section 1(1) of the Courts Act 2003 and the tribunals listed in section 39(1) of the Tribunals, Courts and Enforcement Act 2007.

(5) A fee prescribed by virtue of subsection (1) under section 58(4)(b) of the Mental Capacity Act 2005 must be used to finance the efficient and effective discharge of functions of the Public Guardian.

(6) A fee prescribed by virtue of subsection (1) under any other enactment specified in subsection (2) must be used to finance an efficient and effective system of courts and tribunals.

(7) A statutory instrument—

(a) containing an order or regulations under an enactment specified in subsection (2), and

(b) setting a fee in excess of the cost of anything in respect of which the fee is charged,

may not be made unless a draft of the instrument has been laid before both Houses of Parliament and approved by a resolution of each House.

(8) But subsection (7) does not apply if the statutory instrument only adjusts a fee to reflect changes in the value of money.

PART 14

GENERAL

181 Amendments

(1) Schedule 11 (minor and consequential amendments) has effect.

(2) The Secretary of State may by order make consequential amendments to provisions contained in or made under any Act.

"Consequential amendments" here means amendments that are consequential on any provision of this Act, other than the provisions listed in subsection (4) as they apply in Wales.

(3) The Secretary of State may by order make amendments to sections 136 and 142 of the Sexual Offences Act 2003 that are consequential on the coming into force of any amendment of Part 2 of that Act made by the Criminal Justice Act (Northern Ireland) 2013.

(4) The Welsh Ministers may by order make consequential amendments to provisions contained in or made under any Act or any Measure or Act of the National Assembly for Wales.

"Consequential amendments" here means amendments that are consequential on any of the following provisions as they apply in Wales—

(a) sections 94 to 98 and Schedule 3;

(b) section 100;

(c) paragraphs 2, 7 to 10, 12 to 14, 15(4), 16, 18 to 20, 47(4) and 48 of Schedule 11.

182 Orders and regulations

(1) A power under this Act to make an order or regulations is exercisable by statutory instrument, but this does not apply to a power of the Scottish Ministers to make an order under section 185.

(2) A statutory instrument containing—

(a) an order under section 5(5),

(b) an order under section 53(4),

(c) regulations under section 116(5)(b), or

(d) an order under section 181(2) that amends an Act,

may not be made unless a draft of the instrument has been laid before both Houses of Parliament and approved by a resolution of each House.

(3) A statutory instrument containing an order under section 181(4) that amends an Act or a Measure or Act of the National Assembly for Wales may not be made unless a draft of the instrument has been laid before and approved by a resolution of the National Assembly for Wales.

(4) A statutory instrument containing—

(a) an order under this Act made by the Secretary of State, other than an order within subsection (2) or an order under section 181(3) or 185, or

(b) regulations under this Act made by the Secretary of State, other than regulations within subsection (2),

is subject to annulment in pursuance of a resolution of either House of Parliament.

(5) A statutory instrument containing—

(a) an order under this Act made by the Welsh Ministers, other than an order within subsection (3) or an order under section 185, or

(b) regulations under this Act made by the Welsh Ministers,

is subject to annulment in pursuance of a resolution of the National Assembly for Wales.

(6) An order or regulations under this Act (other than an order under section 185) may make saving, transitional, transitory, supplementary or consequential provision.

183 Financial provision

There is to be paid out of money provided by Parliament any increase attributable to this Act in the sums payable under any other Act out of money so provided.

184 Extent

(1) The following provisions extend to England and Wales only—

(a) Parts 1 to 6;

(b) section 106 except subsections (2)(a)(ii) and (6);

(c) section 114;

(d) sections 116 to 119;

(e) sections 120 and 121;

(f) sections 123 to 130;

(g) section 133(1), (2) and (4);

(h) sections 135 to 143;

(i) sections 144, 145 and 146(1);

(j) sections 149 and 151;

(k) section 152 and Schedule 10;

(l) sections 153 and 154;
(m) sections 166, 171 and 174;
(n) section 176 except subsection (7);
(o) sections 177 and 179.

(2) The following provisions extend to England and Wales and Scotland (but not Northern Ireland)—
(a) sections 106(2)(a)(ii) and (6) and 107;
(b) sections 108 to 110 and 112;
(c) section 133(3);
(d) section 178.

(3) The following provisions extend to England and Wales and Northern Ireland (but not Scotland)—
(a) section 115 and Schedule 6;
(b) section 132 and Schedule 7;
(c) section 175.

(4) The following provisions extend to England and Wales, Scotland and Northern Ireland—
(a) section 111;
(b) section 113 and Schedule 5;
(c) section 131;
(d) section 133(5);
(e) section 146(2);
(f) section 147 and Schedule 8;
(g) section 148 and Schedule 9;
(h) section 150;
(i) Part 12, except sections 166 and 171 to 174;
(j) section 180.

(5) Sections 122 and 172 extend only to Scotland.

(6) Sections 134 and 173 extend only to Northern Ireland.

(7) Section 176(7) has the same extent as section 84 of the Armed Forces Act 2006, and the powers conferred by section 384 of that Act (power to extend Act to the Channel Islands and powers to make provisions of that Act apply with modifications in relation to the Channel Islands, British overseas territories and the Isle of Man) are exercisable in relation to the amendment of that Act made by section 176(7) of this Act.

(8) An amendment, repeal or revocation made by Schedule 11 has the same extent as the relevant part of the Act or instrument amended, repealed or revoked.

(9) The powers conferred by sections 177, 178 and 222 of the Extradition Act 2003 (powers to make provisions of that Act apply in relation to British overseas territories, the Channel Islands and the Isle of Man) are exercisable in relation to any amendment of that Act made by this Act.

185 Commencement

(1) This Act comes into force on whatever day or days the Secretary of State appoints by order.

(2) Subsection (1) does not apply to—

(a) sections 150, 175, 180, 181(2) and (4) and 182 to 186, which come into force on the day on which this Act is passed;

(b) sections 151 and 177, which come into force at the end of the period of 2 months beginning with that day;

(c) the provisions listed in subsection (3) as they apply in Wales;

(d) section 149;

(e) section 122.

(3) The following provisions, as they apply in Wales, come into force on whatever day or days the Welsh Ministers appoint by order—

(a) sections 94 to 98 and Schedule 3;

(b) section 100;

(c) paragraphs 2, 7 to 10, 12 to 14, 15(4), 16, 18 to 20, 47(4) and 48 of Schedule 11 (and section 181(1) so far as it relates to those paragraphs).

(4) Different days may be appointed under subsection (1) or (3) for different purposes or different areas.

(5) Section 149 comes into force on whatever day the Attorney General appoints by order.

(6) Section 122 comes into force on whatever day the Scottish Ministers appoint by order.

(7) The Secretary of State may by order make whatever saving, transitional or transitory provision (in addition to the provision in sections 21, 33, 42, 58 and 93) the Secretary of State thinks appropriate in connection with the coming into force of any provision of this Act, other than the provisions listed in subsection (3) as they apply in Wales.

(8) The Welsh Ministers may by order make whatever saving, transitional or transitory provision they think appropriate in connection with the coming into force in Wales of the provisions listed in subsection (3) as they apply in Wales.

(9) The Scottish Ministers may by order make whatever saving, transitional or transitory provision they think appropriate in connection with the coming into force of section 122.

(10) An order under this section bringing into force on a particular day a provision which refers to the Police Negotiating Board for Scotland may, if it appears to the Secretary of State that no body of that name will be in existence on that day, bring the provision into force subject to whatever consequential amendment or transitional provision the Secretary of State thinks appropriate.

186 Short title

This Act may be cited as the Anti-social Behaviour, Crime and Policing Act 2014.

SCHEDULES

SCHEDULE 1

Section 11

REMANDS UNDER SECTIONS 9 AND 10

Introductory

1 (1) This Schedule applies where—

(a) a judge has power to remand a person under section 9(5),

(b) a justice of the peace is required to remand a person under section 9(6), or

(c) a court has power to remand a person under section 10(8).

(2) A reference in the following paragraphs of this Schedule to a judge is to be read as including a justice of the peace.

Remand in custody or on bail

2 (1) The judge or the court may remand the person—

(a) in custody, or

(b) on bail.

But a person aged under 18 may not be remanded in custody unless paragraph 6 applies.

(2) A reference in this Schedule to remanding a person in custody is a reference to committing the person to custody to be brought before the court at the end of the period of remand or at whatever earlier time the court may require.

(3) The judge or the court may remand the person on bail—

(a) by taking from the person a recognizance, with or without sureties, conditioned as provided in paragraph 3, or

(b) by fixing the amount of the recognizances with a view to their being taken subsequently and, in the meantime, committing the person to custody as mentioned in sub-paragraph (2).

(4) Where a person is brought before the court after remand, the court may further remand the person.

3 (1) Where a person is remanded on bail, the judge or the court may direct that the person's recognizance be conditioned for his or her appearance—

(a) before the court at the end of the period of remand, or

(b) at every time and place to which during the course of the proceedings the hearing may from time to time be adjourned.

(2) Where a recognizance is conditioned for a person's appearance as mentioned in sub-paragraph (1)(b), the fixing of a time for the person next to appear is to be treated as a remand.

(3) Nothing in this paragraph affects the power of the court at any subsequent hearing to remand the person afresh.

4 (1) The judge or the court may not remand a person for a period exceeding 8 clear days unless—

(a) paragraph 5 or 6 applies, or

(b) the person is remanded on bail and both that person and the person who applied for the injunction consent to a longer period.

(2) Where the judge or the court has power to remand a person in custody, the person may be committed to the custody of a constable if the remand is for a period not exceeding 3 clear days.

Remand for medical examination and report

5 (1) This paragraph applies where—

(a) the judge or the court has reason to think that a medical report will be needed, and

(b) the judge or the court remands the person in order to enable a medical examination to take place and a report to be made.

(2) If (in the case of a person aged 18 or over) the person is remanded in custody, the adjournment may not be for more than 3 weeks at a time.

(3) If the person is remanded on bail, the adjournment may not be for more than 4 weeks at a time.

6 (1) If the judge or the court—

(a) is satisfied, on the written or oral evidence of a registered medical practitioner, that there is reason to suspect that the person is suffering from mental disorder, and

(b) is of the opinion that it would be impracticable for a report on the person's mental condition to be made if he or she were remanded on bail,

the judge or the court may remand the person to a hospital or registered establishment specified by the judge or the court for such a report to be made.

(2) In sub-paragraph (1)—

"hospital" has the meaning given by section 145(1) of the Mental Health Act 1983;

"mental disorder" has the meaning given by section 1 of that Act (reading subsection (2B) of that section as if it included a reference to sub-paragraph (1) above);

"registered establishment" has the meaning given by 34(1) of that Act.

(3) Subsections (4) to (10) of section 35 of the Mental Health Act 1983 apply for the purposes of sub-paragraph (1) with any necessary modifications (in particular, with references to the accused person being read as references to the person mentioned in that sub-paragraph, and references to the court being read as references to the judge or the court).

Further remand

7 (1) If the court is satisfied that a person who has been remanded is unable by reason of illness or accident to appear or be brought before the court at the end of the period of remand, the court may further remand the person in his or her absence.

(2) The power in sub-paragraph (1) may, in the case of a person who was remanded on bail, be exercised by enlarging the person's recognizance and those of any sureties for the person to a later time.

(3) Where a person remanded on bail is bound to appear before the court at any time and the court has no power to remand the person under sub-paragraph (1), the court may (in the person's absence) enlarge the person's recognizance and those of any sureties for the person to a later time.

(4) The enlargement of the person's recognizance is to be treated as a further remand.

(5) Paragraph 4(1) (limit of remand) does not apply to the exercise of the powers conferred by this paragraph.

Postponement of taking recognizance

8 Where under paragraph 2(3)(b) the court fixes the amount in which the principal and the sureties, if any, are to be bound, the recognizance may afterwards be taken by a person prescribed by rules of court, with the same consequences as if it had been entered into before the court.

Requirements imposed on remand on bail

9 The court may when remanding a person on bail under this Schedule require the person to comply, before release on bail or later, with any requirements that appear to the court to be necessary to secure that the person does not interfere with witnesses or otherwise obstruct the course of justice.

SCHEDULE 2

Section 12

BREACH OF INJUNCTIONS: POWERS OF COURT IN RESPECT OF UNDER-18S

PART 1

INTRODUCTORY

Power to make supervision order or detention order

1 (1) A youth court, if satisfied beyond reasonable doubt that a person aged under 18 is in breach of a provision of an injunction under section 1 to which he or she is subject, may make in respect of the person—

(a) a supervision order (see Part 2 of this Schedule), or

(b) a detention order (see Part 3 of this Schedule).

(2) An order under sub-paragraph (1) may be made only on the application of the person who applied for the injunction.

(3) A person making an application for an order under sub-paragraph (1) must before doing so—

(a) consult any youth offending team specified under section 3(1) or, if a youth offending team is not specified under that subsection, the local youth offending team within the meaning of section 14;

(b) inform any other body or individual the applicant thinks appropriate.

(4) In considering whether and how to exercise its powers under this paragraph, the court must consider any representations made by the youth offending team referred to in sub-paragraph (3)(a).

(5) A detention order may not be made under sub-paragraph (1) in respect of a person aged under 14.

(6) The court may not make a detention order under sub-paragraph (1) unless it is satisfied that, in view of the severity or extent of the breach, no other power available to the court is appropriate.

PART 2

SUPERVISION ORDERS

Supervision orders

2 (1) A supervision order is an order imposing on the person in respect of whom it is made ("the defaulter") one or more of the following requirements—

(a) a supervision requirement (see paragraph 3);

(b) an activity requirement (see paragraph 4);

(c) a curfew requirement (see paragraph 5).

(2) Before making a supervision order the court must obtain and consider information about the defaulter's family circumstances and the likely effect of a supervision order on those circumstances.

(3) Before making a supervision order imposing two or more requirements, the court must consider their compatibility with each other.

(4) The court must ensure, as far as practicable, that requirements imposed by a supervision order are such as to avoid—

(a) any interference with the times, if any, at which the defaulter normally works or attends school or any other educational establishment;

(b) any conflict with the requirements of any other court order or injunction to which the defaulter may be subject.

(5) A supervision order must for the purposes of this Schedule specify a maximum period for the operation of any requirement contained in the order.

(6) The period specified under sub-paragraph (5) may not exceed 6 months (not counting the day on which the order is made).

(7) A supervision order must for the purposes of this Schedule specify—

(a) the youth offending team in whose area it appears to the court that the respondent will live during the period specified under sub-paragraph (5), or

(b) if it appears to the court that the defaulter will live in more than one such area, whichever of the relevant youth offending teams the court decides.

Supervision requirements

3 (1) In this Schedule "supervision requirement", in relation to a supervision order, means a requirement that the defaulter attend appointments with—

(a) the responsible officer (see paragraph 7), or

(b) another person decided by the responsible officer,

at whatever times and places the responsible officer instructs.

(2) The appointments must be within the period for the time being specified in the order under paragraph 2(5).

Activity requirements

4 (1) In this Schedule "activity requirement", in relation to a supervision order, means a requirement that the defaulter do any or all of the following within the period for the time being specified in the order under paragraph 2(5)—

(a) participate, on however many days are specified in the order, in activities at a place or places specified in it;

(b) participate in an activity or activities specified in the order on however many days are specified in it;

(c) participate in one or more residential exercises for a continuous period or periods comprising however many days are specified in the order;

(d) in accordance with sub-paragraphs (8) to (10), engage in activities in accordance with instructions of the responsible officer on however many days are specified in the order.

(2) The aggregate number of days specified in a supervision order in relation to an activity requirement must not be less than 12 or more than 24.

(3) A requirement referred to in sub-paragraph (1)(a) operates to require the defaulter, in accordance with instructions given by the responsible officer, on the number of days specified in the order in relation to the requirement—

(a) to present himself or herself at a place specified in the order to a person of a description specified in it;

(b) on each day, to comply with instructions given by, or under the authority of, the person in charge of the place.

(4) A requirement referred to in sub-paragraph (1)(b) operates to require the defaulter, in accordance with instructions given by the responsible officer, on the number of days specified in the order in relation to the requirement—

(a) to participate in an activity specified in the order;

(b) on each day, to comply with instructions given by, or under the authority of, the person in charge of the activity.

(5) Where the order includes a requirement referred to in sub-paragraph (1)(c) to participate in a residential exercise, it must specify either—

(a) a place, or

(b) an activity,

in relation to the exercise.

(6) A requirement under sub-paragraph (1)(c) to participate in a residential exercise in relation to which a place is specified under sub-paragraph (5) operates to require the defaulter, in accordance with instructions given by the responsible officer—

(a) to present himself or herself at the beginning of the period specified in the order in relation to the exercise, at the place specified in it, to a person of a description specified in the instructions;

(b) to live there for that period;

(c) during that period to comply with instructions given by, or under the authority of, the person in charge of the place.

(7) A requirement under sub-paragraph (1)(c) to participate in a residential exercise in relation to which an activity is specified under sub-paragraph (5) operates to require the defaulter, in accordance with instructions given by the responsible officer—

(a) to participate, for the period specified in the order in relation to the exercise, in the activity specified in it;

(b) during that period to comply with instructions given by, or under the authority of, the person in charge of the activity.

(8) Subject to sub-paragraph (9), instructions under sub-paragraph (1)(d) relating to any particular day must require the defaulter to do either of the following—

(a) to present himself or herself to a person of a description specified in the instructions at a place specified in them;

(b) to participate in an activity specified in the instructions.

The instructions operate to require the defaulter, on that day or while participating in that activity, to comply with instructions given by, or under the authority of, the person in charge of the place or activity.

(9) If the supervision order so provides, instructions under sub-paragraph (1)(d) may require the defaulter to participate in a residential exercise for a period comprising not more than seven days, and for that purpose—

(a) to present himself or herself at the beginning of that period to a person of a description specified in the instructions at a place specified in them, and to live there for that period, or

(b) to participate for that period in an activity specified in the instructions.

(10) Instructions of the kind mentioned in sub-paragraph (9)—

(a) may not be given except with the consent of a parent or guardian of the defaulter;

(b) operate to require the defaulter, during the period specified under that sub-paragraph, to comply with instructions given by, or under the authority of, the person in charge of the place or activity specified under paragraph (a) or (b) of that sub-paragraph.

(11) Instructions given by, or under the authority of, a person in charge of a place under sub-paragraph (3)(b), (6)(c), (8) or (10)(b) may require the defaulter to engage in activities otherwise than at that place.

(12) Where a supervision order contains an activity requirement, the court may, on the application of the original applicant or the defaulter, amend the order by substituting for a number of days, place, activity, period or description of persons specified in the order a new number of days, place, activity, period or description (subject, in the case of a number of days, to sub-paragraph (2)).

(13) A court may include an activity requirement in a supervision order or vary an activity requirement under sub-paragraph (12) only if—

(a) it has consulted the youth offending team that is to be, or is, specified in the order,

(b) it is satisfied that it is feasible to secure compliance with the requirement, or the requirement as varied,

(c) it is satisfied that provision for the defaulter to participate in the activities proposed can be made under the arrangements for persons to participate in those activities which exist in the area of the youth offending team that is to be, or is, specified in the order, and

(d) in a case where the requirement, or the requirement as varied, would involve the co-operation of a person other than the defaulter and the responsible officer, that person consents to its inclusion or variation.

(14) In sub-paragraph (10) "guardian" has the same meaning as in the Children and Young Persons Act 1933.

But where a local authority has parental responsibility (within the meaning given by section 3 of the Children Act 1989) for a defaulter who—

(a) is in the authority's care, or

(b) is provided with accommodation by the authority in the exercise of social services functions (within the meaning given by section 1A of the Local Authority Social Services Act 1970),

the reference to "guardian" in sub-paragraph (10) is to be read as a reference to that authority.

Curfew requirements

5 (1) In this Schedule "curfew requirement", in relation to a supervision order, means a requirement that the defaulter remain at a place specified in the order for the periods specified in it.

(2) A supervision order imposing a curfew requirement may specify different places or different periods for different days.

(3) The periods specified under sub-paragraph (1)—

(a) must be within the period for the time being specified in the order under paragraph 2(5);

(b) may not amount to less than 2 or more than 8 hours in any day.

(4) Before specifying a place under sub-paragraph (1), the court making the order must obtain and consider information about the place proposed to be specified (including information as to the attitude of persons likely to be affected by the enforced presence there of the defaulter).

(5) Where a supervision order contains a curfew requirement, the court may, on the application of the original applicant or the defaulter, amend the order by—

(a) substituting new periods for the periods specified in the order under this paragraph (subject to sub-paragraph (3));

(b) substituting a new place for the place specified in the order under this paragraph (subject to sub-paragraph (4)).

Electronic monitoring requirements

6 (1) A supervision order containing a curfew requirement may also contain a requirement (an "electronic monitoring requirement") for securing the electronic monitoring of compliance with the curfew requirement during a period—

(a) specified in the order, or

(b) determined by the responsible officer in accordance with the order.

(2) In the case referred to in sub-paragraph (1)(b), the responsible officer must, before the beginning of the period when the electronic monitoring requirement is to take effect, notify—

(a) the defaulter,

(b) the person responsible for the monitoring, and

(c) any person within sub-paragraph (3)(b),

of the time when that period is to begin.

(3) Where—

(a) it is proposed to include an electronic monitoring requirement in a supervision order, but

(b) there is a person (other than the defaulter) without whose co-operation it will not be practicable to secure that the monitoring takes place,

the requirement may not be included in the order without that person's consent.

(4) A supervision order imposing an electronic monitoring requirement must include provision for making a person responsible for the monitoring.

(5) An electronic monitoring requirement may not be included in a supervision order unless the court making the order—

(a) has been notified by the youth offending team for the time being specified in the order that arrangements for electronic monitoring are available in the area that includes the place the court proposes to specify in the order for the purposes of the curfew requirement, and

(b) is satisfied that the necessary provision can be made under the arrangements currently available.

(6) Where a supervision order contains an electronic monitoring requirement, the court may, on the application of the original applicant or the defaulter, amend the order by substituting a new period for the period specified in the order under this paragraph.

(7) Sub-paragraph (3) applies in relation to the variation of an electronic monitoring requirement under sub-paragraph (6) as it applies in relation to the inclusion of a requirement.

"Responsible officer"

7 (1) For the purposes of this Part of this Schedule, the "responsible officer", in relation to a supervision order, means—

(a) in a case where the order imposes a curfew requirement and an electronic monitoring requirement, but does not impose an activity or supervision requirement, the person who under paragraph 6(4) is responsible for the electronic monitoring;

(b) in any other case, the member of the youth offending team for the time being specified in the order who is for the time being responsible for discharging the functions conferred by this Schedule on the responsible officer.

(2) Where a supervision order has been made, it is the duty of the responsible officer—

(a) to make any arrangements that are necessary in connection with the requirements contained in the order;

(b) to promote the defaulter's compliance with those requirements.

(3) The responsible officer must ensure, so far as practicable, that any instructions given by the officer under a supervision order are such as to avoid the things referred to in paragraph 2(4).

(4) A defaulter in respect of whom a supervision order is made must—

(a) keep in touch with the responsible officer, in accordance with any instructions given by the responsible officer from time to time;

(b) notify the responsible officer of any change of address.

These obligations have effect as requirements of the order.

Amendment of operative period

8 (1) The court may, on the application of the original applicant, amend a supervision order by substituting a new period for the one specified in the order for the time being under paragraph 2(5) (subject to paragraph 2(6)).

(2) A court amending a supervision order under sub-paragraph (1) may make whatever other amendments to the order the court considers appropriate in relation to a requirement imposed by the order.

Amendment on change of area of residence

9 (1) This paragraph applies where, on an application made in relation to a supervision order by the original applicant or the defaulter, the court is satisfied that the defaulter proposes to live, or is living, in the area of a youth offending team other than the team for the time being specified in the order.

(2) If the application is made by the defaulter, the court may amend the order by substituting for the youth offending team specified in the order the youth offending team for the area referred to in sub-paragraph (1) (or, if there is more than one youth offending team for that area, whichever of them the court decides).

(3) If the application is made by the original applicant, the court must amend the order in the way mentioned in sub-paragraph (2) (subject to sub-paragraph (5)).

(4) Where a court amends the supervision order under sub-paragraph (2) or (3) but the order contains a requirement that, in the opinion of the court, cannot reasonably be complied with if the defaulter lives in the area referred to in sub-paragraph (1), the court must also amend the order by—

(a) removing that requirement, or

(b) substituting for that requirement a new requirement that can reasonably be complied with if the defaulter lives in that area.

(5) Sub-paragraph (3) does not require a court to amend the supervision order if in its opinion sub-paragraph (4) would produce an inappropriate result.

(6) The original applicant must consult the youth offending team for the time being specified in the order before making an application under sub-paragraph (1).

Revocation of supervision order

10 (1) The original applicant or the defaulter may apply to a youth court—

(a) to revoke a supervision order;

(b) to amend a supervision order by removing a requirement from it.

(2) If it appears to the court to be in the interests of justice to do so, having regard to circumstances that have arisen since the supervision order was made, the court may grant an application under sub-paragraph (1) and revoke or amend the order accordingly.

(3) The circumstances referred to in sub-paragraph (2) include the conduct of the defaulter.

(4) If an application under this paragraph is dismissed, the party by which the dismissed application was made may make no further application under this paragraph without—

(a) the consent of the court, or

(b) the agreement of the other party.

(5) The original applicant must consult the youth offending team for the time being specified in the supervision order before making an application under sub-paragraph (1).

Compliance with supervision order

11 If the responsible officer considers that the defaulter has complied with all the requirements of the supervision order, the officer must inform the original applicant.

Non-compliance with supervision order

12 (1) If the responsible officer considers that the defaulter has failed to comply with a requirement of the supervision order, the officer must inform the original applicant.

(2) On being informed under sub-paragraph (1) the original applicant may apply to a youth court.

(3) Before making an application under sub-paragraph (2) the original applicant must—

(a) consult the youth offending team for the time being specified in the order;

(b) inform any other body or individual the original applicant thinks appropriate.

(4) If on an application under sub-paragraph (2) the court is satisfied beyond reasonable doubt that the defaulter has without reasonable excuse failed to comply with a requirement of the supervision order, the court may—

(a) revoke the supervision order and make a new one;

(b) revoke the order and make a detention order (see Part 3 of this Schedule).

(5) The powers in sub-paragraph (4)—

(a) may not be exercised after the defaulter reaches the age of 18;

(b) are in addition to any other power of the court in relation to the breach of the supervision order.

(6) The court must consider any representations made by the youth offending team for the time being specified in the order before exercising its powers under this paragraph.

Copies of supervision order etc

13 (1) A court that makes a supervision order must straight away provide a copy of the order to—

(a) the defaulter;

(b) the youth offending team for the time being specified in the order.

(2) Where a supervision order is made, the original applicant must straight away provide a copy of so much of the order as is relevant—

(a) in a case where the order includes an activity requirement specifying a place under paragraph 4(1)(a), to the person in charge of that place;

(b) in a case where the order includes an activity requirement specifying an activity under paragraph 4(1)(b), to the person in charge of that activity;

(c) in a case where the order includes an activity requirement specifying a residential exercise under paragraph 4(1)(c), to the person in charge of the place or activity specified under paragraph 4(5) in relation to that residential exercise;

(d) in a case where the order contains an electronic monitoring requirement, to—

(i) any person who by virtue of paragraph 6(4) will be responsible for the electronic monitoring, and

(ii) any person without whose consent that requirement could not have been included in the order.

(3) A court that revokes or amends a supervision order must straight away provide a copy of the revoking order, or of the order as amended, to—

(a) the defaulter;

(b) the youth offending team for the time being specified in the order.

(4) Where—

(a) a copy of a supervision order (or part of a supervision order) has been given to a person under sub-paragraph (2) by virtue of a requirement contained in the order, and

(b) the order is revoked, or amended in respect of that requirement,

the original applicant must straight away give a copy of the revoking order, or of so much of the order as amended as is relevant, to that person.

PART 3

DETENTION ORDERS

Detention orders

14 (1) A detention order is an order that the person in respect of whom it is made ("the defaulter") be detained for a period specified in the order in whatever youth detention accommodation the Secretary of State decides.

(2) The period specified under sub-paragraph (1) may not exceed the period of 3 months (not counting the day on which the order is made).

(3) In sub-paragraph (1) "youth detention accommodation" means—

(a) a secure training centre;

(b) a young offender institution;

(c) secure accommodation, as defined by section 23(12) of the Children and Young Persons Act 1969.

(4) The function of the Secretary of State under sub-paragraph (1) is exercisable concurrently with the Youth Justice Board.

(5) A person detained under a detention order is in legal custody.

Revocation of detention order

15 (1) Where a detention order is made, the original applicant or the defaulter may apply to a youth court to revoke it.

(2) If it appears to the court to be in the interests of justice to do so, having regard to circumstances that have arisen since the detention order was made, the court may grant an application under sub-paragraph (1) and revoke the order accordingly.

(3) The circumstances referred to in sub-paragraph (2) include the conduct of the defaulter.

(4) If an application under this paragraph is dismissed, the party by which the dismissed application was made may make no further application under this paragraph without—

(a) the consent of the court, or

(b) the agreement of the other party.

(5) A person making an application under this paragraph in relation to a detention order made under paragraph 1 must before doing so consult any youth offending team specified in the injunction under section 3(1) or, if none is specified, the local youth offending team within the meaning of section 14.

(6) A person making an application under this paragraph in relation to a detention order made under paragraph 12(4)(b) must before doing so consult the youth offending team for the time being specified in the relevant supervision order.

SCHEDULE 3

Section 94(2)

SCHEDULE TO BE INSERTED AS SCHEDULE 2A TO THE HOUSING ACT 1985

"SCHEDULE 2A

Section 84A(9)

ABSOLUTE GROUND FOR POSSESSION FOR ANTI-SOCIAL BEHAVIOUR: SERIOUS OFFENCES

1 Violent offences

1 Murder.

2 Manslaughter.

3 Kidnapping.

4 False imprisonment.

5 An offence under any of the following sections of the Offences against the Person Act 1861—

(a) section 4 (soliciting murder),
(b) section 16 (threats to kill),
(c) section 18 (wounding with intent to cause grievous bodily harm),
(d) section 20 (malicious wounding),
(e) section 21 (attempting to choke, suffocate or strangle in order to commit or assist in committing an indictable offence),
(f) section 22 (using chloroform etc. to commit or assist in the committing of any indictable offence),
(g) section 23 (maliciously administering poison etc. so as to endanger life or inflict grievous bodily harm),
(h) section 24 (maliciously administering poison etc. with intent to injure, aggrieve or annoy any other person),
(i) section 27 (abandoning or exposing children whereby life is endangered or health permanently injured),
(j) section 28 (causing bodily injury by explosives),
(k) section 29 (using explosives etc. with intent to do grievous bodily harm),
(l) section 30 (placing explosives with intent to do bodily injury),
(m) section 31 (setting spring guns etc. with intent to do grievous bodily harm),
(n) section 38 (assault with intent to resist arrest),
(o) section 47 (assault occasioning actual bodily harm).

6 An offence under any of the following sections of the Explosive Substances Act 1883—

(a) section 2 (causing explosion likely to endanger life or property),
(b) section 3 (attempt to cause explosion, or making or keeping explosive with intent to endanger life or property),
(c) section 4 (making or possession of explosive under suspicious circumstances).

7 An offence under section 1 of the Infant Life (Preservation) Act 1929 (child destruction).

8 An offence under section 1 of the Children and Young Persons Act 1933 (cruelty to children).

9 An offence under section 1 of the Infanticide Act 1938 (infanticide).

10 An offence under any of the following sections of the Public Order Act 1986—

(a) section 1 (riot),
(b) section 2 (violent disorder),
(c) section 3 (affray).

11 An offence under either of the following sections of the Protection from Harassment Act 1997—

(a) section 4 (putting people in fear of violence),
(b) section 4A (stalking involving fear of violence or serious alarm or distress).

12 An offence under any of the following provisions of the Crime and Disorder Act 1998—

(a) section 29 (racially or religiously aggravated assaults),
(b) section 31(1)(a) or (b) (racially or religiously aggravated offences under section 4 or 4A of the Public Order Act 1986),
(c) section 32 (racially or religiously aggravated harassment etc.).

13 An offence under either of the following sections of the Female Genital Mutilation Act 2003—

(a) section 1 (female genital mutilation),
(b) section 2 (assisting a girl to mutilate her own genitalia).

14 An offence under section 5 of the Domestic Violence, Crime and Victims Act 2004 (causing or allowing the death of a child or vulnerable adult).

15 Sexual offences

15 An offence under section 33A of the Sexual Offences Act 1956 (keeping a brothel used for prostitution).

16 An offence under section 1 of the Protection of Children Act 1978 (indecent photographs of children).

17 An offence under section 160 of the Criminal Justice Act 1988 (possession of indecent photograph of a child).

18 An indictable offence under Part 1 of the Sexual Offences Act 2003 (sexual offences).

19 Offensive weapons

19 An offence under either of the following sections of the Prevention of Crime Act 1953—

(a) section 1 (prohibition of the carrying of offensive weapons without lawful authority or reasonable excuse),
(b) section 1A (threatening with offensive weapon in public).

20 An offence under any of the following provisions of the Firearms Act 1968—

(a) section 16 (possession of firearm with intent to endanger life),
(b) section 16A (possession of firearm with intent to cause fear of violence),
(c) section 17(1) (use of firearm to resist arrest),

(d) section 17(2) (possession of firearm at time of committing or being arrested for offence specified in Schedule 1 to the Act of 1968),
(e) section 18 (carrying a firearm with criminal intent),
(f) section 19 (carrying a firearm in a public place),
(g) section 20 (trespassing with firearm),
(h) section 21 (possession of firearms by persons previously convicted of crime).

21 An offence under either of the following sections of the Criminal Justice Act 1988—
(a) section 139 (having article with blade or point in public place),
(b) section 139AA (threatening with article with blade or point or offensive weapon).

22 Offences against property

22 An offence under any of the following sections of the Theft Act 1968—
(a) section 8 (robbery or assault with intent to rob),
(b) section 9 (burglary),
(c) section 10 (aggravated burglary).

23 An offence under section 1 of the Criminal Damage Act 1971 (destroying or damaging property).

24 An offence under section 30 of the Crime and Disorder Act 1998 (racially or religiously aggravated criminal damage).

25 Road traffic offences

25 An offence under section 35 of the Offences against the Person Act 1861 (injuring persons by furious driving).

26 An offence under section 12A of the Theft Act 1968 (aggravated vehicle-taking involving an accident which caused the death of any person).

27 An offence under any of the following sections of the Road Traffic Act 1988—
(a) section 1 (causing death by dangerous driving),
(b) section 1A (causing serious injury by dangerous driving),
(c) section 3A (causing death by careless driving when under influence of drink or drugs).

28 Drug-related offences

28 An offence under any of the following provisions of the Misuse of Drugs Act 1971—
(a) section 4 (restriction of production and supply of controlled drugs),
(b) section 5(3) (possession of controlled drugs with intent to supply),
(c) section 8(a) or (b) (occupiers etc. of premises to be punishable for permitting unlawful production or supply etc. of controlled drugs there).

29 An offence under section 6 of that Act (restrictions of cultivation of cannabis plant) where the cultivation is for profit and the whole or a substantial part of the dwelling-house concerned is used for the cultivation.

30 Inchoate offences

30 (1) An offence of attempting or conspiring the commission of an offence specified or described in this Schedule.

(2) An offence under Part 2 of the Serious Crime Act 2007 (encouraging or assisting) where the offence (or one of the offences) which the person in question intends or believes would be committed is an offence specified or described in this Schedule.

(3) An offence of aiding, abetting, counselling or procuring the commission of an offence specified or described in this Schedule.

31 Scope of offences

31 Where this Schedule refers to offences which are offences under the law of England and Wales and another country or territory, the reference is to be read as limited to the offences so far as they are offences under the law of England and Wales."

SCHEDULE 4

Section 104

ASB CASE REVIEWS: SUPPLEMENTARY PROVISION

PART 1

MAKING AND REVISING REVIEW PROCEDURES ETC

Consultation: local policing bodies

1 (1) In making and revising the review procedures, the relevant bodies in a local government area must consult the local policing body for the relevant police area.

(2) The "relevant police area" is the police area which consists of, or includes, the local government area.

Consultation: local providers of social housing

2 In making and revising the review procedures, the relevant bodies in a local government area must consult such local providers of social housing as they consider appropriate.

Dissatisfaction with ASB case reviews

3 The review procedures must include provision about what is to happen where an applicant is dissatisfied with the way in which the relevant bodies have—

(a) dealt with an application for an ASB case review, or
(b) carried out an ASB case review.

Assessment and revision of review procedures

4 The review procedures must include provision about—

(a) the assessment of the effectiveness of those procedures, and

(b) the revision of those procedures.

PART 2

INCLUSION OF LOCAL PROVIDERS OF SOCIAL HOUSING AMONG RELEVANT BODIES

Co-option arrangements

5 (1) The responsible authorities in a local government area must make arrangements ("co-option arrangements") for the inclusion of local providers of social housing among the relevant bodies in that area.

(2) In this paragraph "responsible authorities" means—

(a) in relation to a local government area in England—

(i) the relevant district council or the unitary authority,

(ii) the chief officer of police for the police area which that local government area is within, and

(iii) each clinical commissioning group established under section 14V of the National Health Service Act 2006 whose area is wholly or partly within that local government area;

(b) in relation to a local government area in Wales—

(i) the council for the area,

(ii) the chief officer of police for the police area which that local government area is within, and

(iii) each Local Health Board whose area is wholly or partly within that local government area.

PART 3

ASB CASE REVIEWS

Consultation and co-operation: local providers of social housing

6 (1) The relevant bodies in a local government area must consult such local providers of social housing as they consider appropriate in carrying out ASB case reviews.

(2) The local providers of social housing must co-operate with the relevant bodies in the local government area in any matters specified by the relevant bodies that concern ASB case reviews.

Information

7 (1) The relevant bodies in a local government area may request any person to disclose information for a purpose connected with the carrying out of an ASB case review.

(2) If such a request is made to a person that exercises public functions, and that person possesses the requested information in connection with the exercise of such functions, the person must (subject to sub-paragraph (4)) comply with the request.

(3) If such a request is made to a person who is not required by sub-paragraph (2) to disclose the requested information, the person may (subject to sub-paragraph (4)) comply with the request.

(4) This paragraph does not require or authorise—

(a) a disclosure, in contravention of any provisions of the Data Protection Act 1998, of personal data which are not exempt from those provisions, or

(b) a disclosure which is prohibited by Part 1 of the Regulation of Investigatory Powers Act 2000.

(5) Subject to that, a disclosure under this paragraph does not breach—

(a) any obligation of confidence owed by the person making the disclosure, or

(b) any other restriction on the disclosure of information (however imposed).

PART 4

GENERAL

Joint review procedures or co-option arrangements

8 (1) The relevant bodies in two or more local government areas—

(a) may jointly make review procedures applicable to those areas;

(b) must secure that such jointly-made review procedures are in place if co-option arrangements applicable to those areas have been jointly made under sub-paragraph (2).

(2) The responsible authorities in two or more local government areas—

(a) may jointly make co-option arrangements applicable to those areas;

(b) must secure that such jointly-made co-option arrangements are in place if review procedures applicable to those areas have been jointly made under sub-paragraph (1).

(3) In a case where review procedures or co-option arrangements are made jointly in accordance with this paragraph, a reference to any of the following in section 104, section 105 or this Schedule is to be read accordingly—

(a) the relevant bodies (in the case of review procedures) or the responsible authorities (in the case of co-option arrangements);

(b) the local government area or the relevant police area (in either case).

Different review procedures or co-option arrangements for different parts of an area etc

9 (1) Review procedures may make different provision in relation to different parts of a local government area.

(2) Review procedures or co-option arrangements made jointly in accordance with paragraph 8 may make different provision in relation to—

(a) different local government areas to which the procedures or arrangements are applicable, or

(b) different parts of such areas.

SCHEDULE 5

Section 113

AMENDMENTS OF PARTS 2 AND 3 OF THE SEXUAL OFFENCES ACT 2003

Introduction

1 Part 2 of the Sexual Offences Act 2003 (notification and orders) is amended as set out in paragraphs 2 to 6.

Sexual harm prevention orders

2 After section 103 there is inserted—

"Sexual harm prevention orders (England and Wales)

103A Sexual harm prevention orders: applications and grounds

103A Sexual harm prevention orders: applications and grounds

(1) A court may make an order under this section (a "sexual harm prevention order") in respect of a person ("the defendant") where subsection (2) or (3) applies to the defendant.

(2) This subsection applies to the defendant where—

(a) the court deals with the defendant in respect of—

(i) an offence listed in Schedule 3 or 5, or

(ii) a finding that the defendant is not guilty of an offence listed in Schedule 3 or 5 by reason of insanity, or

(iii) a finding that the defendant is under a disability and has done the act charged against the defendant in respect of an offence listed in Schedule 3 or 5,

and

(b) the court is satisfied that it is necessary to make a sexual harm prevention order, for the purpose of—

(i) protecting the public or any particular members of the public from sexual harm from the defendant, or

(ii) protecting children or vulnerable adults generally, or any particular children or vulnerable adults, from sexual harm from the defendant outside the United Kingdom.

(3) This subsection applies to the defendant where—

(a) an application under subsection (4) has been made in respect of the defendant and it is proved on the application that the defendant is a qualifying offender, and

(b) the court is satisfied that the defendant's behaviour since the appropriate date makes it necessary to make a sexual harm prevention order, for the purpose of—

(i) protecting the public or any particular members of the public from sexual harm from the defendant, or

(ii) protecting children or vulnerable adults generally, or any particular children or vulnerable adults, from sexual harm from the defendant outside the United Kingdom.

(4) A chief officer of police or the Director General of the National Crime Agency ("the Director General") may by complaint to a magistrates' court apply for a sexual harm prevention order in respect of a person if it appears to the chief officer or the Director General that—

(a) the person is a qualifying offender, and

(b) the person has since the appropriate date acted in such a way as to give reasonable cause to believe that it is necessary for such an order to be made.

(5) A chief officer of police may make an application under subsection (4) only in respect of a person—

(a) who resides in the chief officer's police area, or

(b) who the chief officer believes is in that area or is intending to come to it.

(6) An application under subsection (4) may be made to any magistrates' court acting for a local justice area that includes—

(a) any part of a relevant police area, or

(b) any place where it is alleged that the person acted in a way mentioned in subsection (4)(b).

(7) The Director General must as soon as practicable notify the chief officer of police for a relevant police area of any application that the Director has made under subsection (4).

(8) Where the defendant is a child, a reference in this section to a magistrates' court is to be taken as referring to a youth court (subject to any rules of court made under section 103K(1)).

(9) In this section "relevant police area" means—

(a) where the applicant is a chief officer of police, the officer's police area;

(b) where the applicant is the Director General—

(i) the police area where the person in question resides, or

(ii) a police area which the Director General believes the person is in or is intending to come to.

103B Section 103A: supplemental

103B Section 103A: supplemental

(1) In section 103A—

"appropriate date", in relation to a qualifying offender, means the date or (as the case may be) the first date on which the offender was convicted, found or cautioned as mentioned in subsection (2) or (3) below;

"child" means a person under 18;

"the public" means the public in the United Kingdom;

"sexual harm" from a person means physical or psychological harm caused—

(a) by the person committing one or more offences listed in Schedule 3, or

(b) (in the context of harm outside the United Kingdom) by the person doing, outside the United Kingdom, anything which would constitute an offence listed in Schedule 3 if done in any part of the United Kingdom;

"qualifying offender" means a person within subsection (2) or (3) below;

"vulnerable adult" means a person aged 18 or over whose ability to protect himself or herself from physical or psychological harm is significantly impaired through physical or mental disability or illness, through old age or otherwise.

(2) A person is within this subsection if, whether before or after the commencement of this Part, the person—

(a) has been convicted of an offence listed in Schedule 3 (other than at paragraph 60) or in Schedule 5,

(b) has been found not guilty of such an offence by reason of insanity,

(c) has been found to be under a disability and to have done the act charged against him in respect of such an offence, or

(d) has been cautioned in respect of such an offence.

(3) A person is within this subsection if, under the law in force in a country outside the United Kingdom and whether before or after the commencement of this Part—

(a) the person has been convicted of a relevant offence (whether or not the person has been punished for it),

(b) a court exercising jurisdiction under that law has made in respect of a relevant offence a finding equivalent to a finding that the person is not guilty by reason of insanity,

(c) such a court has made in respect of a relevant offence a finding equivalent to a finding that the person is under a disability and did the act charged against the person in respect of the offence, or

(d) the person has been cautioned in respect of a relevant offence.

(4) In subsection (3), "relevant offence" means an act which—

(a) constituted an offence under the law in force in the country concerned, and

(b) would have constituted an offence listed in Schedule 3 (other than at paragraph 60) or in Schedule 5 if it had been done in any part of the United Kingdom.

For this purpose an act punishable under the law in force in a country outside the United Kingdom constitutes an offence under that law, however it is described in that law.

(5) For the purposes of section 103A, acts, behaviour, convictions and findings include those occurring before the commencement of this Part.

(6) Subject to subsection (7), on an application under section 103A(4) the condition in subsection (4)(b) above (where relevant) is to be taken as met unless, not later than rules of court may provide, the defendant serves on the applicant a notice—

(a) stating that, on the facts as alleged with respect to the act concerned, the condition is not in the defendant's opinion met,

(b) showing the grounds for that opinion, and

(c) requiring the applicant to prove that the condition is met.

(7) The court, if it thinks fit, may permit the defendant to require the applicant to prove that the condition is met without service of a notice under subsection (6).

(8) Subsection (9) applies for the purposes of section 103A and this section.

(9) In construing any reference to an offence listed in Schedule 3, any condition subject to which an offence is so listed that relates—

(a) to the way in which the defendant is dealt with in respect of an offence so listed or a relevant finding (as defined by section 132(9)), or

(b) to the age of any person,

is to be disregarded.

SHPOs: effect

SHPOs: effect

(1) A sexual harm prevention order prohibits the defendant from doing anything described in the order.

(2) Subject to section 103D(1), a prohibition contained in a sexual harm prevention order has effect—

(a) for a fixed period, specified in the order, of at least 5 years, or

(b) until further order.

(3) A sexual harm prevention order—

(a) may specify that some of its prohibitions have effect until further order and some for a fixed period;

(b) may specify different periods for different prohibitions.

(4) The only prohibitions that may be included in a sexual harm prevention order are those necessary for the purpose of—

(a) protecting the public or any particular members of the public from sexual harm from the defendant, or

(b) protecting children or vulnerable adults generally, or any particular children or vulnerable adults, from sexual harm from the defendant outside the United Kingdom.

(5) In subsection (4) "the public", "sexual harm", "child" and "vulnerable adult" each has the meaning given in section 103B(1).

(6) Where a court makes a sexual harm prevention order in relation to a person who is already subject to such an order (whether made by that court or another), the earlier order ceases to have effect.

103D SHPOs: prohibitions on foreign travel

103D SHPOs: prohibitions on foreign travel

(1) A prohibition on foreign travel contained in a sexual harm prevention order must be for a fixed period of not more than 5 years.

(2) A "prohibition on foreign travel" means—

- (a) a prohibition on travelling to any country outside the United Kingdom named or described in the order,
- (b) a prohibition on travelling to any country outside the United Kingdom other than a country named or described in the order, or
- (c) a prohibition on travelling to any country outside the United Kingdom.

(3) Subsection (1) does not prevent a prohibition on foreign travel from being extended for a further period (of no more than 5 years each time) under section 103E.

(4) A sexual harm prevention order that contains a prohibition within subsection (2)(c) must require the defendant to surrender all of the defendant's passports at a police station specified in the order—

- (a) on or before the date when the prohibition takes effect, or
- (b) within a period specified in the order.

(5) Any passports surrendered must be returned as soon as reasonably practicable after the person ceases to be subject to a sexual harm prevention order containing a prohibition within subsection (2)(c) (unless the person is subject to an equivalent prohibition under another order).

(6) Subsection (5) does not apply in relation to—

- (a) a passport issued by or on behalf of the authorities of a country outside the United Kingdom if the passport has been returned to those authorities;
- (b) a passport issued by or on behalf of an international organisation if the passport has been returned to that organisation.

(7) In this section "passport" means—

- (a) a United Kingdom passport within the meaning of the Immigration Act 1971;
- (b) a passport issued by or on behalf of the authorities of a country outside the United Kingdom, or by or on behalf of an international organisation;
- (c) a document that can be used (in some or all circumstances) instead of a passport.

103E SHPOs: variations, renewals and discharges

103E SHPOs: variations, renewals and discharges

(1) A person within subsection (2) may apply to the appropriate court for an order varying, renewing or discharging a sexual harm prevention order.

(2) The persons are—

(a) the defendant;

(b) the chief officer of police for the area in which the defendant resides;

(c) a chief officer of police who believes that the defendant is in, or is intending to come to, that officer's police area;

(d) where the order was made on an application by a chief officer of police under section 103A(4), that officer.

(3) An application under subsection (1) may be made—

(a) where the appropriate court is the Crown Court, in accordance with rules of court;

(b) in any other case, by complaint.

(4) Subject to subsections (5) and (7), on the application the court, after hearing the person making the application and (if they wish to be heard) the other persons mentioned in subsection (2), may make any order, varying, renewing or discharging the sexual harm prevention order, that the court considers appropriate.

(5) An order may be renewed, or varied so as to impose additional prohibitions on the defendant, only if it is necessary to do so for the purpose of—

(a) protecting the public or any particular members of the public from sexual harm from the defendant, or

(b) protecting children or vulnerable adults generally, or any particular children or vulnerable adults, from sexual harm from the defendant outside the United Kingdom.

Any renewed or varied order may contain only such prohibitions as are necessary for this purpose.

(6) In subsection (5) "the public", "sexual harm", "child" and "vulnerable adult" each has the meaning given in section 103B(1).

(7) The court must not discharge an order before the end of 5 years beginning with the day on which the order was made, without the consent of the defendant and—

(a) where the application is made by a chief officer of police, that chief officer, or

(b) in any other case, the chief officer of police for the area in which the defendant resides.

(8) Subsection (7) does not apply to an order containing a prohibition on foreign travel and no other prohibitions.

(9) In this section "the appropriate court" means—

(a) where the Crown Court or the Court of Appeal made the sexual harm prevention order, the Crown Court;

(b) where an adult magistrates' court made the order, that court, an adult magistrates' court for the area in which the defendant resides or, where the application is made by a chief officer of police, any adult magistrates' court acting for a local justice area that includes any part of the chief officer's police area;

(c) where a youth court made the order and the defendant is under the age of 18, that court, a youth court for the area in which the defendant resides or, where the application is made by a chief officer of police, any youth court acting for a local justice area that includes any part of the chief officer's police area;

(d) where a youth court made the order and the defendant is aged 18 or over, an adult magistrates' court for the area in which the defendant resides or, where the application is made by a chief officer of police, any adult magistrates' court acting for a local justice area that includes any part of the chief officer's police area.

In this subsection "adult magistrates' court" means a magistrates' court that is not a youth court.

103F Interim SHPOs

103F Interim SHPOs

(1) This section applies where an application under section 103A(4) ("the main application") has not been determined.

(2) An application for an order under this section ("an interim sexual harm prevention order")—

(a) may be made by the complaint by which the main application is made, or

(b) if the main application has been made, may be made by the person who has made that application, by complaint to the court to which that application has been made.

(3) The court may, if it considers it just to do so, make an interim sexual harm prevention order, prohibiting the defendant from doing anything described in the order.

(4) Such an order—

(a) has effect only for a fixed period, specified in the order;

(b) ceases to have effect, if it has not already done so, on the determination of the main application.

(5) The applicant or the defendant may by complaint apply to the court that made the interim sexual harm prevention order for the order to be varied, renewed or discharged.

103G SHPOs and interim SHPOs: notification requirements

103G SHPOs and interim SHPOs: notification requirements

(1) Where—

(a) a sexual harm prevention order is made in respect of a defendant who was a relevant offender immediately before the making of the order, and

(b) the defendant would (apart from this subsection) cease to be subject to the notification requirements of this Part while the order (as renewed from time to time) has effect,

the defendant remains subject to the notification requirements.

(2) Where a sexual harm prevention order is made in respect of a defendant who was not a relevant offender immediately before the making of the order—

(a) the order causes the defendant to become subject to the notification requirements of this Part from the making of the order until the order (as renewed from time to time) ceases to have effect, and

(b) this Part applies to the defendant, subject to the modification set out in subsection (3).

(3) The "relevant date" is the date of service of the order.

(4) Subsections (1) to (3) apply to an interim sexual harm prevention order as if references to a sexual harm prevention order were references to an interim sexual harm prevention order, and with the omission of "(as renewed from time to time)" in both places.

(5) Where—

(a) a sexual harm prevention order is in effect in relation to a relevant sex offender (within the meaning of section 88A), and

(b) by virtue of section 88F or 88G the relevant sex offender ceases to be subject to the notification requirements of this Part,

the sexual harm prevention order ceases to have effect.

(6) On an application for a sexual harm prevention order made by a chief officer of police, the court must make a notification order in respect of the defendant (either in addition to or instead of a sexual harm prevention order) if—

(a) the applicant invites the court to do so, and

(b) it is proved that the conditions in section 97(2) to (4) are met.

(7) On an application for an interim sexual harm prevention order made by a chief officer of police, the court may, if it considers it just to do so, make an interim notification order (either in addition to or instead of an interim sexual harm prevention order).

103H SHPOs and interim SHPOs: appeals

103H SHPOs and interim SHPOs: appeals

(1) A defendant may appeal against the making of a sexual harm prevention order—

(a) where the order was made by virtue of section 103A(2)(a)(i), as if the order were a sentence passed on the defendant for the offence;

(b) where the order was made by virtue of section 103A(2)(a)(ii) or (iii), as if the defendant had been convicted of the offence and the order were a sentence passed on the defendant for that offence;

(c) where the order was made on an application under section 103A(4), to the Crown Court.

(2) A defendant may appeal to the Crown Court against the making of an interim sexual harm prevention order.

(3) A defendant may appeal against the making of an order under section 103E, or the refusal to make such an order—

(a) where the application for such an order was made to the Crown Court, to the Court of Appeal;

(b) in any other case, to the Crown Court.

(4) On an appeal under subsection (1)(c), (2) or (3)(b), the Crown Court may make such orders as may be necessary to give effect to its determination of the appeal, and may also make such incidental or consequential orders as appear to it to be just.

(5) Any order made by the Crown Court on an appeal under subsection (1)(c) or (2) (other than an order directing that an application be re-heard by a magistrates' court) is for the purposes of section 103E(9) or 103F(5) (respectively) to be treated as if it were an order of the court from which the appeal was brought (and not an order of the Crown Court).

103I Offence: breach of SHPO or interim SHPO etc

103I Offence: breach of SHPO or interim SHPO etc

(1) A person who, without reasonable excuse, does anything that the person is prohibited from doing by—

(a) a sexual harm prevention order,

(b) an interim sexual harm prevention order,

(c) a sexual offences prevention order,

(d) an interim sexual offences prevention order, or

(e) a foreign travel order,

commits an offence.

(2) A person commits an offence if, without reasonable excuse, the person fails to comply with a requirement imposed under section 103D(4).

(3) A person guilty of an offence under this section is liable—

(a) on summary conviction, to imprisonment for a term not exceeding 6 months or a fine or both;

(b) on conviction on indictment, to imprisonment for a term not exceeding 5 years.

(4) Where a person is convicted of an offence under this section, it is not open to the court by or before which the person is convicted to make, in respect of the offence, an order for conditional discharge.

103J SHPOs and interim SHPOs: guidance

103J SHPOs and interim SHPOs: guidance

(1) The Secretary of State must issue guidance to chief officers of police and to the Director General of the National Crime Agency in relation to the exercise by them of their powers with regard to sexual harm prevention orders and interim sexual harm prevention orders.

(2) The Secretary of State may, from time to time, revise the guidance issued under subsection (1).

(3) The Secretary of State must arrange for any guidance issued or revised under this section to be published in such manner as the Secretary of State considers appropriate.

103K SHPOs and interim SHPOs: supplementary

103K SHPOs and interim SHPOs: supplementary

(1) Rules of court—

(a) may provide for a youth court to give permission for an application under section 103A(4) against a person aged 18 or over to be made to the youth court if—

(i) an application to the youth court has been made, or is to be made, under that section against a person aged under 18, and

(ii) the youth court thinks that it would be in the interests of justice for the applications to be heard together;

(b) may, in relation to a person attaining the age of 18 after proceedings against that person by virtue of section 103A, 103E, 103F or 103G(6) or (7) have begun—

(i) prescribe circumstances in which the proceedings may or must remain in the youth court;

(ii) make provision for the transfer of the proceedings from the youth court to a magistrates' court that is not a youth court (including provision applying section 103F with modifications).

(2) A person's age is treated for the purposes of sections 103A to 103J and this section as being that which it appears to the court to be after considering any available evidence."

Sexual offences prevention orders and foreign travel orders

3 (1) Sections 104 to 122 (sexual offences prevention orders and foreign travel orders) are repealed.

(2) This paragraph extends only to England and Wales.

Sexual risk orders

4 Before section 123 there is inserted—

"Sexual risk orders (England and Wales)

122A Sexual risk orders: applications, grounds and effect

122A Sexual risk orders: applications, grounds and effect

(1) A chief officer of police or the Director General of the National Crime Agency ("the Director General") may by complaint to a magistrates' court apply for an order under this section (a "sexual risk order") in respect of a person ("the defendant") if it appears to the chief officer or the Director General that the following condition is met.

(2) The condition is that the defendant has, whether before or after the commencement of this Part, done an act of a sexual nature as a result of which there is reasonable cause to believe that it is necessary for a sexual risk order to be made.

(3) A chief officer of police may make an application under subsection (1) only in respect of a person—

- (a) who resides in the chief officer's police area, or
- (b) who the chief officer believes is in that area or is intending to come to it.

(4) An application under subsection (1) may be made to any magistrates' court acting for a local justice area that includes—

- (a) any part of a relevant police area, or
- (b) any place where it is alleged that the person acted in a way mentioned in subsection (2).

(5) The Director General must as soon as practicable notify the chief officer of police for a relevant police area of any application that the Director has made under subsection (1).

(6) On an application under subsection (1), the court may make a sexual risk order if it is satisfied that the defendant has, whether before or after the commencement of this Part, done an act of a sexual nature as a result of which it is necessary to make such an order for the purpose of—

- (a) protecting the public or any particular members of the public from harm from the defendant, or
- (b) protecting children or vulnerable adults generally, or any particular children or vulnerable adults, from harm from the defendant outside the United Kingdom.

(7) Such an order—

- (a) prohibits the defendant from doing anything described in the order;
- (b) has effect for a fixed period (not less than 2 years) specified in the order or until further order.

(8) A sexual risk order may specify different periods for different prohibitions.

(9) The only prohibitions that may be imposed are those necessary for the purpose of—

(a) protecting the public or any particular members of the public from harm from the defendant, or

(b) protecting children or vulnerable adults generally, or any particular children or vulnerable adults, from harm from the defendant outside the United Kingdom.

(10) Where a court makes a sexual risk order in relation to a person who is already subject to such an order (whether made by that court or another), the earlier order ceases to have effect.

122B Section 122A: interpretation

122B Section 122A: interpretation

(1) In section 122A—

"child" means a person under 18;

"harm" from the defendant means physical or psychological harm caused by the defendant doing an act of a sexual nature;

"the public" means the public in the United Kingdom;

"vulnerable adult" means a person aged 18 or over whose ability to protect himself or herself from physical or psychological harm is significantly impaired through physical or mental disability or illness, through old age or otherwise.

(2) Where the defendant is a child, a reference in that section to a magistrates' court is to be taken as referring to a youth court (subject to any rules of court made under section 122K(1)).

(3) In that section "relevant police area" means—

(a) where the applicant is a chief officer of police, the officer's police area;

(b) where the applicant is the Director General of the National Crime Agency—

(i) the police area where the person in question resides, or

(ii) a police area which the Director General believes the person is in or is intending to come to.

122C Sexual risk orders: prohibitions on foreign travel

122C Sexual risk orders: prohibitions on foreign travel

(1) A prohibition on foreign travel contained in a sexual risk order must not be for a period of more than 5 years.

(2) A "prohibition on foreign travel" means—

(a) a prohibition on travelling to any country outside the United Kingdom named or described in the order,

(b) a prohibition on travelling to any country outside the United Kingdom other than a country named or described in the order, or

(c) a prohibition on travelling to any country outside the United Kingdom.

(3) Subsection (1) does not prevent a prohibition on foreign travel from being extended for a further period (of no more than 5 years each time) under section 122D.

(4) A sexual risk order that contains a prohibition within subsection (2)(c) must require the defendant to surrender all of the defendant's passports at a police station specified in the order—

(a) on or before the date when the prohibition takes effect, or

(b) within a period specified in the order.

(5) Any passports surrendered must be returned as soon as reasonably practicable after the person ceases to be subject to a sexual risk order containing such a prohibition (unless the person is subject to an equivalent prohibition under another order).

(6) Subsection (5) does not apply in relation to—

(a) a passport issued by or on behalf of the authorities of a country outside the United Kingdom if the passport has been returned to those authorities;

(b) a passport issued by or on behalf of an international organisation if the passport has been returned to that organisation.

(7) In this section "passport" means—

(a) a United Kingdom passport within the meaning of the Immigration Act 1971;

(b) a passport issued by or on behalf of the authorities of a country outside the United Kingdom, or by or on behalf of an international organisation;

(c) a document that can be used (in some or all circumstances) instead of a passport.

122D Sexual risk order: variations, renewals and discharges

122D Sexual risk order: variations, renewals and discharges

(1) A person within subsection (2) may by complaint to the appropriate court apply for an order varying, renewing or discharging a sexual risk order.

(2) The persons are—

(a) the defendant;

(b) the chief officer of police for the area in which the defendant resides;

(c) a chief officer of police who believes that the defendant is in, or is intending to come to, that officer's police area;

(d) where the order was made on an application by a chief officer of police, that officer.

(3) Subject to subsections (4) and (5), on the application the court, after hearing the person making the application and (if they wish to be heard) the other persons mentioned in subsection (2), may make any order, varying, renewing or discharging the sexual risk order, that the court considers appropriate.

(4) An order may be renewed, or varied so as to impose additional prohibitions on the defendant, only if it is necessary to do so for the purpose of—

(a) protecting the public or any particular members of the public from harm from the defendant, or

(b) protecting children or vulnerable adults generally, or any particular children or vulnerable adults, from harm from the defendant outside the United Kingdom.

Any renewed or varied order may contain only such prohibitions as are necessary for this purpose.

(5) The court must not discharge an order before the end of 2 years beginning with the day on which the order was made, without the consent of the defendant and—

(a) where the application is made by a chief officer of police, that chief officer, or

(b) in any other case, the chief officer of police for the area in which the defendant resides.

(6) Section 122B(1) applies for the purposes of this section.

(7) In this section "the appropriate court" means—

(a) where an adult magistrates' court made the sexual risk order, that court, any adult magistrates' court for the area in which the defendant resides or, where the application is made by a chief officer of police, any adult magistrates' court acting for a local justice area that includes any part of the chief officer's police area;

(b) where a youth court made the order and the defendant is under the age of 18, that court, a youth court for the area in which the defendant resides or, where the application is made by a chief officer of police, any youth court acting for a local justice area that includes any part of the chief officer's police area;

(c) where a youth court made the order and the defendant is aged 18 or over, an adult magistrates' court for the area in which the defendant resides or, where the application is made by a chief officer of police, any adult magistrates' court acting for a local justice area that includes any part of the chief officer's police area.

In this subsection "adult magistrates' court" means a magistrates' court that is not a youth court.

122E Interim sexual risk orders

122E Interim sexual risk orders

(1) This section applies where an application for a sexual risk order ("the main application") has not been determined.

(2) An application for an order under this section ("an interim sexual risk order") —

(a) may be made by the complaint by which the main application is made, or

(b) if the main application has been made, may be made by the person who has made that application, by complaint to the court to which that application has been made.

(3) The court may, if it considers it just to do so, make an interim sexual risk order, prohibiting the defendant from doing anything described in the order.

(4) Such an order—

(a) has effect only for a fixed period, specified in the order;

(b) ceases to have effect, if it has not already done so, on the determination of the main application.

(5) The applicant or the defendant may by complaint apply to the court that made the interim sexual risk order for the order to be varied, renewed or discharged.

122F Sexual risk orders and interim sexual risk orders: notification requirements

122F Sexual risk orders and interim sexual risk orders: notification requirements

(1) A person in respect of whom a court makes—

(a) a sexual risk order (other than one that replaces an interim sexual risk order), or

(b) an interim sexual risk order,

must, within the period of 3 days beginning with the date of service of the order, notify to the police the information set out in subsection (2) (unless the person is subject to the notification requirements of this Part on that date).

(2) The information is—

(a) the person's name and, where the person uses one or more other names, each of those names;

(b) the person's home address.

(3) A person who—

(a) is subject to a sexual risk order or an interim sexual risk order (but is not subject to the notification requirements of this Part), and

(b) uses a name which has not been notified under this section (or under any other provision of this Part), or changes home address,

must, within the period of 3 days beginning with the date on which that happens, notify to the police that name or (as the case may be) the new home address.

(4) Sections 87 (method of notification and related matters) and 91 (offences relating to notification) apply for the purposes of this section—

(a) with references to section 83(1) being read as references to subsection (1) above,

(b) with references to section 84(1) being read as references to subsection (3) above, and

(c) with the omission of section 87(2)(b).

122G Sexual risk orders and interim sexual risk orders: appeals

122G Sexual risk orders and interim sexual risk orders: appeals

(1) A defendant may appeal to the Crown Court—
- (a) against the making of a sexual risk order;
- (b) against the making of an interim sexual risk order; or
- (c) against the making of an order under section 122D, or the refusal to make such an order.

(2) On any such appeal, the Crown Court may make such orders as may be necessary to give effect to its determination of the appeal, and may also make such incidental or consequential orders as appear to it to be just.

(3) Any order made by the Crown Court on an appeal under subsection (1)(a) or (b) (other than an order directing that an application be re-heard by a magistrates' court) is for the purposes of section 122D(7) or 122E(5) (respectively) to be treated as if it were an order of the court from which the appeal was brought (and not an order of the Crown Court).

122H Offence: breach of sexual risk order or interim sexual risk order etc

122H Offence: breach of sexual risk order or interim sexual risk order etc

(1) A person who, without reasonable excuse, does anything that the person is prohibited from doing by—
- (a) a sexual risk order,
- (b) an interim sexual risk order,
- (c) a risk of sexual harm order,
- (d) an interim risk of sexual harm order,
- (e) an order under section 2 of the Protection of Children and Prevention of Sexual Offences (Scotland) Act 2005 (risk of sexual harm orders in Scotland), or
- (f) an order under section 5 of that Act (interim risk of sexual harm orders in Scotland),

commits an offence.

(2) A person commits an offence if, without reasonable excuse, the person fails to comply with a requirement imposed under section 122C(4).

(3) A person guilty of an offence under this section is liable—
- (a) on summary conviction, to imprisonment for a term not exceeding 6 months or a fine or both;
- (b) on conviction on indictment, to imprisonment for a term not exceeding 5 years.

(4) Where a person is convicted of an offence under this section, it is not open to the court by or before which the person is convicted to make, in respect of the offence, an order for conditional discharge.

122I Effect of conviction etc of an offence under section 122H etc

122I Effect of conviction etc of an offence under section 122H etc

(1) This section applies to a person ("the defendant") who—
- (a) is convicted of an offence mentioned in subsection (2);
- (b) is found not guilty of such an offence by reason of insanity;
- (c) is found to be under a disability and to have done the act charged against him in respect of such an offence; or
- (d) is cautioned in respect of such an offence.

(2) Those offences are—
- (a) an offence under section 122H or 128 of this Act;
- (b) an offence under section 7 of the Protection of Children and Prevention of Sexual Offences (Scotland) Act 2005 (contravention of risk of sexual harm order or interim risk of sexual harm order in Scotland).

(3) Where—
- (a) a defendant was a relevant offender immediately before this section applied to the defendant, and
- (b) the defendant would (apart from this subsection) cease to be subject to the notification requirements of this Part while the relevant order (as renewed from time to time) has effect,

the defendant remains subject to the notification requirements.

(4) Where the defendant was not a relevant offender immediately before this section applied to the defendant—
- (a) this section causes the defendant to become subject to the notification requirements of this Part from the time the section first applies to the defendant until the relevant order (as renewed from time to time) ceases to have effect, and
- (b) this Part applies to the defendant, subject to the modification set out in subsection (5).

(5) The "relevant date" is the date on which this section first applies to the defendant.

(6) In this section "relevant order" means—
- (a) where the conviction, finding or caution within subsection (1) is in respect of a breach of a sexual risk order or a risk of sexual harm order, that order;
- (b) where the conviction, finding or caution within subsection (1) is in respect of a breach of an interim sexual risk order or an interim risk of sexual harm order, any sexual risk order or risk of sexual harm order made on the hearing of the application to which the interim order relates or, if no such order is made, the interim order.

(7) In subsection (6) "risk of sexual harm order" and "interim risk of sexual harm order" include orders under sections 2 and 5 (respectively) of the Protection of Children and Prevention of Sexual Offences (Scotland) Act 2005.

122J Sexual risk orders and interim sexual risk orders: guidance

122J Sexual risk orders and interim sexual risk orders: guidance

(1) The Secretary of State must issue guidance to chief officers of police and to the Director General of the National Crime Agency in relation to the exercise by them of their powers with regard to sexual risk orders and interim sexual risk orders.

(2) The Secretary of State may, from time to time, revise the guidance issued under subsection (1).

(3) The Secretary of State must arrange for any guidance issued or revised under this section to be published in such manner as the Secretary of State considers appropriate.

122K Sexual risk orders and interim sexual risk orders: supplementary

122K Sexual risk orders and interim sexual risk orders: supplementary

(1) Rules of court—

(a) may provide for a youth court to give permission for an application under section 122A against a person aged 18 or over to be made to the youth court if—

(i) an application to the youth court has been made, or is to be made, under that section against a person aged under 18, and

(ii) the youth court thinks that it would be in the interests of justice for the applications to be heard together;

(b) may, in relation to a person attaining the age of 18 after proceedings against that person by virtue of section 122A, 122D or 122E have begun—

(i) prescribe circumstances in which the proceedings may or must remain in the youth court;

(ii) make provision for the transfer of the proceedings from the youth court to a magistrates' court that is not a youth court (including provision applying section 122E with modifications).

(2) A person's age is treated for the purposes of sections 122A to 122J and this section as being that which it appears to the court to be after considering any available evidence."

Risk of sexual harm orders

5 (1) Sections 123 to 129 (risk of sexual harm orders) are repealed.

(2) This paragraph extends only to England and Wales.

Application etc of orders

6 After section 136 there is inserted—

"136ZA Application of orders throughout the United Kingdom

"136ZA Application of orders throughout the United Kingdom

(1) In this section "relevant order" means—

(a) a sexual harm prevention order;

(b) an interim sexual harm prevention order;

(c) a sexual offences prevention order;

(d) an interim sexual offences prevention order;

(e) a foreign travel order;

(f) a sexual risk order;

(g) an interim sexual risk order;

(h) a risk of sexual harm order;

(i) an interim risk of sexual harm order;

(j) an order under section 2 of the Protection of Children and Prevention of Sexual Offences (Scotland) Act 2005 (risk of sexual harm orders in Scotland);

(k) an order under section 5 of that Act (interim risk of sexual harm orders in Scotland).

(2) For the purposes of sections 103I, 113, 122, 122H and 128, prohibitions imposed by a relevant order made in one part of the United Kingdom apply (unless expressly confined to particular localities) throughout that and every other part of the United Kingdom.

136ZB Order ceases to have effect when new order made

136ZB Order ceases to have effect when new order made

(1) Where a court in England and Wales makes an order listed in the first column of the following Table in relation to a person who is already subject to an order listed opposite it in the second column, the earlier order ceases to have effect (whichever part of the United Kingdom it was made in) unless the court orders otherwise.

New order	*Earlier order*
Sexual harm prevention order	— sexual offences prevention order; — foreign travel order.
Sexual risk order	— risk of sexual harm order; — foreign travel order.

(2) Where a court in Northern Ireland or Scotland makes an order listed in the first column of the following Table in relation to a person who is already subject to an order or prohibition listed opposite it in the second column, the earlier order or prohibition ceases to have effect (even though it was made or imposed by a court in England and Wales) unless the court orders otherwise.

New order	*Earlier order or prohibition*
Sexual offences prevention order	— sexual harm prevention order not containing a prohibition on foreign travel; — in the case of a sexual harm prevention order containing a prohibition on foreign travel, each of its other prohibitions.
Foreign travel order	— prohibition on foreign travel contained in a sexual harm prevention order.
Risk of sexual harm order	— sexual risk order not containing a prohibition on foreign travel; — in the case of a sexual risk order containing a prohibition on foreign travel, each of its other prohibitions.

(3) In this section—

(a) "court", in Scotland, includes sheriff;

(b) "risk of sexual harm order" includes an order under section 2 of the Protection of Children and Prevention of Sexual Offences (Scotland) Act 2005.

136ZC Variation of sexual harm prevention order by court in Northern Ireland

136ZC Variation of sexual harm prevention order by court in Northern Ireland

(1) This section applies where a sexual harm prevention order has been made in respect of a person who now—

(a) is residing in Northern Ireland, or

(b) is in or is intending to come to Northern Ireland.

(2) An application may be made to the appropriate court in Northern Ireland—

(a) by the defendant, or

(b) by the Chief Constable,

for an order varying the sexual harm prevention order.

(3) An application under subsection (2) may be made—

(a) where the appropriate court is the Crown Court, in accordance with rules of court;

(b) in any other case, by complaint.

(4) Subject to subsections (5) and (6), on the application the court, after hearing the person making the application and the other person mentioned in subsection (2) (if that person wishes to be heard), may make any order varying the sexual harm prevention order that the court considers appropriate.

(5) An order may be varied so as to impose additional prohibitions on the defendant only if it is necessary to do so for the purpose of—

(a) protecting the public in Northern Ireland, or any particular members of the public in Northern Ireland, from sexual harm from the defendant, or

(b) protecting children or vulnerable adults generally, or any particular children or vulnerable adults, from sexual harm from the defendant outside the United Kingdom.

(6) An order as varied under this section may contain only such prohibitions as are necessary for the purpose of—

(a) protecting the public or any particular members of the public from sexual harm from the defendant, or

(b) protecting children or vulnerable adults generally, or any particular children or vulnerable adults, from sexual harm from the defendant outside the United Kingdom.

(7) The defendant may appeal against the making of an order under this section, or the refusal to make such an order—

(a) where the application for such an order was made to the Crown Court, to the Court of Appeal in Northern Ireland;

(b) in any other case, to a county court in Northern Ireland.

(8) On an appeal under subsection (7)(b), the county court may make such orders as may be necessary to give effect to its determination of the appeal, and may also make such incidental or consequential orders as appear to it to be just.

(9) In this section—

"the appropriate court" means—

(a) where the sexual harm prevention order was made by—

(i) the Crown Court, otherwise than on appeal from a magistrates' court, or

(ii) the Court of Appeal,

the Crown Court (in Northern Ireland);

(b) where—

(i) the sexual harm prevention order was made by a magistrates' court, or by the Crown Court on appeal from a magistrates' court, and

(ii) the defendant is aged 18 or over,

any court of summary jurisdiction in Northern Ireland;

(c) where—

(i) the defendant is aged under 18, and

(ii) paragraph (a) does not apply,

any youth court in Northern Ireland;

"the Chief Constable" means the Chief Constable of the Police Service of Northern Ireland;

"sexual harm", "child" and "vulnerable adult" each has the meaning given in section 103B(1).

136ZD Variation of sexual risk order by court in Northern Ireland

136ZD Variation of sexual risk order by court in Northern Ireland

(1) This section applies where a sexual risk order has been made in respect of a person who now—

(a) is residing in Northern Ireland, or

(b) is in or is intending to come to Northern Ireland.

(2) An application may be made to the appropriate court in Northern Ireland—

(a) by the defendant, or

(b) by the Chief Constable,

for an order varying the sexual risk order.

(3) Subject to subsections (4) and (5), on the application the court, after hearing the person making the application and the other person mentioned in subsection (2) (if that person wishes to be heard), may make any order varying the sexual risk order that the court considers appropriate.

(4) An order may be varied so as to impose additional prohibitions on the defendant only if it is necessary to do so for the purpose of—

(a) protecting the public in Northern Ireland, or any particular members of the public in Northern Ireland, from harm from the defendant, or

(b) protecting children or vulnerable adults generally, or any particular children or vulnerable adults, from harm from the defendant outside the United Kingdom.

(5) An order as varied under this section may contain only such prohibitions as are necessary for the purpose of—

(a) protecting the public or any particular members of the public from harm from the defendant, or

(b) protecting children or vulnerable adults generally, or any particular children or vulnerable adults, from harm from the defendant outside the United Kingdom.

(6) The defendant may appeal against the making of an order under this section, or the refusal to make such an order, to a county court in Northern Ireland.

(7) On an appeal under subsection (6), the county court may make such orders as may be necessary to give effect to its determination of the appeal, and may also make such incidental or consequential orders as appear to it to be just.

(8) In this section—

"the appropriate court" means—

(a) where the defendant is aged 18 or over, any court of summary jurisdiction in Northern Ireland;

(b) where the defendant is aged under 18, any youth court in Northern Ireland;

"the Chief Constable" means the Chief Constable of the Police Service of Northern Ireland;

"harm", "child" and "vulnerable adult" each has the meaning given in section 122B(1)."

Service courts

7 (1) Section 137 of the Sexual Offences Act 2003 (service courts) is amended as follows.

(2) In subsection (2), for "104(1)" there is substituted "103A(1)".

(3) For subsection (3) there is substituted—

"(3) Where the court making a sexual harm prevention order is a service court—

(a) sections 103A(3) to (9), 103F and 103J do not apply;

(b) sections 103A(1) and (2), 103B to 103E and 103G to 103I apply—

(i) subject to paragraphs (c) and (d), and

(ii) as if they extended to the whole of the United Kingdom;

(c) in relation to an application under section 103E in respect of a defendant who at the time of the application is a person subject to service law or a civilian subject to service discipline—

(i) the application may be made only by the defendant or a Provost Martial, and must be made to the Court Martial;

(ii) consent under section 103E(7) must be the consent of the defendant and a Provost Martial;

(iii) an appeal against the making of an order under section 103E, or the refusal to make such an order, must be made to the Court Martial Appeal Court;

(d) in relation to an application under section 103E in respect of a defendant who at the time of the application is neither a person subject to service law nor a civilian subject to service discipline—

(i) the application must be made to the Crown Court in England and Wales;

(ii) an appeal against the making of an order under section 103E, or the refusal to make such an order, must be made to the Court of Appeal in England and Wales."

(4) In subsection (4)—

(a) for "section "service court" means" there is substituted "section—

"civilian subject to service discipline" has the same meaning as in the Armed Forces Act 2006 (see section 370 of that Act);

"service court" means";

(b) at the end there is inserted—

"""subject to service law" has the same meaning as in the Armed Forces Act 2006 (see section 374 of that Act)."

(5) After subsection (5) there is inserted—

"(6) Paragraphs (c)(i) and (d)(i) of subsection (3) have effect, in relation to a sexual harm prevention order made by the Court Martial Appeal Court, as if the reference to a service court in that subsection included a reference to that court."

SCHEDULE 6

Section 115

AMENDMENTS OF PART 2A OF THE SEXUAL OFFENCES ACT 2003

1 Part 2A of the Sexual Offences Act 2003 (closure orders) is amended as follows.

2 (1) Section 136A (meaning of specified prostitution offence etc) is amended as follows.

(2) In subsection (2)—

(a) in paragraph (a) the words "section 47 of this Act or" are omitted;
(b) in paragraph (b) the words "section 48 of this Act, or" are omitted;
(c) in paragraph (c) the words "section 49 of this Act, or" are omitted;
(d) in paragraph (d) the words "section 50 of this Act, or" are omitted.

(3) In subsection (3)—

(a) in paragraph (a) the words "section 48 of this Act, or" are omitted;
(b) in paragraph (b) the words "section 49 of this Act, or" are omitted;
(c) in paragraph (c) the words "section 50 of this Act, or" are omitted.

(4) After that subsection there is inserted—

"(3A) The specified child sex offences are—

(a) an offence under any of the following sections of this Act—
sections 5 to 13;
sections 16 to 19;
sections 25 and 26;
sections 47 to 50;
(b) an offence under section 1 of the Protection of Children Act 1978 (indecent photographs of children);
(c) an offence under any of the following sections of this Act committed against a person under 18—
sections 1 to 4;
sections 30 to 41;
section 59A;
section 61;
sections 66 and 67."

(5) In subsection (4)(a)—

(a) the words "section 47 of this Act or" are omitted;
(b) the words "subsection (1)(a) of that section or, as the case may be," are omitted.

(6) After subsection (5) there is inserted—

"(5A) Premises are being used for activities related to a specified child sex offence at any time when the premises are used—

(a) to commit the offence, or
(b) for activities intended to arrange or facilitate the commission of the offence."

3 In section 136B (power to authorise issue of closure notice), in the heading, for "**notice**" there is substituted "**notice: prostitution or pornography offences**".

4 After that section there is inserted—

"136BA Power to authorise issue of closure notice: child sex offences in England and Wales

"136BA "136BA Power to authorise issue of closure notice: child sex offences in England and Wales

(1) A member of a police force not below the rank of superintendent ("the authorising officer") may authorise the issue of a closure notice in respect of any premises in England and Wales if three conditions are met.

(2) The first condition is that the officer has reasonable grounds for believing that—

(a) during the relevant period, the premises were used for activities related to one or more specified child sex offences, or

(b) the premises are likely to be used (unless a closure order is made) for activities related to one or more specified child sex offences.

(3) In subsection (2)(a), "the relevant period" means the period of 3 months ending with the day on which the officer is considering whether to authorise the issue of the notice.

(4) The second condition is that the officer has reasonable grounds for believing that the making of a closure order under section 136D is necessary to prevent the premises being used for activities related to one or more specified child sex offences.

(5) For the purposes of the second condition, it does not matter whether the officer believes that the offence or offences in question have been committed or that they will be committed (or will be committed unless a closure order is made).

(6) The third condition is that the officer is satisfied that reasonable efforts have been made—

(a) to consult the local authority for the area in which the premises are situated, and

(b) to establish the identity of any person who resides on the premises or who has control of or responsibility for or an interest in the premises.

(7) If the local authority has not been consulted when the notice is issued, it must be consulted as soon as possible afterwards.

(8) An authorisation under subsection (1) may be given orally or in writing, but if it is given orally the authorising officer must confirm it in writing as soon as it is practicable.

(9) The issue of a closure notice may be authorised whether or not a person has been convicted of any specified child sex offence that the authorising officer believes has been committed.

(10) The Secretary of State may by regulations specify premises or descriptions of premises to which this section does not apply."

5 (1) Section 136C (contents and service of closure notice) is amended as follows.

(2) In subsection (1)(c), after "section 136B" there is inserted "or 136BA".

(3) In subsection (3)(d), after "section 136B(7)(b)" there is inserted "or 136BA(6)(b)".

6 (1) Section 136D (power to make a closure order) is amended as follows.

(2) In subsection (5), for "either subsection (6) or subsection (7) (or both)" there is substituted "at least one of subsections (6), (7) and (7A)".

(3) After subsection (7) there is inserted—

"(7A) This subsection applies if—

(a) during the relevant period, the premises were used for activities related to one or more specified child sex offences, or

(b) the premises are likely to be used (unless a closure order is made) for activities related to one or more specified child sex offences."

(4) In subsection (8), for "subsections (6) and (7)" there is substituted "subsections (6), (7) and (7A)(a)".

(5) In subsection (9), for "prostitution or pornography offences" there is substituted "prostitution, pornography or child sex offences".

(6) In subsection (10)(a), after "section 136B(7)(b)" there is inserted "or 136BA(6)(b)".

(7) In subsection (12), for "prostitution or pornography offences" there is substituted "prostitution, pornography or child sex offences".

7 In section 136H (applications for extension of closure order), in subsection (4), for "prostitution or pornography offences" there is substituted "prostitution, pornography or child sex offences".

8 In section 136I (orders extending closure orders), in subsection (2), for "prostitution or pornography offences" there is substituted "prostitution, pornography or child sex offences".

9 In section 136J (discharge of closure order), in subsection (3), for "prostitution or pornography offences" there is substituted "prostitution, pornography or child sex offences".

10 In section 136O (compensation), in subsection (5)(a), after "section 136B" there is inserted "or 136BA".

11 (1) Section 136R (interpretation) is amended as follows.

(2) In subsection (2), after "section 136B" there is inserted "or 136BA".

(3) After subsection (14) there is inserted—

"(15) In the application of this Part to England and Wales, references to specified pornography offences are to be ignored.

(16) "Specified child sex offence" means an offence listed in section 136A(3A).

(17) In the application of this Part to Northern Ireland, references to specified child sex offences and to section 136BA are to be ignored."

SCHEDULE 7

Section 132

SCHEDULE TO BE INSERTED AS SCHEDULE 4B TO THE POLICE ACT 1996

"SCHEDULE 4B

Section 64A

THE POLICE REMUNERATION REVIEW BODY

1 Interpretation

1 In this Schedule "review body" means the Police Remuneration Review Body.

2 Members of the review body

2 The Secretary of State shall determine how many members the review body should have and what kinds of experience the members should possess.

3 Members shall hold and vacate office in accordance with the terms of their appointment.

4 Members shall adhere to any statement of principles issued by the Secretary of State as to their conduct as members.

5 Resignation of members

5 (1) The chair of the review body may resign by giving written notice to the Prime Minister.

(2) Resignation may be either—

(a) as chair, or

(b) as both chair and member.

6 (1) The deputy chair of the review body may resign by giving written notice to the Secretary of State.

(2) Resignation may be either—

(a) as deputy chair, or

(b) as both deputy chair and member.

7 A member other than the chair or deputy chair may resign by giving written notice to the Secretary of State.

8 Dismissal of members

8 (1) The Prime Minister may by written notice dismiss the chair on the ground that—

(a) the chair has been adjudged bankrupt, has been made the subject of a debt relief order (under Part 7A of the Insolvency Act 1986) or has made an arrangement with creditors;

(b) in the opinion of the Prime Minister the chair is unable, unfit or unwilling to perform—

(i) the functions of chair, or

(ii) the functions of a member.

(2) Dismissal may be either—

(a) as chair, or

(b) as both chair and member (but only if sub-paragraph (1)(a) or (b)(ii) applies).

9 (1) The Secretary of State may by written notice dismiss the deputy chair on the ground that—

(a) the deputy chair has been adjudged bankrupt, has been made the subject of a debt relief order (under Part 7A of the Insolvency Act 1986) or has made an arrangement with creditors;

(b) in the opinion of the Secretary of State the deputy chair is unable, unfit or unwilling to perform—

(i) the functions of deputy chair, or

(ii) the functions of a member.

(2) Dismissal may be either—

(a) as deputy chair, or

(b) as both deputy chair and member (but only if sub-paragraph (1)(a) or (b)(ii) applies).

10 The Secretary of State may by written notice dismiss a member other than the chair or deputy chair on the ground that—

(a) the member has been adjudged bankrupt, has been made the subject of a debt relief order (under Part 7A of the Insolvency Act 1986) or has made an arrangement with creditors, or

(b) in the opinion of the Secretary of State the member is unable, unfit or unwilling to perform the functions of a member.

11 Procedure

11 (1) Subject to sub-paragraph (2), the review body shall determine its own procedure.

(2) The Secretary of State may give directions to the review body as to its procedure, including in particular directions about—

(a) the persons from whom the review body is to obtain evidence;

(b) the procedure for obtaining evidence.

(3) The validity of proceedings of the review body is not affected by—

(a) a vacancy in its membership (including a vacancy in the position of chair);

(b) a defect in a person's appointment.

12 Matters to be considered

12 The Secretary of State may give directions to the review body about the matters that it is to consider when making decisions.

13 Consultation

13 (1) The Secretary of State shall consult with the persons and bodies listed in sub-paragraph (2), and any others that the Secretary of State thinks fit, before—

(a) making or revising a determination under paragraph 2;

(b) issuing or revising a statement of principles under paragraph 4;

(c) giving or revising a direction under paragraph 11(2) or 12.

(2) The persons and bodies are—

(a) the Department of Justice in Northern Ireland;

(b) persons whom the Secretary of State considers to represent the views of chief officers of police and of the Chief Constable of the Police Service of Northern Ireland;

(c) persons whom the Secretary of State considers to represent the interests of members of police forces;

(d) persons whom the Secretary of State considers to represent the interests of members of the Police Service of Northern Ireland;

(e) persons whom the Secretary of State considers to represent the views of the persons and bodies who between them maintain the police forces in England and Wales;

(f) the Northern Ireland Policing Board.

(3) The Minister shall consult with the Department of Justice in Northern Ireland before exercising a power of dismissal under paragraph 8, 9 or 10.

14 Publication

14 The Secretary of State shall arrange for the publication of—

(a) a statement of any determination made under paragraph 2 (and of any revised determination);

(b) any statement of principles issued under paragraph 4 (and any revised statement);

(c) any direction given under paragraph 11(2) or 12 (and any revised direction).

15 Money

15 The Secretary of State or the Department of Justice in Northern Ireland—

(a) may defray expenses incurred by the review body;

(b) may pay remuneration and allowances to members;

(c) may make payments to or in respect of a member by way of or in connection with—

(i) a pension;

(ii) an allowance or gratuity on retirement or death;

(d) may pay compensation to a person who ceases to be a member if it seems to the Secretary of State or the Department to be right to do so by reason of special circumstances."

SCHEDULE 8

Section 147

POWERS TO SEIZE INVALID PASSPORTS ETC

Interpretation

1 (1) In this Schedule "examining officer" means—

(a) a constable,

(b) a person appointed as an immigration officer under paragraph 1 of Schedule 2 to the Immigration Act 1971, or

(c) a general customs official designated under section 3(1) of the Borders, Citizenship and Immigration Act 2009.

(2) In this Schedule "travel document" means anything that is, or appears to be, a passport or other document which—

(a) has been issued by or for Her Majesty's Government, or the government of another state, and

(b) enables or facilitates travel from one state to another.

(3) For the purposes of this Schedule a travel document is "invalid" if—

(a) it has been cancelled,

(b) it has expired,

(c) it was not issued by the government or authority by which it purports to have been issued, or

(d) it has undergone an unauthorised alteration.

(4) In this Schedule "port" means—

(a) an airport,

(b) a sea port,

(c) a hoverport,

(d) a heliport,

(e) a railway station where passenger trains depart for, or arrive from, places outside the United Kingdom, or

(f) any other place at which a person is able, or attempting, to get on or off any craft, vessel or vehicle in connection with entering or leaving Great Britain or Northern Ireland.

Powers of search and seizure etc: ports

2 (1) An examining officer may exercise any of the powers under this paragraph in the case of a person at a port whom the officer believes to be there in connection with—

(a) entering or leaving Great Britain or Northern Ireland, or

(b) travelling by air within Great Britain or within Northern Ireland.

(2) The powers are—

(a) to require the person to hand over all travel documents in his or her possession for inspection by the examining officer;

(b) to search for travel documents and to take possession of any that the officer finds;

(c) to inspect any travel document taken from the person and to retain it while its validity is checked;

(d) (subject to paragraph 4) to retain any travel document taken from the person that the examining officer believes to be invalid.

(3) The power under sub-paragraph (2)(b) is a power to search—

(a) the person;

(b) anything that the person has with him or her;

(c) any vehicle in which the examining officer believes the person to have been travelling or to be about to travel.

(4) An examining officer—
- (a) may stop a person or vehicle for the purposes of exercising a power under this paragraph;
- (b) may if necessary use reasonable force for the purpose of exercising a power under this paragraph;
- (c) may authorise a person to carry out on the officer's behalf a search under this paragraph.

Powers of search and seizure etc: constables

3 (1) A constable may exercise any of the powers under this paragraph, at a place that is not a port, in the case of a person whom the constable reasonably believes to be in possession of a passport to which this paragraph applies.

(2) This paragraph applies to a passport if—
- (a) the passport was issued by or for Her Majesty's Government,
- (b) the Secretary of State has cancelled the passport on the basis that the person to whom it was issued has or may have been, or will or may become, involved in activities so undesirable that it is contrary to the public interest for the person to have access to passport facilities, and
- (c) the passport is specified in an authorisation issued by the Secretary of State for the use of the powers under this paragraph.

(3) The powers are—
- (a) to require the person to hand over all travel documents in his or her possession for inspection by the constable;
- (b) to search for travel documents and to take possession of any that the constable finds;
- (c) to inspect any travel document taken from the person and to retain it while its validity is checked;
- (d) (subject to paragraph 4) to retain any travel document taken from the person that the constable believes to be invalid.

(4) The power under sub-paragraph (3)(b) is a power to search—
- (a) the person;
- (b) anything that the person has with him or her;
- (c) any vehicle in which the constable believes the person to have been travelling or to be about to travel;
- (d) any premises on which the constable is lawfully present.

(5) A constable—
- (a) may if necessary use reasonable force for the purpose of exercising a power under this paragraph;
- (b) may authorise a person to carry out on the constable's behalf a search under this paragraph.

Retention or return of documents seized

4 (1) If a travel document is retained under paragraph 2(2)(c) or 3(3)(c) while its validity is checked, the checking must be carried out as soon as possible.

(2) If it is established that a travel document taken from a person under paragraph 2 or 3—

(a) is valid, or

(b) is invalid only because it has expired,

it must be returned to the person straight away.

(3) A travel document taken from a person under paragraph 2 or 3 must be returned to the person before the end of the period of 7 days beginning with the day on which it was taken, unless during that period it is established that the document is invalid for some reason other than expiry.

(4) A requirement under sub-paragraph (2)(b) or (3) to return an expired travel document does not apply where the officer concerned reasonably believes that the person from whom he or she took the document, or some other person, intends to use it for purposes for which it is no longer valid.

(5) A requirement under sub-paragraph (2) or (3) to return a travel document has effect subject to any provision not in this Schedule under which the document may be lawfully retained.

Offences

5 (1) A person who is required under paragraph 2(2)(a) or 3(3)(a) to hand over all travel documents in the person's possession commits an offence if he or she fails without reasonable excuse to do so.

(2) A person who intentionally obstructs, or seeks to frustrate, a search under paragraph 2 or 3 commits an offence.

(3) A person guilty of an offence under this paragraph is liable on summary conviction—

(a) to imprisonment for a term not exceeding 6 months, or

(b) to a fine, which in Scotland or Northern Ireland may not exceed £5,000,

or to both.

6 An examining officer, other than a constable, exercising a power under paragraph 2 has the same powers of arrest without warrant as a constable in relation to an offence under—

(a) paragraph 5, or

(b) section 4 or 6 of the Identity Documents Act 2010.

SCHEDULE 9

Section 148

PORT AND BORDER CONTROLS

Examining officers

1 (1) Schedule 7 to the Terrorism Act 2000 is amended as follows.

(2) In paragraph 1(1)(b), after "officer" there is inserted "who is designated for the purpose of this Schedule by the Secretary of State".

(3) After paragraph 1 there is inserted—

"1A Examining officers etc

1A (1) The Secretary of State must under paragraph 6 of Schedule 14 issue a code of practice about—

(a) training to be undertaken by constables, immigration officers and customs officers who are to act as examining officers or exercise other functions under this Schedule, and

(b) the procedure for making designations under paragraph 1(1)(b) and (c).

(2) In particular, the code must make provision for consultation with the relevant chief officer of police before designations are made under paragraph 1(1)(b) or (c).

(3) "Relevant chief officer of police" means—

(a) in England and Wales, the chief officer of police for the police area in which the persons designated would act as examining officers,

(b) in Scotland, the Chief Constable of the Police Service of Scotland, and

(c) in Northern Ireland, the Chief Constable of the Police Service of Northern Ireland."

Time limits on examination without detention and on detention

2 (1) Schedule 7 to the Terrorism Act 2000 is amended as follows.

(2) Paragraph 6(4) is repealed.

(3) After paragraph 6 there is inserted—

"6A (1) This paragraph applies where a person is questioned under paragraph 2 or 3.

(2) After the end of the 1 hour period, the person may not be questioned under either of those paragraphs unless the person is detained under paragraph 6.

(3) If the person is detained under paragraph 6 the person must be released not later than the end of the 6 hour period (unless detained under another power).

(4) In this paragraph—

"the 1 hour period" is the period of 1 hour beginning with the time the person is first questioned under paragraph 2 or 3;

"the 6 hour period" is the period of 6 hours beginning with that time."

Powers to search persons

3 In paragraph 8 of Schedule 7 to the Terrorism Act 2000, after sub-paragraph (3) there is inserted—

"(4) An intimate search of a person may not be carried out under this paragraph.

(5) A strip search of a person may not be carried out under this paragraph unless—

(a) the person is detained under paragraph 6,

(b) the examining officer has reasonable grounds to suspect that the person is concealing something which may be evidence that the person falls within section 40(1)(b), and

(c) the search is authorised by a senior officer who has not been directly involved in questioning the person.

(6) "Senior officer" means—

(a) where the examining officer is a constable, a constable of a higher rank than the examining officer,

(b) where the examining officer is an immigration officer, an immigration officer of a higher grade than the examining officer, and

(c) where the examining officer is a customs officer, a customs officer of a higher grade than the examining officer.

(7) In this paragraph—

"intimate search" means a search which consists of a physical examination of a person's body orifices other than the mouth;

"strip search" means a search which is not an intimate search but involves the removal of an article of clothing which—

(a) is being worn wholly or partly on the trunk, and

(b) is being so worn either next to the skin or next to an article of underwear."

Power to make and retain copies

4 In Schedule 7 to the Terrorism Act 2000, after paragraph 11 there is inserted—

"11A Power to make and retain copies

11A (1) This paragraph applies where the examining officer is a constable.

(2) The examining officer may copy anything which—

(a) is given to the examining officer in accordance with paragraph 5,

(b) is searched or found on a search under paragraph 8, or

(c) is examined under paragraph 9.

(3) The copy may be retained—

(a) for so long as is necessary for the purpose of determining whether a person falls within section 40(1)(b),

(b) while the examining officer believes that it may be needed for use as evidence in criminal proceedings, or

(c) while the examining officer believes that it may be needed in connection with a decision by the Secretary of State whether to make a deportation order under the Immigration Act 1971."

Right of person detained under Schedule 7 to have someone informed and to consult a solicitor

5 (1) Schedule 8 to the Terrorism Act 2000 is amended as follows.

(2) In paragraph 1(5) (definition of examining officer) for "paragraph" there is substituted "Schedule".

(3) In paragraph 2(2)(d), the words "(within the meaning of that Schedule)" are omitted.

(4) In paragraph 6, for "police station", in each place, there is substituted "place".

(5) In paragraph 7(1) the words "at a police station" are omitted.

(6) After paragraph 7 there is inserted—

"7A (1) This paragraph applies where a person detained under Schedule 7 requests to consult a solicitor.

(2) The examining officer may not question the detained person under paragraph 2 or 3 of Schedule 7 until the person has consulted a solicitor (or no longer wishes to do so).

(3) Sub-paragraph (2) does not apply if the examining officer reasonably believes that postponing the questioning until then would be likely to prejudice determination of the relevant matters.

(4) The powers given by paragraph 8 of Schedule 7 (search powers where a person is questioned under paragraph 2 of Schedule 7) may be used when questioning is postponed because of sub-paragraph (2).

(5) The detained person is entitled to consult a solicitor in person.

(6) Sub-paragraph (5) does not apply if the examining officer reasonably believes that the time it would take to consult a solicitor in person would be likely to prejudice determination of the relevant matters.

(7) In that case the examining officer may require any consultation to take place in another way.

(8) In this paragraph "the relevant matters" means the matters the examining officer seeks to determine under paragraph 2 or 3 of Schedule 7."

(7) In paragraph 8(1), for "an officer" there is substituted "a police officer".

(8) In paragraph 9(2)(a) and (b)—

(a) the words "at a police station" are omitted;

(b) for "an officer" there is substituted "a police officer".

(9) In paragraph 16—

(a) in sub-paragraphs (1) and (3), in each place, for "police station" there is substituted "place";

(b) in sub-paragraph (6), after "detained" there is inserted "as mentioned in sub-paragraph (1)".

(10) After paragraph 16 there is inserted—

"16A (1) This paragraph applies where a person detained under Schedule 7 requests to consult a solicitor.

(2) The examining officer may not question the detained person under paragraph 2 or 3 of Schedule 7 until the person has consulted a solicitor (or no longer wishes to do so).

(3) Sub-paragraph (2) does not apply if the examining officer reasonably believes that postponing the questioning until then would be likely to prejudice determination of the relevant matters.

(4) The powers given by paragraph 8 of Schedule 7 (search powers where a person is questioned under paragraph 2 of Schedule 7) may be used when questioning is postponed because of sub-paragraph (2).

(5) The detained person is entitled to consult a solicitor in person.

(6) Sub-paragraph (5) does not apply if the examining officer reasonably believes that the time it would take to consult a solicitor in person would be likely to prejudice determination of the relevant matters.

(7) In that case the examining officer may require any consultation to take place in another way.

(8) In this paragraph "the relevant matters" means the matters the examining officer seeks to determine under paragraph 2 or 3 of Schedule 7."

(11) In paragraph 17(1)—

(a) for "An officer" there is substituted "A police officer";

(b) after "uniformed" there is inserted "police".

(12) In paragraph 18—

(a) in sub-paragraph (1), for "and" there is substituted "to";

(b) in sub-paragraph (2), for "police station" there is substituted "place";

(c) after sub-paragraph (2) there is inserted—

"(3) In relation to a person detained under Schedule 7 at a place other than a police station—

(a) sub-paragraph (2), and

(b) section 15(4) of the Criminal Procedure (Scotland) Act 1995 as applied by that sub-paragraph,

apply as if references to a constable included an examining officer."

Biometrics

6 (1) Paragraph 10 of Schedule 8 to the Terrorism Act 2000 is amended as follows.

(2) In sub-paragraph (5), for "the detained person only" there is substituted "a person detained under section 41, but only".

(3) In sub-paragraph (6)(b), after "in any case" there is inserted "in which an authorisation under that sub-paragraph may be given".

Review of detention under Schedule 7

7 (1) The Terrorism Act 2000 is amended as follows.

(2) In paragraph 6(3) of Schedule 7 (provisions of Schedule 8 applying to detention under Schedule 7)—

(a) for "Part I" there is substituted "Parts 1 and 1A";

(b) after "treatment" there is inserted "and review of detention".

(3) In Schedule 8, after Part 1 there is inserted—

"**PART 1A**

REVIEW OF DETENTION UNDER SCHEDULE 7

20K General requirements

20K General requirements

(1) A person's detention under Schedule 7 must be periodically reviewed by a review officer.

(2) The first review must be carried out before the end of the period of one hour beginning with the person's detention under that Schedule.

(3) Subsequent reviews must be carried out at intervals of not more than two hours.

(4) The review officer may authorise a person's continued detention under Schedule 7 only if satisfied that it is necessary for the purposes of exercising a power under paragraph 2 or 3 of that Schedule.

(5) If on a review under this paragraph the review officer does not authorise a person's continued detention, the person must be released (unless detained under another power).

(6) In this Part of this Schedule "review officer" means a senior officer who has not been directly involved in questioning the detained person under paragraph 2 or 3 of Schedule 7.

(7) "Senior officer" means—

(a) where the examining officer is a constable, a constable of a higher rank than the examining officer,

(b) where the examining officer is an immigration officer, an immigration officer of a higher grade than the examining officer, and

(c) where the examining officer is a customs officer, a customs officer of a higher grade than the examining officer.

(8) The Secretary of State must under paragraph 6 of Schedule 14 issue a code of practice about reviews under this Part of this Schedule.

(9) The code of practice must include provision about training to be undertaken by persons who are to act as review officers.

20L Representations

20L Representations

(1) Before determining whether to authorise a person's continued detention, a review officer must give either of the following persons an opportunity to make representations about the detention—

(a) the detained person, or

(b) a solicitor representing the detained person who is available at the time of the review.

(2) Representations may be oral or written.

(3) A review officer may refuse to hear oral representations from the detained person if the officer considers that the detained person is unfit to make representations because of the detained person's condition or behaviour.

20M Rights

20M Rights

(1) Where a review officer authorises continued detention the officer must inform the detained person—

(a) of any of the detained person's rights under paragraphs 6 and 7 which have not yet been exercised, and

(b) if the exercise of any of those rights is being delayed in accordance with the provisions of paragraph 8, of the fact that it is being delayed.

(2) Where a review of a person's detention is being carried out at a time when the person's exercise of a right under paragraph 6 or 7 is being delayed—

(a) the review officer must consider whether the reason or reasons for which the delay was authorised continue to subsist, and

(b) if in the review officer's opinion the reason or reasons have ceased to subsist, the review officer must inform the officer who authorised the delay of that opinion (unless the review officer was that officer).

(3) In the application of this paragraph to Scotland, for the references to paragraphs 6, 7 and 8 substitute references to paragraph 16.

20N Record

20N Record

(1) A review officer carrying out a review must make a written record of the outcome of the review and of any of the following which apply—

(a) the fact that the officer is satisfied that continued detention is necessary for the purposes of exercising a power under paragraph 2 or 3 of Schedule 7,

(b) the fact that the detained person has been informed as required under paragraph 20M(1),

(c) the officer's conclusion on the matter considered under paragraph 20M(2)(a), and

(d) the fact that the officer has taken action under paragraph 20M(2)(b).

(2) The review officer must inform the detained person whether the officer is authorising continued detention, and if so that the officer is satisfied that continued detention is necessary for the purposes of exercising a power under paragraph 2 or 3 of Schedule 7.

(3) Sub-paragraph (2) does not apply where the detained person is—

(a) incapable of understanding what is said,

(b) violent or likely to become violent, or

(c) in urgent need of medical attention."

Codes of practice

8 (1) Schedule 14 to the Terrorism Act 2000 (exercise of powers—codes of practice etc) is amended as follows.

(2) In paragraph 1, after ""officer" means" there is inserted "(subject to paragraph 6A)".

(3) After paragraph 6 there is inserted—

"6A In paragraphs 5 and 6, "officer" includes a constable, immigration officer or customs officer who—

(a) has functions under Schedule 7, or

(b) has functions under Schedule 8 in relation to a person detained under Schedule 7,

otherwise than as an examining officer."

SCHEDULE 10

Section 152

POWERS OF COMMUNITY SUPPORT OFFICERS

Introduction

1 Part 1 of Schedule 4 to the Police Reform Act 2002 (powers of community support officers) is amended as follows.

Additional powers to issue fixed penalty notices

2 (1) In paragraph 1 (powers to issue fixed penalty notices), in sub-paragraph (2)(b), for the words after "in respect of an offence" there is substituted "listed in sub-paragraph (2B)".

(2) In sub-paragraph (2) of that paragraph, after paragraph (ca) there is inserted—

"(cb) the power of an authorised officer of a borough council to give a notice under section 15 of the London Local Authorities Act 2004 in respect of an offence under section 38(1) of the London Local Authorities Act 1990 or section 27(1) of the City of Westminster Act 1999 (unlicensed street trading);".

(3) After sub-paragraph (2A) of that paragraph there is inserted—

"(2B) The offences referred to in sub-paragraph (2)(b) are—

(a) an offence under section 72 of the Highway Act 1835 (riding on a footway) committed by cycling;

(b) an offence under section 5(1) or 8(1) of the Road Traffic Regulation Act 1984 involving a contravention of a prohibition or restriction that relates to—

(i) stopping, waiting or parking at or near a school entrance,

(ii) one-way traffic on a road, or

(iii) lanes or routes for use only by cycles, only by buses or only by cycles and buses;

(c) an offence under section 24 of the Road Traffic Act 1988 (more than one person on a one-person bicycle);

(d) an offence under section 35 of that Act (failing to comply with traffic directions) committed by the rider of a cycle;

(e) an offence under section 36 of that Act (failing to comply with traffic signs) committed by the rider of a cycle who fails to comply with the indication given by a red traffic light;

(f) an offence under section 42 of that Act of contravening or failing to comply with a construction or use requirement about—

(i) lighting equipment or reflectors for cycles,

(ii) the use on a road of a motor vehicle in a way that causes excessive noise,

(iii) stopping the action of a stationary vehicle's machinery,

(iv) the use of a vehicle's horn on a road while the vehicle is stationary or on a restricted road at night, or

(v) opening a vehicle's door on a road so as to injure or endanger a person;

(g) an offence under section 163 of that Act (failing to stop vehicle or cycle when required to do so by constable or traffic officer)."

(4) After sub-paragraph (4) of that paragraph there is inserted—

"(5) In this paragraph "cycle" has the same meaning as in the Road Traffic Act 1988 (see section 192(1) of that Act)."

Powers to issue fixed penalty notices: consultation with local authorities

3 In paragraph 1, after sub-paragraph (2B) (inserted by paragraph 2(3) above) there is inserted—

"(2C) Before a chief officer of police makes a designation applying this paragraph to any person and specifying or describing an offence listed in sub-paragraph (2B)(b)(i), the officer shall consult every local authority any part of whose area lies within the officer's police area.

(2D) In paragraph (2C) "local authority" means—

(a) in relation to England, a district council, a London borough council, the Common Council of the City of London or the Council of the Isles of Scilly; and

(b) in relation to Wales, a county council or a county borough council."

General power of seizure

4 After paragraph 2A there is inserted—

"2B General power of seizure

2B Where a designation applies this paragraph to any person—

(a) that person shall, when lawfully on any premises in the relevant police area, have the same powers as a constable under section 19 of the 1984 Act (general powers of seizure) to seize things;

(b) that person shall also have the powers of a constable to impose a requirement by virtue of subsection (4) of that section in relation to information accessible from such premises;

(c) subsection (6) of that section (protection for legally privileged material from seizure) shall have effect in relation to the seizure of anything by that person by virtue of sub-paragraph (a) as it has effect in relation to the seizure of anything by a constable;

(d) section 21(1) and (2) of that Act (provision of record of seizure) shall have effect in relation to the seizure of anything by that person in exercise of the power conferred on him by virtue of sub-paragraph (a) as if the references to a constable and to an officer included references to that person; and

(e) sections 21(3) to (8) and 22 of that Act (access, copying and retention) shall have effect in relation to anything seized by that person in exercise of that power or taken away by him following the imposition of a requirement by virtue of sub-paragraph (b)—

(i) as they have effect in relation to anything seized in exercise of the power conferred on a constable by section 19(2) or (3) of that Act or taken away by a constable following the imposition of a requirement by virtue of section 19(4) of that Act; and

(ii) as if the references to a constable in subsections (3), (4) and (5) of section 21 included references to a person to whom this paragraph applies."

Powers with regard to charity collectors

5 After paragraph 3A there is inserted—

"3B Power to require name and address etc: charity collectors

3B Where a designation applies this paragraph to any person, that person shall, in the relevant police area, have the powers of a constable—

(a) under section 6 of the House to House Collections Act 1939 to require a person to give his name and address and to sign his name; and

(b) under regulations under section 4 of that Act to require a person to produce his certificate of authority."

Power to stop cycles

6 In paragraph 11A (power to stop cycles), in sub-paragraph (2), for the words after "has committed an offence" there is substituted "listed in paragraph 1(2B)(a) to (e), (f)(i) or (g)".

SCHEDULE 11

Section 181

MINOR AND CONSEQUENTIAL AMENDMENTS

PART 1

AMENDMENTS RELATING TO PARTS 1 TO 6

Magistrates' Courts Act 1980 (c. 43)

1 In section 143(2) of the Magistrates' Courts Act 1980 (provisions in which sums may be altered) paragraph (da) is omitted.

Housing Act 1980 (c. 51)

2 In Schedule 9 to the Housing Act 1980 (provisions relating to housing association and housing trust tenancies under Rent Act 1977), in paragraph 5, after "83" there is inserted "or 83ZA".

Highways Act 1980 (c. 66)

3 Sections 129A to 129G of the Highways Act 1980 (restriction of rights over highway) are repealed.

Police and Criminal Evidence Act 1984 (c. 60)

4 In section 64A of the Police and Criminal Evidence Act 1984 (photographing of suspects etc), for paragraph (ca) of subsection (1B) there is substituted—

"(ca) given a direction by a constable under section 35 of the Anti-social Behaviour, Crime and Policing Act 2014;".

Prosecution of Offences Act 1985 (c. 23)

5 (1) In section 3 of the Prosecution of Offences Act 1985 (functions of DPP), subsection (2) is amended as follows.

(2) In paragraph (fa), for the words from "section 1C" to "proceedings)" there is substituted "section 22 of the Anti-social Behaviour, Crime and Policing Act 2014 (criminal behaviour orders made on conviction)".

(3) In paragraph (fb)—

(a) for "section 1CA(3) of the Crime and Disorder Act 1998" there is substituted "section 27 of the Anti-social Behaviour, Crime and Policing Act 2014";
(b) for "section 1C" there is substituted "section 22".

(4) In paragraph (fc)—
(a) for "section 1CA" there is substituted "section 27";
(b) for "section 1C" there is substituted "section 22".

(5) Paragraphs (fd) and (fe) are omitted.

Housing Act 1985 (c. 68)

6 (1) Section 82A of the Housing Act 1985 (demotion because of anti-social behaviour) is amended as follows.

(2) In subsection (4)(a), for sub-paragraphs (i) and (ii) there is substituted—
"(i) conduct that is capable of causing nuisance or annoyance to some person (who need not be a particular identified person) and that directly or indirectly relates to or affects the landlord's housing management functions, or
(ii) conduct that consists of or involves using housing accommodation owned or managed by the landlord for an unlawful purpose, and".

(3) For subsection (7A) there is substituted—

"(7A) In subsection (4)(a)(ii) "housing accommodation" includes—
(a) flats, lodging-houses and hostels;
(b) any yard, garden, outhouses and appurtenances belonging to the accommodation or usually enjoyed with it;
(c) any common areas used in connection with the accommodation."

7 (1) Section 83 of that Act (proceedings for possession or termination: notice requirements) is amended as follows.

(2) In the heading, after "**termination:**" there is inserted "**general**".

(3) Before subsection (1) there is inserted—

"(A1) This section applies in relation to proceedings for an order mentioned in section 82(1A) other than—
(a) proceedings for possession of a dwelling-house under section 84A (absolute ground for possession for anti-social behaviour), including proceedings where possession is also sought on one or more of the grounds set out in Schedule 2, or
(b) proceedings for possession of a dwelling-house under section 107D (recovery of possession on expiry of flexible tenancy)."

(4) In subsection (1), for the words from "proceedings for" to "tenancy)," there is substituted "proceedings to which this section applies".

8 (1) Section 83A of that Act (additional requirements in relation to certain proceedings for possession) is amended as follows.

(2) In subsection (2)(a), after "83" there is inserted "or 83ZA".

(3) In subsection (2)(b), for "subsection (4)(a) of that section" there is substituted "section 83(4)(a) or section 83ZA(9)(a)".

(4) In subsection (3)(a), after "83" there is inserted "or 83ZA".

(5) In subsection (4)(a), after "83" there is inserted "or 83ZA".

(6) In subsection (5)—

(a) for "the notice" there is substituted "a notice";

(b) after "83" there is inserted "or a notice is served under section 83ZA".

9 (1) Section 84 of that Act (grounds and orders for possession) is amended as follows.

(2) In subsection (1), after "in accordance with" there is inserted "section 84A (absolute ground for possession for anti-social behaviour) or".

(3) In subsection (2)(a), for "that Schedule" there is substituted "Schedule 2".

(4) In subsection (3)—

(a) after "83" there is inserted "or 83ZA";

(b) for "such an order on any of those grounds above" there is substituted "an order on any of the grounds mentioned in subsection (2)".

10 In the heading of section 85A of that Act (proceedings for possession: anti-social behaviour) after "**possession**" there is inserted "**on non-absolute grounds**".

11 (1) Section 121A of that Act (order suspending right to buy because of anti-social behaviour) is amended as follows.

(2) In subsection (3)(a), for sub-paragraphs (i) and (ii) there is substituted—

"(i) conduct that is capable of causing nuisance or annoyance to some person (who need not be a particular identified person) and that directly or indirectly relates to or affects the landlord's housing management functions, or

(ii) conduct that consists of or involves using housing accommodation owned or managed by the landlord for an unlawful purpose, and".

(3) In subsection (7)(a), for sub-paragraphs (i) and (ii) there is substituted—

"(i) conduct that is capable of causing nuisance or annoyance to some person (who need not be a particular identified person) and that directly or indirectly relates to or affects the landlord's housing management functions, or

(ii) conduct that consists of or involves using housing accommodation owned or managed by the landlord for an unlawful purpose, and".

(4) For subsection (10) there is substituted—

"(10) In this section "housing accommodation" includes—

(a) flats, lodging-houses and hostels;

(b) any yard, garden, outhouses and appurtenances belonging to the accommodation or usually enjoyed with it;

(c) any common areas used in connection with the accommodation."

12 (1) In Schedule 1 to that Act (tenancies which are not secure tenancies), paragraph 4ZA (family intervention tenancies) is amended as follows.

(2) In sub-paragraph (3)(a)—

(a) in the opening words, for "possession order under section 84" there is substituted "relevant possession order";

(b) in sub-paragraph (i) the words ", on ground 2 or 2A of Part 1 of Schedule 2" are omitted.

(3) In sub-paragraph (12), after the definition of "the new tenant" there is inserted—

""relevant possession order" means—

(a) a possession order under section 84 that is made on ground 2, 2ZA or 2A of Part 1 of Schedule 2, or

(b) a possession order under section 84A;".

13 In Part 5 of Schedule 2 to that Act (approval of redevelopment schemes for purposes of Ground 10A), in paragraph 5(3), after "83" there is inserted "or 83ZA".

14 In Schedule 3 to that Act (grounds for withholding consent to assignment by way of exchange), in Ground 2, after "83" there is inserted "or 83ZA".

15 (1) In that Schedule, Ground 2A is amended as follows.

(2) In paragraph (a), for "or suspended Ground 2 or 14 possession order" there is substituted ", a suspended anti-social behaviour possession order or a suspended riot-related possession order".

(3) In paragraph (b), for "or a Ground 2 or 14 possession order" there is substituted ", an anti-social behaviour possession order or a riot-related possession order".

(4) In the definition of "relevant order"—

(a) the word "or" before the final entry is omitted;

(b) in the final entry, after "section 91 of the Anti-social Behaviour Act 2003" there is inserted "or section 27 of the Police and Justice Act 2006";

(c) at the end there is inserted—

"an injunction under section 1 of the Anti-social Behaviour, Crime and Policing Act 2014;

an order under section 22 of that Act."

(5) After the definition of "relevant order" there is inserted—

"An "anti-social behaviour possession order" means an order for possession under Ground 2 in Schedule 2 to this Act or Ground 14 in Schedule 2 to the Housing Act 1988."

(6) After the definition of "demotion order" there is inserted—

"A "riot-related possession order" means an order for possession under Ground 2ZA in Schedule 2 to this Act or Ground 14ZA in Schedule 2 to the Housing Act 1988."

(7) The definition of a "Ground 2 or 14 possession order" is omitted.

16 After Ground 2A in that Schedule there is inserted—

"Ground 2B

The dwelling-house is subject to a closure notice or closure order under Chapter 3 of Part 4 of the Anti-social Behaviour, Crime and Policing Act 2014."

Housing Act 1988 (c. 50)

17 (1) Section 6A of the Housing Act 1988 (demotion because of anti-social behaviour) is amended as follows.

(2) In subsection (4), for paragraph (a) there is substituted—

"(a) that the tenant or a person residing in or visiting the dwelling-house has engaged or has threatened to engage in—

(i) conduct that is capable of causing nuisance or annoyance to some person (who need not be a particular identified person) and that directly or indirectly relates to or affects the landlord's housing management functions, or

(ii) conduct that consists of or involves using housing accommodation owned or managed by the landlord for an unlawful purpose, and".

(3) After subsection (10) there is inserted—

"(10A) In subsection (4)(a)(ii) "housing accommodation" includes—

(a) flats, lodging-houses and hostels;

(b) any yard, garden, outhouses and appurtenances belonging to the accommodation or usually enjoyed with it;

(c) any common areas used in connection with the accommodation."

18 (1) Section 7 of that Act (orders for possession) is amended as follows.

(2) In subsection (3), after "below" there is inserted "(and to any available defence based on the tenant's Convention rights, within the meaning of the Human Rights Act 1998)".

(3) In subsection (5A)(a), for "and 5" there is substituted ", 5 and 7A".

(4) In subsection (6)(a), after "Ground 2" there is inserted ", Ground 7A".

19 In the heading of section 9A of that Act (proceedings for possession: anti-social behaviour) after "**possession**" there is inserted "**on non-absolute grounds**".

20 In Schedule 1 to that Act (tenancies which cannot be assured tenancies), in paragraph 12ZA (family intervention tenancies), in sub-paragraph (3)(a)(i), for "ground 14" there is substituted "ground 7A of Part 1 of Schedule 2 or ground 14, 14ZA".

Environmental Protection Act 1990 (c. 43)

21 In the Environmental Protection Act 1990, sections 92 to 94A (litter abatement notices, litter clearing notices and street litter control notices) are repealed.

Housing Act 1996 (c. 52)

22 In the Housing Act 1996, sections 153A to 158 and Schedule 15 (injunctions against housing-related anti-social behaviour) are repealed.

23 In section 218A of that Act (anti-social behaviour: landlords' policies and procedures), for subsections (8) and (8A) there is substituted—

"(8) Anti-social behaviour is—

(a) conduct that is capable of causing nuisance or annoyance to some person (who need not be a particular identified person) and that directly or indirectly relates to or affects the landlord's housing management functions, or

(b) conduct that consists of or involves using or threatening to use housing accommodation owned or managed by the landlord for an unlawful purpose."

Crime and Disorder Act 1998 (c. 37)

24 The following provisions of the Crime and Disorder Act 1998 are repealed—

(a) sections 1 to 1K (anti-social behaviour orders etc);

(b) section 4 (appeals against orders);

(c) section 8A (parenting orders on breach of anti-social behaviour order).

25 (1) Section 8 of that Act (parenting orders) is amended as follows.

(2) In subsection (1)(b), for "an anti-social behaviour order or" there is substituted "an injunction is granted under section 1 of the Anti-social Behaviour, Crime and Policing Act 2014, an order is made under section 22 of that Act or a".

(3) In subsection (1)(c) the words ", except in a case where section 8A below applies (parenting order on breach of anti-social behaviour order)" are omitted.

(4) In subsection (6)(a), for the words after "behaviour which led to" there is substituted "the order being made or the injunction granted".

26 (1) Section 9 of that Act (parenting orders: supplemental) is amended as follows.

(2) In subsection (1) the words ", other than an offence under section 1(10) above in respect of an anti-social behaviour order," are omitted.

(3) In subsection (1B)—

(a) for "an anti-social behaviour order" there is substituted "an injunction under section 1 of the Anti-social Behaviour, Crime and Policing Act 2014 is granted or an order is made under section 22 of that Act";

(b) after "which" there is inserted "grants the injunction or".

(4) In subsection (2)—

(a) paragraph (d) and the word "or" before it are omitted;

(b) in the text after paragraph (d) the words "(including any report prepared under section 1(1C))" are omitted.

(5) Subsection (2AA) is repealed.

27 (1) Section 18 of that Act (interpretation etc) is amended as follows.

(2) In subsection (1)—

(a) the definitions of "anti-social behaviour order" and "individual support order" are omitted;

(b) paragraph (za) of the definition of "responsible officer" is omitted.

(3) In subsection (4)—

(a) the words "an individual support order or" are omitted;

(b) for "the child, defendant or parent, as the case may be" there is substituted "the child or, as the case may be, the parent".

28 In section 38 of that Act (local provision of youth justice services), in subsection (4)(f) the words "individual support orders," are omitted.

29 In section 114 of that Act (orders and regulations), in subsection (2) "(1A), (1G)" is omitted.

Criminal Justice and Police Act 2001 (c. 16)

30 Sections 12 to 16 of the Criminal Justice and Police Act 2001 (alcohol consumption in designated public places) are repealed.

Police Reform Act 2002 (c. 30)

31 (1) Section 50 of the Police Reform Act 2002 (power of constable to require person acting in an anti-social manner to give name and address) is amended as follows.

(2) In subsection (1) the words "(within the meaning of section 1 of the Crime and Disorder Act 1998 (c. 37) (anti-social behaviour orders)" are omitted.

(3) After that subsection there is inserted—

"(1A) In subsection (1) "anti-social behaviour" has the meaning given by section 2 of the Anti-social Behaviour, Crime and Policing Act 2014 (ignoring subsection (2) of that section)."

32 In Part 1 of Schedule 4 to that Act (powers exercisable by community support officers), paragraph 1(2)(e) (powers to issue fixed penalty notices in respect of offences under dog control orders) and the word "and" before it are omitted.

33 In Schedule 5 to that Act (powers exercisable by accredited persons), in paragraph 1(2), paragraph (d) and the word "and" before it are omitted.

Licensing Act 2003 (c. 17)

34 Sections 161 to 166 of the Licensing Act 2003 (closure orders of identified premises) are repealed.

35 (1) Section 167 of that Act (review of premise licence following closure order) is amended as follows.

(2) In subsection (1)(a), for "a closure order has come into force" there is substituted "a magistrates' court has made a closure order under section 80 of the Anti-social Behaviour, Crime and Policing Act 2014, or the Crown Court has made a closure order on appeal under section 84 of that Act,".

(3) In subsection (1)(b), for the words after "the relevant licensing authority has" there is substituted "accordingly received a notice under section 80(9) or 84(7) of that Act".

(4) In subsection (4)(a), for the words after "notice of" there is substituted "the review and of the order mentioned in subsection (1)(a)".

(5) In subsection (5)(a), for the words after "to consider" there is substituted "the order mentioned in subsection (1)(a) and any relevant representations;".

36 In section 168 of that Act (provisions about decisions under section 167), in subsections (3)(b) and (6)(b), for the words after "the premises to which the licence relates" there is substituted "are closed at the time of the decision by virtue of an closure order made under section 80 or 84 of the Anti-social Behaviour, Crime and Policing Act 2014".

37 Section 169 of that Act (enforcement of closure order) is repealed.

38 (1) Section 170 of that Act (exemption of police from liability for damages) is amended as follows.

(2) In subsection (1) the words "of his functions in relation to a closure order or any extension of it or" are omitted.

(3) Paragraph (b) of subsection (2) is omitted.

39 (1) Section 171 of that Act (interpretation of Part 8) is amended as follows.

(2) In subsection (2), for "Relevant premises" there is substituted "Premises".

(3) In subsection (3) the word "relevant" is omitted.

(4) In subsection (5)—

(a) in the definition of "appropriate person" the word "relevant" is omitted;

(b) the definitions of "closure order", "extension", "relevant magistrates' court", "relevant premises", "responsible senior police officer" and "senior police officer" are omitted.

40 In Schedule 3 to that Act (matters to be entered in licensing register), for the words after "any notice given to it under" in paragraph (z) there is substituted "section 80(9) or 84(7) of the Anti-social Behaviour, Crime and Policing Act 2014 (notification by court of closure order)".

Anti-social Behaviour Act 2003 (c. 38)

41 The following provisions of the Anti-social Behaviour Act 2003 are repealed—

(a) Part 1 (closure of premises where drugs used unlawfully);

(b) Part 1A (closure of premises associated with persistent disorder or nuisance);

(c) Part 4 (dispersal of groups etc);

(d) sections 40 and 41 (closure of noisy premises);

(e) sections 48 to 52 (removal of graffiti and fly-posting) and the cross-heading before section 48.

Clean Neighbourhoods and Environment Act 2005 (c. 16)

42 Sections 55 to 64, 66 and 67 of the Clean Neighbourhoods and Environment Act 2005 are repealed.

Government of Wales Act 2006 (c. 32)

43 In Schedule 7 to the Government of Wales Act 2006 (legislative competence of Welsh Assembly), in the list of exceptions in paragraph 12, for "Anti-social behaviour orders" there is substituted "Orders to protect people from behaviour that causes or is likely to cause harassment, alarm or distress".

Violent Crime Reduction Act 2006 (c. 38)

44 The following provisions of the Violent Crime Reduction Act 2006 (which relate to drinking banning orders) are repealed—

(a) sections 1 to 7;

(b) section 8(1) to (6);

(c) sections 9 to 14.

45 Section 27 of that Act (directions to individuals who represent a risk of disorder) is repealed.

Crime and Security Act 2010 (c. 17)

46 Sections 40 and 41 of the Crime and Security Act 2010 (anti-social behaviour orders: report on family circumstances and parenting orders on breach) are repealed.

Localism Act 2011 (c. 20)

47 (1) In Schedule 14 to the Localism Act 2011 (grounds on which landlord may refuse to surrender and grant tenancies under section 158 of that Act), paragraph 6 (Ground 6) is amended as follows.

(2) In sub-paragraph (2), for "or suspended Ground 2 or 14 possession order" there is substituted ", a suspended anti-social behaviour possession order or a suspended riot-related possession order".

(3) In sub-paragraph (3), for "or a Ground 2 or 14 possession order" there is substituted ", an anti-social behaviour possession order or a riot-related possession order".

(4) In sub-paragraph (4), in the definition of "relevant order"—

(a) the word "or" before paragraph (e) is omitted;

(b) in paragraph (e), after "section 91 of the Anti-social Behaviour Act 2003" there is inserted "or section 27 of the Police and Justice Act 2006";

(c) at the end there is inserted—

"(f) an injunction under section 1 of the Anti-social Behaviour, Crime and Policing Act 2014, or

(g) an order under section 22 of that Act;".

(5) After the definition of "relevant order" in that sub-paragraph there is inserted—

"An "anti-social behaviour possession order" means an order for possession under Ground 2 in Schedule 2 to the Housing Act 1985 or Ground 14 in Schedule 2 to the Housing Act 1988."

(6) After the definition of "demotion order" in that sub-paragraph there is inserted—

"A "riot-related possession order" means an order for possession under Ground 2ZA in Schedule 2 to the Housing Act 1985 or Ground 14ZA in Schedule 2 to the Housing Act 1988."

(7) The definition of "Ground 2 or 14 possession order" in that sub-paragraph is omitted.

48 After paragraph 6 of that Schedule there is inserted—

"6A Ground 6A

6A This ground is that a dwelling-house let on an existing tenancy is subject to a closure notice or closure order under Chapter 3 of Part 4 of the Anti-social Behaviour, Crime and Policing Act 2014."

Legal Aid, Sentencing and Punishment of Offenders Act 2012 (c. 10)

49 (1) Schedule 1 to the Legal Aid, Sentencing and Punishment of Offenders Act 2012 (legal aid for civil legal services) is amended as follows.

(2) In paragraph 36 of Part 1 (anti-social behaviour), in sub-paragraph (1), for the words after "in relation to" there is substituted "an application for, or proceedings in respect of, an injunction against the individual under section 1 of the Anti-social Behaviour, Crime and Policing Act 2014."

(3) In paragraph 7 of Part 3 (certain advocacy services in a magistrates' court excepted from the advocacy exclusion), for "and 15 to 18" there is substituted ", 15 to 18 and 36".

Repeal of spent provisions etc

50 The following provisions are repealed.

Short title and chapter	*Extent of repeal*
Crime and Disorder Act 1998 (c. 37)	Section 40(2).
Powers of Criminal Courts(Sentencing) Act 2000 (c. 6)	In Schedule 9, paragraph 192.
Police Reform Act 2002 (c. 30)	Sections 61 to 66.
Licensing Act 2003 (c. 17)	Section 155(2).
	In Schedule 6, paragraphs 121 to 125.
Anti-social Behaviour Act 2003 (c. 38)	Section 13.
	Section 14(3)(a).
	Section 56(1).
	Section 85(2) to (7) and (9) to (11).
	Section 86(1) to (4).
Sexual Offences Act 2003 (c. 42)	In Schedule 6, paragraph 38(3).
Criminal Justice Act 2003 (c. 44)	Sections 322 and 323.
	In Schedule 26, paragraph 59.
Children Act 2004 (c. 31)	In Schedule 2, paragraph 8.
Serious Organised Crime andPolice Act 2005 (c. 15)	Section 139(1) to (9).
	Section 140(1) to (4).

Short title and chapter	*Extent of repeal*
	Sections 141 to 143.
	In Schedule 7, paragraph 36.
	In Schedule 10, paragraph 3(3)(b).
Clean Neighbourhoods and Environment Act 2005 (c. 16)	Section 2.
	Section 20(2).
	Section 21.
	Section 22.
	Section 31.
	In Schedule 4, paragraphs 7, 13 and 16 to 19.
Drugs Act 2005 (c. 17)	Section 20.
	In Schedule 1, paragraph 7.
Violent Crime Reduction Act2006 (c. 38)	Section 8(7).
	Section 26.
	Section 59(1).
Police and Justice Act 2006 (c. 48)	Section 26.
	In Schedule 14, paragraphs 12(3), 13(3), 15, 32 and 33.
Mental Health Act 2007 (c. 12)	In Schedule 1, paragraph 21.
Criminal Justice and Immigration Act 2008 (c. 4)	Section 118.
	Section 123.
	Section 124.
	Schedule 20.
Transport for London Act 2008 (c. i)	Section 29(a).
Coroners and Justice Act 2009 (c. 25)	In Schedule 21, paragraph 72.
Policing and Crime Act 2009 (c. 26)	Section 31.
Police Reform and Social Responsibility Act 2011 (c. 13)	In Schedule 16, paragraphs 307 to 309.
Localism Act 2011 (c. 20)	Section 155(1).

PART 2

AMENDMENTS RELATING TO PART 9

Criminal Procedure (Scotland) Act 1995 (c. 46)

51 In section 19AA of the Criminal Procedure (Scotland) Act 1995 (samples etc from sex offenders), in subsection (1)(c), after "an order under section" there is inserted "122A or".

52 In section 19AB of that Act (supplementary provision in risk of sexual harm order cases), in subsection (7), at the end of the definition of "risk of sexual harm order" there is inserted—

"and also includes an order under section 122A of the 2003 Act (sexual risk orders);".

Police Act 1997 (c. 50)

53 (1) Section 113CA of the Police Act 1997 (suitability information relating to children) is amended as follows.

(2) After paragraph (f) of subsection (2) there is inserted—

"(fa) if a sexual harm prevention order, made under section 103A of the Sexual Offences Act 2003, is in effect in respect of the applicant—

(i) the prohibitions described in that order;

(ii) the date of that order;

(iii) the period for which the prohibitions have effect by virtue of section 103C(2) or 103D(1) of that Act;

(iv) details as to whether the order has been varied or renewed under section 103E(5) of that Act;

(fb) if an interim sexual harm prevention order, made under section 103F of the Sexual Offences Act 2003, is in effect in respect of the applicant—

(i) the prohibitions described in that order;

(ii) the date of that order;

(iii) the period for which that order has effect by virtue of section 103F(4) of that Act;

(iv) details as to whether the order has been varied or renewed under section 103F(5) of that Act;".

(3) After paragraph (i) of that subsection there is inserted—

"(ia) if a sexual risk order, made under section 122A of the Sexual Offences Act 2003, is in effect in respect of the applicant—

(i) the prohibitions described in that order;

(ii) the date of that order;

(iii) the period for which the prohibitions have effect by virtue of section 122A(7) or 122C(1) of that Act;

(iv) details as to whether the order has been varied or renewed under section 122D(4) of that Act;

(ib) if an interim sexual risk order, made under section 122E of the Sexual Offences Act 2003, is in effect in respect of the applicant—

(i) the prohibitions described in that order;
(ii) the date of that order;
(iii) the period for which that order has effect by virtue of section 122E(4) of that Act;
(iv) details as to whether the order has been varied or renewed under section 122E(5) of that Act;".

54 (1) Section 113CB of that Act (suitability information relating to protected adults) is amended as follows.

(2) After paragraph (f) of subsection (2) there is inserted—

"(fa) if a sexual harm prevention order, made under section 103A of the Sexual Offences Act 2003, is in effect in respect of the applicant—
(i) the prohibitions described in that order;
(ii) the date of that order;
(iii) the period for which the prohibitions have effect by virtue of section 103C(2) or 103D(1) of that Act;
(iv) details as to whether the order has been varied or renewed under section 103E(5) of that Act;

(fb) if an interim sexual harm prevention order, made under section 103F of the Sexual Offences Act 2003, is in effect in respect of the applicant—
(i) the prohibitions described in that order;
(ii) the date of that order;
(iii) the period for which that order has effect by virtue of section 103F(4) of that Act;
(iv) details as to whether the order has been varied or renewed under section 103F(5) of that Act;".

(3) After paragraph (i) of that subsection there is inserted—

"(ia) if a sexual risk order, made under section 122A of the Sexual Offences Act 2003, is in effect in respect of the applicant—
(i) the prohibitions described in that order;
(ii) the date of that order;
(iii) the period for which the prohibitions have effect by virtue of section 122A(7) or 122C(1) of that Act;
(iv) details as to whether the order has been varied or renewed under section 122D(4) of that Act;

(ib) if an interim sexual risk order, made under section 122E of the Sexual Offences Act 2003, is in effect in respect of the applicant—
(i) the prohibitions described in that order;
(ii) the date of that order;
(iii) the period for which that order has effect by virtue of section 122E(4) of that Act;
(iv) details as to whether the order has been varied or renewed under section 122E(5) of that Act;".

Crime and Disorder Act 1998 (c. 37)

55 (1) Section 8 of the Crime and Disorder Act 1998 (parenting orders) is amended as follows.

(2) For "sexual offences prevention order" there is substituted "sexual harm prevention order"—

(a) in subsection (1)(b);

(b) in subsection (6)(a).

(3) For subsection (9) there is substituted—

"(9) In this section "sexual harm prevention order" means an order under section 103A of the Sexual Offences Act 2003 (sexual harm prevention orders)."

Sexual Offences Act 2003 (c. 42)

56 In section 88 of the Sexual Offences Act 2003 (section 87: interpretation), in subsection (4)(c), after "interim notification order," there is inserted "sexual harm prevention order, interim sexual harm prevention order,".

57 In section 89 of that Act (young offenders: parental directions), in the Table in subsection (1), after "interim notification order," there is inserted "sexual harm prevention order, interim sexual harm prevention order,".

58 In section 91A of that Act (review of indefinite notification requirements: qualifying young offender), in subsection (2)(b), after "not subject to" there is inserted "a sexual harm prevention order under section 103A, an interim sexual harm prevention order under section 103F,".

59 In the cross-heading before section 104 of that Act (sexual offences prevention orders: application and grounds), after "*orders*" there is inserted "*(Scotland and Northern Ireland)*".

60 In section 108 of that Act (SOPOs: variations, renewals and discharges), in subsection (8)(b) the words "2 or" and "England and Wales or" are omitted.

61 In section 109 of that Act (interim SOPOs), in subsection (7)(a) the words "2A or" and "England and Wales or" are omitted.

62 (1) Section 110 of that Act (SOPOs and interim SOPOs: appeals) is amended as follows.

(2) For the heading there is substituted "**Appeals in relation to SOPOs and interim SOPOs: Northern Ireland**".

(3) In subsections (1)(c), (2) and (3)(b), for "the Crown Court" there is substituted "a county court".

(4) In subsection (4), for "the Crown Court" there is substituted "the county court".

(5) For subsection (5) there is substituted—

"(5) Any order made by a county court on an appeal under subsection (1)(c) or (2) (other than an order directing that an application be re-heard by a court of summary jurisdiction) is for the purposes of section 108(7) or 109(6) (respectively) to be treated as if it were an order of the court from which the appeal was brought (and not an order of the county court)."

63 (1) Section 113 of that Act (offence: breach of SOPO or interim SOPO) is amended as follows.

(2) In the heading, at the end there is inserted "**etc**".

(3) In subsection (1), in paragraph (d) the words "2, 2A or" and "in England and Wales and" are omitted.

(4) After that subsection there is inserted—

"(1ZA) A person commits an offence if, without reasonable excuse, he contravenes a prohibition imposed by—

(a) a sexual harm prevention order, or

(b) an interim sexual harm prevention order,

other than a prohibition on foreign travel."

64 In the cross-heading before section 114 of that Act (foreign travel orders: applications and grounds), after "*orders*" there is inserted "*(Scotland and Northern Ireland)*".

65 (1) Section 117A of that Act (foreign travel orders: surrender of passports) is amended as follows.

(2) For the heading there is substituted "**Surrender of passports: Northern Ireland**".

(3) In subsection (2), after "at a police station" there is inserted "in Northern Ireland".

(4) In subsection (3), at the end there is inserted "(unless the person is subject to an equivalent prohibition under another order)".

66 In section 117B of that Act (surrender of passports: Scotland), at the end of subsection (3) there is inserted "(unless the person is subject to an equivalent prohibition under another order)".

67 (1) Section 119 of that Act (foreign travel orders: appeals) is amended as follows.

(2) For the heading there is substituted "**Appeals in relation to foreign travel orders: Northern Ireland**".

(3) In subsection (1), for "the Crown Court" there is substituted "a county court".

(4) In subsection (2), for "the Crown Court" there is substituted "the county court".

(5) For subsection (3) there is substituted—

"(3) Any order made by a county court on an appeal under subsection (1)(a) (other than an order directing that an application be re-heard by a court of summary jurisdiction) is for the purposes of section 118(5) to be treated as if it were an order of the court from which the appeal was brought (and not an order of the county court)."

68 (1) Section 122 (offence: breach of foreign travel order) is amended as follows.

(2) In the heading, at the end there is inserted "**etc**".

(3) In subsection (1)—

(a) for "excuse, he" there is substituted "excuse—

(a) he";

(b) at the end there is inserted ", or

(b) he contravenes a prohibition on foreign travel imposed by a sexual harm prevention order."

(4) In subsection (1B)(a) the words "England and Wales and" are omitted.

69 In the cross-heading before section 123 of that Act, after "*orders*" there is inserted "*(Northern Ireland)*".

70 (1) Section 123 of that Act (risk of sexual harm orders: application, grounds and effect) is amended as follows.

(2) In subsection (1)—

(a) for "A chief officer of police" there is substituted "The Chief Constable of the Police Service of Northern Ireland";

(b) for "a magistrates' court" there is substituted "a court of summary jurisdiction";

(c) for "his police area" (in both places) there is substituted "Northern Ireland";

(d) for "the chief officer" (in both places) there is substituted "the Chief Constable".

(3) Subsection (2) is repealed.

71 (1) Section 125 (RSHOs: variation, renewals and discharges) is amended as follows.

(2) In subsection (2), for paragraphs (b) to (d) there is substituted—

"(b) the Chief Constable of the Police Service of Northern Ireland."

(3) In subsection (3), for "and (if they wish to be heard) the other persons mentioned in subsection (2)" there is substituted ", and the other person mentioned in subsection (2) (if that person wishes to be heard)".

(4) In subsection (5), for the words after "without the consent of the defendant and" there is substituted "the Chief Constable of the Police Service of Northern Ireland".

(5) In subsection (7), for paragraphs (b) and (c) there is substituted—

"(b) a court of summary jurisdiction for the petty sessions district which includes the area where the defendant resides;

(c) where the application is made by the Chief Constable of the Police Service of Northern Ireland, any court of summary jurisdiction."

72 In section 126 (interim RSHOs), in subsection (2)(b), for "the person who has made that application" there is substituted "the Chief Constable of the Police Service of Northern Ireland".

73 (1) Section 127 (RSHOs and interim RSHOs) is amended as follows.

(2) In subsection (1), for "the Crown Court" there is substituted "a county court".

(3) In subsection (2), for "the Crown Court" there is substituted "the county court".

(4) For subsection (3) there is substituted—

"(3) Any order made by a county court on an appeal under subsection (1)(a) or (b) (other than an order directing that an application be re-heard by a court of summary jurisdiction) is for the purposes of section 125(7) or 126(5) (respectively) to be treated as if it were an order of the court from which the appeal was brought (and not an order of the county court)."

74 (1) Section 128 (offence: breach of RSHO or interim RSHO) is amended as follows.

(2) In the heading, after "**interim RSHO**" there is inserted "**etc**".

(3) For subsections (1) and (1A) there is substituted—

"(1) A person who, without reasonable excuse, does anything that the person is prohibited from doing by—

(a) a risk of sexual harm order,

(b) an interim risk of sexual harm order,

(c) a sexual risk order,

(d) an interim sexual risk order,

(e) an order under section 2 of the Protection of Children and Prevention of Sexual Offences (Scotland) Act 2005 (risk of sexual harm orders in Scotland), or

(f) an order under section 5 of that Act (interim risk of sexual harm orders in Scotland),

commits an offence."

75 (1) Section 129 (effect of conviction etc of an offence under section 128) is amended as follows.

(2) In the heading, after "**section 128**" there is inserted "**etc**".

(3) In subsection (1A)(a), after "an offence under section" there is inserted "122H or".

(4) For subsection (5) there is substituted—

"(5) In this section "relevant order" means—

(a) where the conviction, finding or caution within subsection (1) is in respect of a breach of a risk of sexual harm order or a sexual risk order, that order;

(b) where the conviction, finding or caution within subsection (1) is in respect of a breach of an interim risk of sexual harm order or an interim sexual risk order, any risk of sexual harm order or sexual risk order made on the hearing of the application to which the interim order relates or, if no such order is made, the interim order.

(6) In subsection (5)—

"risk of sexual harm order" includes an order under section 2 of the Protection of Children and Prevention of Sexual Offences (Scotland) Act 2005;

"interim risk of sexual harm order" includes an order under section 5 of that Act."

76 (1) Section 133 of that Act (Part 2: general interpretation) is amended as follows.

(2) In subsection (1), at the appropriate places there is inserted—

""interim sexual harm prevention order" has the meaning given by section 103F(2);";

""interim sexual risk order" has the meaning given by section 122E(2);";

""prohibition on foreign travel" has the meaning given by section 103D(2) or 122C(2);";

"""sexual harm prevention order" has the meaning given by section 103A(1);";

"""sexual risk order" has the meaning given by section 122A(1);".

77 In section 136 of that Act (Part 2: Northern Ireland), for subsection (8) there is substituted—

"(8) The reference in section 101 to the Crown Court is to be read as a reference to a county court."

Protection of Children and Prevention of Sexual Offences (Scotland) Act 2005 (asp 9)

78 (1) Section 7 of the Protection of Children and Prevention of Sexual Offences (Scotland) Act 2005 (offence: breach of RSHO or interim RSHO) is amended as follows.

(2) In the heading, after "**interim RSHO**" there is inserted "**etc**".

(3) In subsection (2), after "an order made under" there is inserted "section 122A or 122E or".

79 (1) Section 8 of that Act (effect of conviction etc under section 7 of that Act or section 128 of the Sexual Offences Act 2003) is amended as follows.

(2) In the heading, after "**or section**" there is inserted "**122H or**".

(3) In subsection (1)(a), for the words after "an offence under section 7 above" there is substituted ", section 122H of the 2003 Act (breach of sexual risk order or interim sexual risk order in England and Wales) or section 128 of that Act (breach of risk of sexual harm order or interim risk of sexual harm order in Northern Ireland)".

(4) In subsection (1)(b), after "an offence under section" there is inserted "122H or".

(5) In the definition of "relevant order" in subsection (5)—

(a) in paragraph (a), for "section 123" there is substituted "an order under section 122A or section 123";

(b) in paragraph (b), after "a breach of" there is inserted "a sexual risk order under section 122A of the 2003 Act or";

(c) for paragraphs (c) and (d) there is substituted—

"(c) where the conviction or finding referred to in subsection (1)(a), (c) or (d) above is in respect of a breach of an interim risk of sexual harm order under section 5 above or an interim order under section 122E or 126 of the 2003 Act—

(i) any risk of sexual harm order or sexual risk order made upon the application to which the interim order relates; or

(ii) if no risk of sexual harm order or sexual risk order has been made, the interim order;

(d) where the caution referred to in subsection (1)(b) above is in respect of a breach of an interim order under section 122E or 126 of the 2003 Act—

(i) any order under section 122A or 123 of that Act made upon the application to which the interim order relates; or

(ii) if no order under section 122A or 123 of that Act has been made, the interim order."

Violent Crime Reduction Act 2006 (c. 38)

80 In section 56 of the Violent Crime Reduction Act 2006 (cross-border provisions relating to sexual offences), subsection (2) is repealed.

Armed Forces Act 2006 (c. 52)

81 In Schedule 3A to the Armed Forces Act 2006 (Court Martial sentencing powers where election for trial by that court instead of CO), paragraph 13(2) and (3) (service sexual offences prevention orders) is repealed.

Armed Forces Act 2011 (c. 18)

82 (1) Section 17 of the Armed Forces Act 2011 (service sexual offences prevention orders) is repealed.

(2) In Schedule 4 to that Act (consequential amendments), paragraph 3(3) is repealed.

PART 3

AMENDMENTS RELATING TO PART 11

House of Commons Disqualification Act 1975 (c. 24)

83 In Part 2 of Schedule 1 to the House of Commons Disqualification Act 1975. (bodies of which all members are disqualified) at the appropriate place there is inserted—

"The Police Remuneration Review Body."

Police Pensions Act 1976 (c. 35)

84 In section 7 of the Police Pensions Act 1976 (payment of pensions and contributions), for paragraph (f) of subsection (2) there is substituted—

"(f) a person to whom section 100A of the Police Act 1996 applies (senior police officer appointed as member of staff of College of Policing);".

85 (1) Section 11 of that Act (interpretation) is amended as follows.

(2) For paragraph (e) of subsection (1) there is substituted—

"(e) service, by a person to whom section 100A of the Police Act 1996 applies, as a member of the staff of the College of Policing;".

(3) In subsection (2A)(i) the words "the body known as" are omitted.

(4) In subsection (8A), for "the Chief Executive of the body known as" there is substituted "a member of the staff of".

Police and Criminal Evidence Act 1984 (c. 60)

86 (1) Schedule 2A to the Police and Criminal Evidence Act 1984 (fingerprinting and samples: power to require attendance at police station) is amended as follows.

(2) In paragraph 1 (fingerprinting: persons arrested and released)—

(a) in sub-paragraph (2), for "section 61(5A)(b)" there is substituted "section 61(5A)(b)(i)";

(b) after sub-paragraph (3) there is inserted—

"(4) The power under sub-paragraph (1) above may not be exercised in a case falling within section 61(5A)(b)(ii) (fingerprints destroyed where investigation interrupted) after the end of the period of six months beginning with the day on which the investigation was resumed."

(3) In paragraph 2 (fingerprinting: persons charged etc)—

(a) in sub-paragraph (2)(b), for "section 61(5B)(b)" there is substituted "section 61(5B)(b)(i)";

(b) at the end of sub-paragraph (2) there is inserted ", or

(c) in a case falling within section 61(5B)(b)(ii) (fingerprints destroyed where investigation interrupted), the day on which the investigation was resumed."

(4) In paragraph 9 (non-intimate samples: persons arrested and released)—

(a) in sub-paragraph (2), for "within section 63(3ZA)(b)" there is substituted "within section 63(3ZA)(b)(i) or (ii)";

(b) after sub-paragraph (3) there is inserted—

"(4) The power under sub-paragraph (1) above may not be exercised in a case falling within section 63(3ZA)(b)(iii) (sample, and any DNA profile, destroyed where investigation interrupted) after the end of the period of six months beginning with the day on which the investigation was resumed."

(5) In paragraph 10 (non-intimate samples: persons charged etc)—

(a) in sub-paragraph (3), for "within section 63(3A)(b)" there is substituted "within section 63(3A)(b)(i) or (ii)";

(b) after sub-paragraph (4) there is inserted—

"(5) The power under sub-paragraph (1) above may not be exercised in a case falling within section 63(3A)(b)(iii) (sample, and any DNA profile, destroyed where investigation interrupted) after the end of the period of six months beginning with the day on which the investigation was resumed."

Police Act 1996 (c. 16)

87 In section 36 of the Police Act 1996 (general duty of Secretary of State), in subsection (2)(c), the words "(other than sections 61 and 62)" are omitted.

88 In section 97 of that Act (police officers engaged on service outside their force), in subsection (1)(i) the words "the body known as" are omitted.

89 In section 105 of that Act (extent), in subsection (3), for "sections 61 and 62" there is substituted "Part 3A".

Police Act 1997 (c. 50)

90 In section 137 of the Police Act 1997 (extent), in subsection (2) (provisions extending to England and Wales only), after "sections" in paragraph (e) there is inserted "125(1A),".

Police (Northern Ireland) Act 2000 (c. 32)

91 In section 49 of the Police (Northern Ireland) Act 2000 (severance arrangements), for subsection (4) there is substituted—

"(4) Sections 25(8) and 26(6) of the Police (Northern Ireland) Act 1998 (requirement to consult the Board and the Police Association before making regulations) shall not apply in relation to regulations made by virtue of this section."

Freedom of Information Act 2000 (c. 36)

92 In Part 6 of Schedule 1 to the Freedom of Information Act 2000 (public authorities), the following entries are inserted at the appropriate places—

"The College of Policing."

"The Police Remuneration Review Body."

Police Reform Act 2002 (c. 30)

93 (1) Section 29 of the Police Reform Act 2002 (interpretation of Part 2) is amended as follows.

(2) In subsection (1), in the definition of "serving with the police", for "12(7)" there is substituted "12(7) to (10)".

(3) In subsection (1A), for "12(7)" there is substituted "12(7) to (10)".

94 In section 39 (police powers for contracted-out staff), subsections (9) to (11) are repealed.

95 (1) Schedule 3 to that Act (handling of complaints and conduct matters etc) is amended as follows.

(2) In paragraph 19, after paragraph (a) of sub-paragraph (7) there is inserted—

"(aa) a body required by section 26BA to enter into an agreement with the Commission, or".

(3) In paragraph 20A(4), at the end there is inserted ", but this is subject to paragraph 19ZD (restriction on disclosure of sensitive information)".

(4) In paragraph 20C(4)—

(a) the words from the beginning to "sub-paragraph (3)," are omitted;

(b) at the end there is inserted ", except so far as—

(a) regulations made by virtue of sub-paragraph (3) provide otherwise, or

(b) the Commission is prevented from doing so by paragraph 19ZD (restriction on disclosure of sensitive information)."

(5) In paragraph 20H(5)—

(a) the words from the beginning to "sub-paragraph (4)," are omitted;

(b) at the end there is inserted ", except so far as—

"(a) regulations made by virtue of sub-paragraph (4) provide otherwise, or

(b) the Commission is prevented from doing so by paragraph 19ZD (restriction on disclosure of sensitive information)."

(6) In paragraph 23(12)—

(a) the words from the beginning to "sub-paragraph (11)," are omitted;

(b) at the end there is inserted ", except so far as—

(a) regulations made by virtue of sub-paragraph (11) provide otherwise, or

(b) the Commission is prevented from doing so by paragraph 19ZD (restriction on disclosure of sensitive information)."

(7) In paragraph 24A(3), after "a report" there is inserted "to the Commission".

(8) In paragraph 24C—

(a) in sub-paragraph (1), for "If" there is substituted "This paragraph applies where";

(b) the words in that sub-paragraph from "it shall make" to the end are omitted;

(c) sub-paragraph (2) is repealed.

(9) In paragraph 27—

(a) in the heading, after "*disciplinary proceedings*" there is inserted "*etc*";

(b) in sub-paragraph (7), after "disciplinary" there is inserted "or other";

(c) in sub-paragraph (9)(a), after "sub-paragraph (1)(b)" there is inserted "or (c)".

Equality Act 2010 (c. 15)

96 In Part 1 of Schedule 19 to the Equality Act 2010 (authorities subject to public sector equality duty), at the appropriate place under the heading "*Police*" there is inserted—

"The College of Policing."

Police Reform and Social Responsibility Act 2011 (c. 13)

97 In section 7 of the Police Reform and Social Responsibility Act 2011 (police and crime plans), for paragraph (f) of subsection (1) there is substituted—

"(ea) the services which are to be provided by virtue of section 143 of the Anti-social Behaviour, Crime and Policing Act 2014;

(f) any grants which the elected local policing body is to make under that section, and the conditions (if any) subject to which any such grants are to be made."

98 Section 9 of that Act (crime and disorder reduction grants) is repealed.

99 In Schedule 2 to that Act (chief constables), paragraph 7(3) is repealed.

100 In Schedule 4 to that Act (Commissioner of Police of the Metropolis), paragraph 4(3) is repealed.

Police and Fire Reform (Scotland) Act 2012 (Consequential Provisions and Modifications) Order 2013 (S.I. 2013/602)

101 In article 14 of the Police and Fire Reform (Scotland) Act 2012 (Consequential Provisions and Modifications) Order 2013 (pensions: special constables and police cadets), in paragraph (2), for "the Police Negotiating Board for the United Kingdom" there is substituted "the Police Negotiating Board for Scotland".

Repeal or revocation of spent provisions etc

102 The following provisions are repealed or revoked—

Title and reference	*Extent of repeal or revocation*
Police Act 1996 (c. 16)	In Schedule 7, paragraph 28.
Police (Northern Ireland) Act 1998 (c. 32)	Section 34.
Greater London Authority Act 1999 (c. 29)	In Schedule 27, paragraph 92(2).
Scotland Act 1998 (Cross-Border Public Authorities) (Specification) Order 1999 (S.I. 1999/1319)	In the Schedule, the entry for the Police Negotiating Board for the United Kingdom.
Scotland Act 1998 (Cross-Border Public Authorities) (Adaptation of Functions etc.) Order 1999 (S.I. 1999/1747)	In Schedule 1, the entry for the Police Negotiating Board for the United Kingdom.
	Schedule 21.
Scotland Act 1998 (Consequential Modifications) (No. 2) Order 1999 (S.I. 1999/1820)	In Schedule 2, paragraph 124.
Police (Northern Ireland) Act 2000 (c. 32)	In Schedule 6, paragraph 12(2).
Freedom of Information Act 2000 (c. 36)	In Part 6 of Schedule 1, the entry for the Police Negotiating Board.
Police Reform Act 2002 (c. 30)	In Schedule 4, in paragraph 1(2), the word "and" at the end of paragraph (ca).
Police and Justice Act 2006 (c. 48)	In Schedule 4, paragraphs 3 and 10.
Police, Public Order and Criminal Justice (Scotland) Act 2006 (asp 10)	In Schedule 6, paragraph 5(3) and (4).
Policing and Crime Act 2009 (c. 26)	Section 12(3).
Northern Ireland Act 1998 (Devolution of Policing and Justice Functions) Order 2010 (S.I. 2010/976)	In Schedule 3, paragraphs 5 to 7.
Police Reform and Social Responsibility Act 2011 (c. 13)	Section 24(2)(a).

Title and reference	*Extent of repeal or revocation*
	In Schedule 16, paragraphs 30(3), 35(3) and 38.
Police and Fire Reform (Scotland) Act 2012 (asp 8)	In Schedule 7, paragraph 13(4).
Police and Fire Reform (Scotland) Act 2012 (Consequential Provisions and Modifications) Order 2013 (S.I. 2013/602)	In Schedule 1, paragraph 5(4) to (6).

PART 4

AMENDMENTS RELATING TO PART 12

Prison Act (Northern Ireland) 1953 (c. 18)

103 In section 38 of the Prison Act (Northern Ireland) 1953 (arrest, etc, of persons unlawfully at large), in subsection (4), for "the last foregoing sub-section" there is substituted "subsection (2)".

Extradition Act 2003 (c. 41)

104 In section 11 of the Extradition Act 2003 (bars to extradition), in subsection (1A), for "by reason of forum only" there is substituted "by reason of—

(a) absence of prosecution decision, or

(b) forum,

only".

105 (1) Section 21 of that Act (human rights) is amended as follows.

(2) For the heading there is substituted "**Person unlawfully at large: human rights**".

(3) In subsection (1) the words "11 or" are omitted.

106 In section 26 of that Act (appeal against extradition order: category 1 territory), in subsection (4), for "Notice of an appeal" there is substituted "Notice of application for leave to appeal".

107 In section 28 of that Act (appeal against discharge at extradition hearing: category 1 territory), in subsection (5), for "Notice of an appeal" there is substituted "Notice of application for leave to appeal".

108 In section 35 of that Act (extradition where there is no appeal), after subsection (4) there is inserted—

"(4A) If the day referred to in paragraph (a) of subsection (4) is earlier than the earliest day on which, by reason of an order under section 36B or 36C, the extradition order may be carried out ("the postponed date"), that paragraph has effect as if it referred instead to the postponed date."

109 In section 36 of that Act (extradition following appeal), after subsection (3) there is inserted—

"(3A) If the day referred to in paragraph (a) of subsection (3) is earlier than the earliest day on which, by reason of an order under section 36B or 36C, the extradition order may be carried out ("the postponed date"), that paragraph has effect as if it referred instead to the postponed date."

110 In section 66 of that Act (supplementary provision for the purposes of sections 64 and 65), in subsection (1), for "(2)" there is substituted "(1A)".

111 In section 103 of that Act (appeal where case sent to Secretary of State), in subsection (9), for "Notice of an appeal" there is substituted "Notice of application for leave to appeal".

112 In section 105 of that Act (appeal against discharge at extradition hearing: category 2 territory), in subsection (5), for "Notice of an appeal" there is substituted "Notice of application for leave to appeal".

113 (1) Section 108 of that Act (appeal against extradition order: category 2 territory) is amended as follows.

(2) In subsection (4), for the words before "is 14 days" there is substituted

"Notice of application for leave to appeal under this section must be given—

(a) in accordance with rules of court, and

(b) subject to subsections (5) and (7A), before the end of the permitted period, which".

(3) In subsection (5)—

(a) for "But notice of an appeal" there is substituted "Notice of application for leave to appeal"

(b) after "if it is an" there is inserted "application for leave to".

(4) In subsection (6), for the words before "before the person is extradited" there is substituted "Notice of application for leave to appeal on human rights grounds given after the end of the permitted period must be given".

(5) In subsection (7)—

(a) for "notice of an appeal" there is substituted "notice of application for leave to appeal";

(b) for "consider the appeal" there is substituted "grant leave";

(c) for "to consider the appeal" there is substituted "for the appeal to be heard".

(6) In subsection (8), for ""appeal on human rights grounds" means an appeal" there is substituted ""to appeal on human rights grounds" means to appeal".

114 In section 110 of that Act (appeal against discharge by Secretary of State), in subsection (5), for "Notice of an appeal" there is substituted "Notice of application for leave to appeal".

115 In section 117 of that Act (extradition where there is no appeal), in subsection (2), for the words after "28 days" there is substituted "starting with—

(a) the day on which the Secretary of State makes the extradition order, or

(b) if an order is made under section 118C or 118D, the earliest day on which the extradition order may be carried out."

116 In section 118 of that Act (extradition following appeal), after subsection (2) there is inserted—

"(2A) But if the day referred to in paragraph (a) or (b) of subsection (3) is earlier than the earliest day on which, by reason of an order under section 118C or 118D, the extradition order may be carried out ("the postponed date"), the required period is 28 days beginning with the postponed date."

117 In section 137 (definition of extradition offence for the purposes of Part 2 of the Act: person not sentenced for offence) subsection (9) is repealed.

118 In section 138 (definition of extradition offence for the purposes of Part 2 of the Act: person sentenced for offence) subsection (9) is repealed.

119 (1) Section 197 of that Act (custody) is amended as follows.

(2) In subsection (1), at the end there is inserted—

"This is subject to the power to order the temporary transfer of a person under section 21B."

(3) After subsection (6) there is inserted—

"(6A) An order for a person's temporary transfer under section 21B is sufficient authority for an appropriate person—

(a) to receive him;

(b) to keep him in custody until he is transferred in accordance with the order;

(c) to convey him to and from the territory to which he is to be transferred;

(d) on his return from that territory, to keep him in custody until he is brought back to the institution to which he was committed."

120 (1) Section 204 of that Act (warrant issued by category 1 territory: transmission by electronic means) is amended as follows.

(2) In subsections (1)(c) and (2)(c), for "a qualifying form" there is substituted "a form in which it is intelligible and which is capable of being used for subsequent reference".

(3) In subsection (6)—

(a) at the end of paragraph (a) there is inserted "and";

(b) paragraph (c) and the word "and" before it are omitted.

121 (1) Section 216 of that Act (interpretative provisions) is amended as set out in sub-paragraphs (2) and (3).

(2) After subsection (10) there is inserted—

"(10A) Human Rights Convention" has the meaning given to "the Convention" by section 21(1) of the Human Rights Act 1998."

(3) After subsection (12) there is inserted—

"(12A) Refugee Convention" means the Convention relating to the Status of Refugees done at Geneva on 28 July 1951 and the Protocol to the Convention."

(4) The following provisions of that Act are repealed in consequence of sub-paragraphs (2) and (3)—

(a) the definition of "the Refugee Convention" in section 40(4);

(b) section 70(2A);

(c) section 153D(3).

122 In section 223 of that Act (orders and regulations), in subsection (6)(a), after the entry for section 173(4) there is inserted—

"section 189D(4);

section 189E(1)(b);".

123 In section 226 of that Act (extent), in subsection (2), after "Sections" there is inserted "151B,".

124 In Part 1 of Schedule 1 to that Act (re-extradition: category 1 territories), in paragraph 3, after "21(3)" there is inserted "and section 21A(5)".

PART 5

AMENDMENTS CONSEQUENTIAL ON ESTABLISHMENT OF POLICE SERVICE OF SCOTLAND

Terrorism Act 2000 (c. 11)

125 (1) Schedule 8 to the Terrorism Act 2000 (detention) is amended as follows.

(2) In paragraph 20B(10), for paragraph (b) of the definition of "a specified chief officer of police" there is substituted—

"(b) the chief constable of the Police Service of Scotland, where—

(i) the person who provided the material, or from whom it was taken, resides in Scotland, or

(ii) the chief constable believes that the person is in, or is intending to come to, Scotland."

(3) In paragraph 20J—

(a) for paragraphs (d) and (e) of the definition of "police force" there is substituted—

"(d) the Police Service of Scotland;

(e) the Scottish Police Authority;";

(b) in the second of the three definitions of "responsible chief officer of police", for the words after "the chief constable of" there is substituted "the Police Service of Scotland".

Counter-Terrorism Act 2008 (c. 28)

126 (1) In section 18D of the Counter-Terrorism Act 2008 (use of retained material), in subsection (2) for "the Scottish Police Services Authority" there is substituted "the Scottish Police Authority".

(2) In section 18E(1) of that Act (interpretation of sections 18 to 18E), for paragraph (d) of the definition of "police force" there is substituted—

"(d) the Police Service of Scotland;".

Adapted and published by GRANGIS under the OGL Licence 3.0.

www.nationalarchives.gov.uk/doc/open-government-licence/version/3/

GRANGIS - UK PUBLISHING 2022.
Thank you for taking the time to leave us a review regarding this version

★★★★★

For further inquiries, contact us at:
www.grangis.com / contact@grangis.com

www.ingramcontent.com/pod-product-compliance
Lightning Source LLC
LaVergne TN
LVHW060211210926
848481LV00008B/2698